Sanctions beyond Borders

Sanctions beyond Borders

Multinational Corporations and U.S. Economic Statecraft

Kenneth A. Rodman

ROWMAN & LITTLEFIELD PUBLISHERS, INC.
Lanham • Boulder • New York • Oxford

ROWMAN & LITTLEFIELD PUBLISHERS, INC.

Published in the United States of America
by Rowman & Littlefield Publishers, Inc.
4720 Boston Way, Lanham, Maryland 20706
www.rowmanlittlefield.com

12 Hid's Copse Road
Cumnor Hill, Oxford OX2 9JJ, England

British Library Cataloguing-in-Publication Information Available

Library of Congress Cataloging-in-Publication Data

Rodman, Kenneth Aaron.
   Sanctions beyond borders : multinational corporations and U.S. economic statecraft /
Kenneth A. Rodman.
     p. cm.
   Includes bibliographical references and index.
   ISBN 0-8476-9307-4 (alk. paper)—ISBN 0-8476-9308-2 (pbk. : alk. paper)
   1. Economic sanctions, American. 2. International business enterprises—Political
aspects—United States. 3. International trade—Political aspects—United States. I. Title.

HF1413.5 .R63 2001
337.73—dc21
                                          2001019884

Printed in the United States of America

∞™ The paper used in this publication meets the minimum requirements of American
National Standard for Information Sciences—Permanence of Paper for Printed Library
Materials, ANSI/NISO Z.39.48-1992.

Contents

Acknowledgments

There are numerous people whose support and assistance were indispensable to this project. I would like to thank Steve Kobrin, who introduced me to the subject of extraterritorial sanctions and provided critical encouragement for some of the early papers that eventually evolved into this book. Bill Cotter, the former president of Colby College, appointed me to the college's South African investment committee and gave me an opportunity to participate in a subject of my scholarship. Ambassador Robert Gelbard was generous with his time in discussing his involvement in these issues and in helping me set up my most important interviews in Washington, D.C. I also acknowledge the assistance of Canada's Department of Foreign Affairs and International Trade (DFAIT), particularly Ted Kelly in the Office of the Historian, for providing me access to classified material. The Department of Foreign Affairs and International Trade has screened and approved my use of this material, as was required by our agreement. Nothing was excised from the original draft.

I am grateful for the assistance of Colby College's Social Science Fund and the Oak Foundation (which endows the William R. Cotter chair) for research funding. The Oak Foundation also provided me with an opportunity to work with some of the human rights activists involved in corporate social responsibility issues through directing the Oak Institute for the Study of International Human Rights. My student research assistants provided invaluable support, particularly Mark Adelman, Flannery Higgins, and Lydia Tomitova, all of whom demonstrated persistence and initiative that went above and beyond the call of duty. Jennifer Knerr and the reviewers at Rowman & Littlefield provided valuable advice in refining and streamlining the theoretical arguments and smoothing the rough edges of my writing. Finally, I would like to thank my parents, who taught me the value of intellectual pursuits from an early age. It is to them I owe my greatest debt.

Introduction

Since the end of the Cold War, the U.S. government has tightened its economic sanctions against "rogue states," such as Cuba, Libya, and Iran. What is noteworthy about these measures is their extraterritorial scope. Prior regulations had already banned nearly all transactions with these countries from the territory of the United States. These new laws reach beyond U.S. borders to extend criminal jurisdiction to the foreign operations of American multinational corporations (MNCs) and attach economic penalties to foreign firms for their dealings with sanctioned countries. Their aim is to broaden the observance of unilateral measures by applying U.S. law to private actors in third countries that have not imposed parallel controls.

If the past is any indication of the future, these efforts are more likely to produce acrimony with allies than to inflict costs on target states. This was the experience of the Reagan administration in 1982 when it imposed the pipeline sanctions after the declaration of martial law and suppression of the Solidarity trade union movement in Poland. Frustrated by the unwillingness of its allies to abandon a Soviet–European project to transport Siberian natural gas to Western Europe, the United States sought to coerce their compliance by extending technology sanctions to the foreign subsidiaries and licensees of U.S. firms. This effort was frustrated by allied governments, which effectively blocked corporate compliance with U.S. regulations, and private actors, including the subsidiaries of U.S. firms, who sided with the host governments. Ultimately, the United States was forced to back down, ending one of the worst crises in the history of the Atlantic alliance.

These pipeline sanctions have been used as the frame of reference for a pessimistic conventional wisdom regarding extraterritorial sanctions. The lesson drawn from this experience was that the United States had lost the unilateral ability to extend sanctions to the foreign activity of its MNCs. First,

1

the global spread of American business and banking placed a substantial proportion of U.S. commercial and financial activity beyond U.S. law. Second, the decline of America's economic dominance over its allies, relative to the early Cold War era, decreased U.S. leverage to obtain foreign compliance with or acquiescence to its sanctions and increased the capacity of host countries to frustrate extraterritorial controls. Drawing on this episode, contemporary critics of extraterritorial sanctions characterized them as attempts to "bully allies that cannot be persuaded"—attempts that will generate high diplomatic costs relative to the prospects for success.[1]

The purpose of this book is to test this conventional wisdom. The introduction draws on the scholarly literature on MNCs and economic sanctions to lay out the hypothesis that hegemonic decline and economic globalization have placed the overseas activities of American MNCs beyond the influence of the American political system. Part I (chapters 1–3) tests this model against the history of extraterritorial sanctions from the early Cold War era—when American business was less global and the United States was more economically dominant—through the pipeline sanctions. Part II tests the generalizability of the pipeline experience for subsequent sanctions and their territorial scope. Chapter 4 assesses efforts to influence the subsidiaries of U.S.-based MNCs in third countries, examining the moderation of this practice in the 1980s and efforts to reverse that trend in the 1990s. Chapter 5 addresses the question of whether the United States can extend its regulations to subsidiaries in the target state or whether their location makes them hostages to the host country and places them beyond the reach of U.S. sanctions. Chapter 6 examines two recent efforts to extend sanctions beyond foreign subsidiaries to wholly foreign firms through the Helms–Burton Act and the Iran–Libya Sanctions Act (ILSA). Chapter 7 asks whether nongovernmental human rights organizations can impose the equivalent of economic sanctions by inducing MNCs to withdraw from repressive regimes through transnational consumer and shareholder pressure, contrasting the antiapartheid movement in the 1980s with attempts to replicate it vis-à-vis Burma and Nigeria in the 1990s.

The findings of this study address a number of important questions central to academic debates in international political economy: To what extent have MNCs become transnational actors increasingly free of their home governments? Has the decline in American economic preponderance since the early post–World War II era diminished the effectiveness of unilateral sanctions or the leverage to induce others to cooperate with its sanctions? Or does the increasing use of extraterritorial coercion indicate a second era of American hegemony? The answers to these questions also have important policy implications. Since the end of the Cold War, the United States has increasingly relied on economic sanctions. In most cases, U.S. restrictions exceeded what its allies were willing to impose. In such circumstances, should the United States resign itself to diplomacy and persuasion, recognizing that sanctions can be no more effective than the multilateral consensus behind them? Or can unilateral pressure broaden multilateral compliance?

THE LESSONS OF THE PIPELINE SANCTIONS

The pipeline sanctions were part of the Reagan administration's "grand strategy" of reasserting U.S. power to maximize pressure on the Soviet Union. It viewed East–West projects, such as the natural gas pipeline, as freeing up resources for its adversary's expansionism and military buildup; cutting those ties would increase the cost of these policies and force the Soviets to turn inward. It also recognized that its European allies did not share this perspective and would resist the expansion of East–West trade restrictions. The Polish crisis provided the administration with the opportunity to coerce allied compliance through extraterritorial sanctions. Why did this policy fail?

The answers given by academics and policy analysts at the time drew, explicitly or implicitly, on two literatures in the international political economy subfield of international relations—theories of transnational relations and the neorealist theory of hegemonic stability. Scholars operating within these traditions have radically different views regarding the continuing relevance of sovereignty in contemporary world politics. Their analyses nonetheless agree that the United States is less able to employ unilateral sanctions—the former, because of economic globalization and the increased independence of the MNC from state control; the latter, because the proportion of economic resources controlled by the United States had diminished relative to other states.

Therefore, the pipeline sanctions were characterized as an assertion of U.S. power that was no longer sustainable given changes in the international system. Extraterritorial sanctions may have been possible in the early Cold War era because of the nationalist orientation of U.S. firms and the preponderant position of the United States in the world economy. The global spread of American business and dispersion of power in the international system constrained those capabilities, predictably frustrating the pipeline sanctions. Contemporary critics of extraterritorial sanctions assume that these conditions have not changed appreciably since the end of the Cold War—that is, economic globalization has expanded, and the United States, its military predominance notwithstanding, has not returned to its economic position in the early Cold War era. The pipeline episode is consequently cited by contemporary scholars and policy analysts to demonstrate why extraterritorial sanctions do not work.

Sanctions at Bay: Transnational Relations and Economic Statecraft

In employing extraterritorial sanctions, the Reagan administration tried to use American MNCs as conduits through which it could extend its sanctions onto the territory of allied countries that opposed U.S. policy. Implicit in this strategy is the realist view that the state is the dominant actor in world politics and its national corporations can be used as diplomatic assets. Washington could consequently "convert the multinationals and their overseas subsidiaries into instruments of American foreign policy."[2]

This premise was challenged at the time by theories of transnational relations, which argued that a growing number of important transactions across national boundaries were conducted by nonstate actors that were increasingly capable of acting independently of the states in which they are based.[3] The most prominent of these actors were the multinational corporations, whose global spread and increasingly cosmopolitan outlook increased their independence from home governments, a view that was shared by many students of the MNC in economics departments and business schools.[4] As a result, American MNCs were no longer instruments of foreign policy, but autonomous actors whose self-interested behavior could undercut strategies of economic statecraft.

This argument has been pushed further in the recent literature on globalization. As the world economy has become increasingly borderless, MNCs have become "footloose," shedding their national identity and relocating wherever they can best promote global profits.[5] This development has led many observers to question whether the self-interest of U.S.-based MNCs automatically advances national goals. Robert Reich, for example, contends that, as American multinationals establish operations abroad and their foreign counterparts invest in the United States, a firm's national identity is no longer a reliable indicator of its contribution to economic growth and employment in the United States.[6]

Parallel arguments have been made with respect to the impact of MNCs on trade and financial controls. Economic sanctions presume that a sender state can ban business between its national corporations and a target state. The globalization of American business makes this relationship less axiomatic. By locating export platforms abroad, U.S.-based MNCs have increased the proportion of commercial activity that takes place outside U.S. territory. Raymond Vernon notes that this development has weakened the impact of trade controls because these subsidiaries are wholly inside the jurisdiction of another country and "out of the control of security planners."[7] Critics of the MNC contend that this enables MNCs to practice a kind of "regulatory arbitrage" in which they can use their transnational network to evade regulations. David Korten notes that this is precisely what Halliburton did when it transferred its Libyan contracts from its Houston to its London office after the imposition of economic sanctions in 1986.[8]

Comparable developments have taken place in international finance. In the early post–World War II era, policymakers could control the flow of American capital abroad because private international lending was generally conducted by banks operating within the boundaries of states and the main source of balance of payments financing came from public sources (i.e., the International Monetary Fund, occasionally supplemented by bilateral assistance to key allies) rather than private ones. This capability was weakened by two developments. First, the emergence of the Eurocurrency market in the late 1950s created a relatively unregulated environment for private international lending. By the mid-1960s, this market had attracted a significant number of U.S. banks that moved offshore to escape U.S. tax and regulatory policy.[9] Second, those markets exploded in the 1970s when the banks recycled the Organization of Petroleum Exporting Countries's (OPEC) petrodollars to oil-importing Third World countries. The end result was what Benjamin Cohen called the "privatization of international finance," as commercial banks surpassed public institutions as the primary conduits for international capital transfers. Since these transactions took place outside the regulatory authority of the U.S. government, private financial decisions reflected calculations of risk and opportunity that were less accountable to diplomatic priorities. Cohen noted that this made it "more difficult [for Washington] to support or reward its friends or thwart or punish its enemies."[10]

While the United States encouraged these developments as consistent with its vision of a liberal world economy, it tried to retain the ability to turn the economic spigot on and off to support its diplomatic and strategic interests. One means of exercising that control was through the extraterritorial extension of American law. The Trading with the Enemy Act and Export Control Act applied U.S. regulations to the foreign subsidiaries of U.S. firms and to foreign purchasers of goods and technology that originated in the United States. Informal pressures were also placed on multinationals, ranging from moral suasion to linking cooperation to eligibility for federal contracts. The aim was to use U.S.-based MNCs as instruments of U.S. power vis-à-vis target states and allies that enacted less restrictive controls. As one former Commerce Department official wrote, "the existence of the multinational enterprise permits the U.S. government to impose its will through a private channel when it is unable to accomplish the same goal diplomatically."[11]

Much of the scholarship on MNCs indicates that the United States was more capable of obtaining private cooperation with its economic statecraft in the early postwar period because of the national orientation of U.S. investors. First, the U.S. market was clearly the most important for U.S.-based MNCs. As a result, public officials could credibly use the threat (actual or implied) of denying the affiliate access or complicating eligibility for federal contracts to secure corporate compliance.[12]

Second, U.S. investors generally adopted an ethnocentric perspective in which they saw themselves as national firms with foreign operations and identified with U.S. interests and values. They were organized to maximize control by the home office and accepted the view that all their operations, foreign as well as domestic, were subject to U.S. jurisdiction.[13] They also shared the prevailing Cold War ethic that trading with the communists was wrong and contrary to their long-term interests. Even when U.S. policy became less restrictive in the 1960s, many firms remained reticent about East–West trade. One State Department survey noted "a reluctance on the part of the American industrial community . . . [to] exploit opportunities legally open to it . . . It is as if the Bloc market has been generally accepted as a dirty market, one in which it is simply immoral to trade."[14] This predisposed MNCs to cooperate with Washington. Jack Behrman's 1970 study found that most firms not only accepted the application of sanctions to foreign subsidiaries but also voluntarily policed affiliate behavior to prevent transactions at variance with U.S. foreign policy.[15]

Much of the subsequent scholarship indicated a shift away from this ethnocentric orientation as the result of globalization. Some business scholars observed that, as foreign operations grew, the home market became just one piece in a large transnational network. Multinational corporations may have initially formed alliances with the states that chartered them, but as they took "a more global view, those alliances may prove to be no more lasting than those of nation-states."[16] This transfer of corporate loyalty has figured prominently in the more recent literature on globalization. It has also been articulated frequently by many corporate officials, such as the chief financial officer of Colgate-Palmolive who stated that "[t]here is no mindset that puts this country first."[17]

One possible outcome is that MNCs will adopt a "polycentric" perspective, identifying with the interests of the host country even when this works at cross-purposes with the aims of the home country.[18] As Vernon noted, a foreign investor places a heavy emphasis on playing the role of good corporate citizen wherever it is located because, like any outsider, it bears "the burden of demonstrating that it is not the agent of some foreign interest, public or private."[19] This was clearly evident in the response to extraterritorial sanctions, which work against the MNC's interest in expanding exports, a goal it shares with the host country. Since the 1970s, corporate trade associations have opposed extraterritorial sanctions, and home offices have increasingly sided with host countries when confronted with conflicts of jurisdiction.[20]

In addition, MNCs often equated their private interests with the stability and economic growth of the countries in which they operated. As a result, several firms acted more as conduits for host rather than home government influence, even if there was an adversarial relationship with the United States. One study found that, after détente in the 1970s, the U.S. business community made an abrupt turnaround from anti-Soviet hostility to "lobbying for relaxing restrictions on economic contacts with the Soviet Union."[21] Similarly, Louis Turner found that U.S. oil companies, when confronted with diplomatic disputes, tended to adapt to host country preferences rather than act as instruments of U.S. policy. During the 1973 oil crisis, for example, U.S. oil companies cooperated with the Arab oil embargo and lobbied the Nixon administration to adopt a less pro-Israeli approach during the 1973 Arab–Israeli war. In the 1980s, U.S. oil companies established businesslike relationships with the Marxist government in Angola and lobbied Congress to ban covert operations against the government at a time when the Reagan administration's preferences were exactly the opposite.[22]

Another alternative is that MNCs will adopt a "geocentric" perspective in which they view themselves as global enterprises with less of an identity with or loyalty to any particular government.[23] These firms seek to maximize worldwide profits and insulate those efforts from manipulation by both home and host governments. The most idealized expression of this was put forward by Carl Gerstacker, the former chairman of Dow Chemical, when he confessed his dream of establishing his corporate headquarters "on the truly neutral ground of . . . an island beholden to no nation."[24] In other words, by shedding one's national identity, MNCs can ignore national boundaries and pursue their global interests without reference to political pressures from home or host countries.

These changes in corporate mind-set make it less likely that public officials can manipulate international business activity. John Purcell's study of MNCs in Central America in the early 1980s found that U.S. investors were averse to cooperating with strategies of economic coercion because they adopted "an ideological outlook that elevates trade, finance, and investment into a generally social good that should not be tampered with lest the tampering produce distortions that would be even more harmful than the original problem."[25] Given this view, MNCs portray their foreign investments as neutral and apolitical, even when dealing with radical regimes or human rights abusers whose policies are at odds with the interests and values promoted by public officials. Chevron's president, George Keller, justified his company's presence in Marxist Angola in the 1980s by stating that it did not "constitute a political endorsement of the political actions of a particular government."[26] Multinational corporations employed similar rationales in justifying their presence in South Africa under apartheid, even during the worst period of repression in the late 1970s and mid-1980s. As a Citicorp official testified, "there is one rule for multinationals wherever they operate. The rule is: Hands Off."[27]

Private lenders adopted a comparable outlook. One survey of international bankers found "a general unwillingness to comply with any attempt by the U.S. government to instruct them on where and when to lend internationally."[28] Another study found that banks had few qualms about lending to unfriendly countries as long as they were able to service their debt. As a result, lending to Eastern Europe continued to grow in the 1970s, even as the United States became disillusioned with détente. The bottom line was that these countries were seen as good credit risks given their apparent (and illusory) stability and the presumed willingness of the Soviet Union to act as lender of last resort should they fall into trouble.[29]

These developments were cited by observers as undercutting the Reagan administration's economic warfare preferences during the Polish crisis. Private bank lending to Poland and Eastern Europe created interdependencies that transformed bankers into advocates of target state interests who favored preserving normal economic relations and claimed that financial sanctions were too risky for the world economy. Technology firms, such as Dresser Industries, tried to insulate their East–West business, such as the pipeline project, from U.S. sanctions. When regulations were applied extraterritorially, Dresser instructed its French subsidiary to ignore U.S. directives and obey the laws of its European hosts.[30] As Stephen Neff concluded, "the cosmopolitanism of the multinational companies plays an important part" in constraining the political manipulation of trade and finance.[31]

Sanctions Entangled: Hegemonic Decline and Coercive Cooperation

The extraterritorial dimensions of the pipeline sanctions represented an exercise in "coercive cooperation," extending unilateral sanctions onto the territory of allies who refused to follow the U.S. lead. The strategy was premised on the assumption that the U.S. economy was so dominant that the threat of denying access to it would induce foreign corporate compliance with U.S. directives and allied acquiescence to that outcome.

One former government official attributed the failure of these extraterritorial regulations to the changed position of the United States in the world economy:

We do have different standards from other people, and in the past we have been able to get away with them. But these days, the United States doesn't have the overwhelming clout it used to, and other nations are protecting their economic interests much more aggressively than they used to.[32]

This line of argument is consistent with the theory of hegemonic stability, which predicts that strong international laws and institutions require an economically dominant power that can either enforce the rules or compensate others for the costs of compliance. As the lead state's position of economic preponderance declines, its ability to procure cooperation with its preferences proportionately diminishes.[33]

While this model has been applied primarily to trade and monetary relations, it has also been used to study economic sanctions, particularly in cases of "coercive cooperation," in which U.S. preferences are not shared by allies.[34] One example of this is the practice of placing the foreign operations of U.S.-based MNCs within the ambit of U.S. sanctions. During the early Cold War era, this was an area in which the United States differed with its allies over questions of policy and law. In terms of policy, it sought to build a multilateral consensus behind strategies of economic warfare against communist adversaries. Its allies preferred to limit embargoes to items of direct military significance while encouraging nonstrategic trade.[35] In terms of law, the United States and its allies disagreed as to whose legal system had final authority over the foreign subsidiaries of U.S. firms. Washington asserted that the nationality of the home office gave it the right to assert jurisdiction if there was an adverse impact on important public interests (the effects doctrine) or national security (the protective principle). Europe and Canada disagreed, maintaining that jurisdiction should be determined by the territory in which a foreign subsidiary was incorporated, not by the nationality of the home country. Extraterritorial regulations were opposed as encroachments on sovereignty.[36]

Despite these differences, the United States persuaded its allies to accede to its position. The hegemonic model attributes this outcome to the U.S. position of structural hegemony, given the devastation of the European and Japanese economies and their acute dependence on the United States for economic recovery and national security. Adler-Karlsson found that the United States was able to use Western Europe's dependence on U.S. aid in the early 1950s to secure compliance with a broader embargo against the Soviet Union.[37] In a similar vein, Kobrin's study of the Trading with the Enemy Act found that allies generally acquiesced to the extraterritorial application of embargoes against targets with whom they favored trade because of their dependence on American aid, markets, and investment.[38]

By the 1970s, the United States was less able to obtain allied cooperation with its sanctions. As allies became less dependent on U.S. economic resources, they were more willing to assert their own interests rather than defer to U.S. leadership. This often meant resistance to Washington, either because allies did not share the same perceptions of threat that triggered U.S. sanctions or because they were more dependent on their foreign economic relations and did not want to jeopardize them in long-term uncertain confrontations.

Opposition to U.S. sanctions extended to the practices of the local affiliates of U.S. firms. Allies more forcefully objected to U.S. presumptions of extraterritoriality, maintaining that U.S.-based firms incorporated within their territory were local firms subject to local law. Several countries, most notably Canada and Great Britain, enacted legislation legally blocking firms on their territory, including the foreign subsidiaries of U.S. MNCs, from complying with foreign directives. Washington ultimately acceded to this view, in practice if not in theory. Kobrin's study found that, by the mid-1970s, host countries were increasingly successful in blocking the extension of U.S. embargoes to foreign subsidiaries. In 1975, this persuaded Washington to remove foreign subsidiary sanctions from the Cuban embargo and limit the territorial scope of subsequent sanctions.[39]

As a result, the failure of the pipeline sanctions can be attributed to changes in the structural position of the United States in the world economy. Unlike the 1950s, the United States lacked the economic clout to either coerce compliance or compensate the Europeans with alternative sources of energy. As a result, the Europeans thwarted the pipeline sanctions by invoking legislation that compelled American affiliates and their European consignees to disregard U.S. regulations and perform their contracts. The ensuing crisis in the alliance dissuaded the Reagan administration from extending subsequent sanctions to third country subsidiaries.[40] Some contemporary critics of extraterritorial sanctions have drawn parallel conclusions, as noted in the following critique of Helms–Burton and ILSA put forward by a former Commerce Department official: "The problem is that sanctions imply a leverage we don't have any more. In 1946, when half of all world trade went through the U.S., we could impose those kinds of controls. Today, when 14 percent goes through the United States, we can't control it."[41]

This argument suggests two other factors that constrain extraterritorial sanctions, both of which were in evidence in the pipeline case. First, hegemonic decline increases the domestic political constraints on attempts to play a leadership role in the world economy. Robert Gilpin notes that the ability of the United States to absorb the domestic political costs of policies that sacrifice short-term economic interests for the sake of the system depends on economic hegemony. When that hegemony erodes, the United States becomes less capable of preventing other states from defecting from the rules. Gilpin predicts that, as the costs of leadership exceed the benefits, "powerful groups will become less and less willing to subordinate their interests to the continuation of the system."[42]

Although Gilpin applies this model to trade liberalization, it can be extrapolated to economic sanctions. Domestic constraints on sanctions were minimal in the early postwar period because U.S. firms were technologically dominant and the U.S. market was the most important for U.S.-based firms. This changed as foreign companies became more competitive and economic opportunities abroad increased relative to those in the United States. U.S. firms came to see unilateral sanctions as ceding markets to foreign competitors without imposing meaningful costs on target states. The routine use of extraterritorial sanctions was also seen as costly because U.S. business could be branded by potential partners as unreliable and excluded from many international ventures because of the political risk of unpredictable U.S. sanctions. It may also legitimize discrimination against U.S. investors abroad since they will be seen in host countries as instruments of a U.S. political agenda at the expense of the host country's economic development goals.

As a result, corporate trade associations became more aggressive in using the political system to set limits on the exercise of sanctions. This was evident during the Polish crisis, when the American business community lobbied heavily against the pipeline sanctions and the House of Representatives came within three votes of overturning them.[43] Shortly thereafter, they succeeded in persuading Congress to amend the Export Administration Act to make it more difficult for the president to abrogate contracts, even during a declared embargo.[44] Therefore, the hegemonic decline model predicts increased interest group and congressional limits on unilateral and extraterritorial sanctions.

A second consequence of hegemonic decline, which will purportedly constrain extraterritorial sanctions, is the increased dependence of the United States on international institutions in areas where it is less capable of achieving objectives on its own. Writing shortly after the pipeline sanctions, Kenneth Oye noted that "In a world of declining American unilateral power, greater reliance on multilateral strategies becomes a necessity."[45] Extraterritorial coercion, however, can be corrosive of those institutions. Michael Mastanduno's study of East–West trade found that the pipeline sanctions strained the cohesiveness of the Atlantic alliance and complicated negotiations to strengthen multilateral controls over technologies that contributed to Soviet military capabilities, an aim which the United States and its allies shared.[46]

Critics of the more recent wave of extraterritorial sanctions have cited comparable impacts on international institutions, particularly in the areas of nonproliferation and trade. Cooperation in the former (e.g., controls over technology associated with ballistic missiles or weapons of mass destruction) represents an area of multilateral consensus that is likely to be frayed by attempts to use coercion in areas where interests are incompatible (e.g., trying to coerce Europeans into energy sanctions vis-à-vis Iran). International trade institutions are weakened when the United States establishes precedents (e.g., extraterritorial jurisdiction and secondary boycotts) that it has condemned when employed by others and refuses to accept international adjudication when challenged.[47] Therefore, the need to preserve and strengthen multilateral institutions ought to set limits on unilateral coercion.

TESTING THE GLOBALIZATION
AND HEGEMONIC DECLINE MODELS

The model depicted in the previous section posits the U.S. government can no longer unilaterally enlist the foreign operations of MNCs as agents of economic pressure. Washington can only succeed in such efforts by building a multilateral consensus that harmonizes economic strategies, as happened with the United Nations' sanctions against Iraq (1990) and Yugoslavia (1993), the Libyan air and arms embargo (1991), and the Haitian oil embargo (1994). Absent that consensus, attempts to apply sanctions beyond borders will be constrained by economic globalization and hegemonic decline. The former has increased the ability and willingness of MNCs to pursue their global economic objectives without reference to their home countries. The latter has increased the countervailing power of host countries to block extraterritorial measures. The analysis above also suggests that attempts to defy these constraints and apply extraterritorial sanctions are likely to trigger domestic opposition and weaken multilateral institutions.

Most observers predicted that these factors would lead the United States to rein in the territorial scope of its sanctions. Much of the evidence in part II supports this prediction. For the most part, the executive branch crafted its postpipeline sanctions to avoid contentious conflicts of jurisdiction. As a result, U.S. MNCs were legally free to act as profit-maximizing transnational actors pursuing their global interests in ways that often worked at cross-purposes with official policy.

Yet there has also been an expansion of extraterritorial sanctions, particularly in the 1990s. In fact, the scope and rigidity of these new measures went beyond what had been done at the zenith of U.S. economic power. In 1992, the Cuban Democracy Act reimposed the Cuban embargo on foreign subsidiaries, denying the executive branch any discretionary authority. In 1996, the Helms–Burton law and the Iran–Libya Sanctions Act took the unprecedented step of extending sanctions to foreign companies with no connection to U.S. persons or technology. The Panamanian and Haitian sanctions sought to reach direct investors in the target states themselves. Pressures on multinationals were also applied by grassroots human rights organizations through consumer and shareholder pressure. Even states and localities tried to reach corporate conduct abroad by linking eligibility for municipal contracts to withdrawal from repressive regimes.

While many of these efforts were frustrated by globalization, they also elicited a greater degree of corporate compliance than would have been predicted in the 1980s. Both formal and informal attempts to reach foreign subsidiaries usually succeeded in cutting off their third country trade with target states. Direct investors within target states initially complied with U.S. directives, at least until they were blocked from doing so by host countries. Secondary sanctions have chilled the business climate in Iran and in Cuba for non-U.S. investors with significant stakes in the United States. Nongovernmental pressures elicited substantial corporate disengagement from South Africa in the 1980s and altered some corporate practices in Burma and Nigeria.

These outcomes raise questions about the theoretical perspectives that inform the lessons of the pipeline sanctions, even if they do not necessarily refute the policy argument against extraterritorial sanctions. First, the findings of this study challenge hegemonic explanation of extraterritorial sanctions. The case studies in part I demonstrate that it overstates the willingness and ability of the United States to enforce its jurisdictional claims even at the height of its economic power. The problem with the hegemonic interpretation is that it applies what David Baldwin calls a "power-as-resources" model, assuming that concentrated resources automatically translate into economic leverage.[48] Yet the United States was reluctant to exercise this leverage because the rules governing East–West trade were only one part of a larger architecture of interests and institutions the United States sought to construct and preserve in the postwar period. As a result, successive administrations favored discreet compromises over unilateral enforcement.[49] In that sense, the Reagan administration's pipeline sanctions represented a departure from traditional diplomatic priorities, not a return to the bygone days of American hegemony.

In addition, the extraterritorial sanctions of the 1990s have secured significant private compliance—terminating foreign subsidiary trade with Cuba and deterring many non-U.S. firms from investing in Cuba and Iran. These findings support those critics of the hegemonic model who contend that it overstates the decline of U.S. economic power even if the United States no longer occupies the same position in the world economy that it did in an earlier era.[50] The United States has the largest and most open economy in the world; the threat of denying access to it or penalizing behavior within it is still a powerful deterrent to U.S. and even foreign companies considering proscribed transactions.

Second, domestic politics provides a better explanation of both the use of extraterritorial sanctions and their likely success than does structural position of the United States in the world economy. In the early days of the Chinese and Cuban embargoes, the United States sought compromise over enforcement because an open dispute with allies would have aroused anticommunist public and congressional sentiment and increased the momentum for legislated reprisals against allies who "traded with the enemy." To avoid damaging confrontations, extraterritorial disputes were settled discreetly with the United States granting waivers from the sanctions in most cases while maintaining its legal right to assert jurisdiction.

Nonetheless, very little foreign subsidiary trade with China or Cuba materialized—less due to the threat of official retaliation than to the risks in the U.S. market given the intensity of anticommunist sentiment. Actively pursuing this trade could have made them targets for policy entrepreneurs in Congress, which was, in the words of one scholar, the "hardest driving force in the embargo policy."[51] Many firms were also deterred by public opinion and the risk of becoming targets of organized protests and boycotts. In 1964, for example, Firestone Tire and Rubber backed out of a deal with the Romanian government to build a rubber plant because of an organized campaign by the Young Americans for Freedom, which included picketing, pressure on dealers to boycott Firestone products, and the threat of a spectacular demonstration against the company at the Indianapolis 500.[52] While such actions emerged independently of, and sometimes against the wishes of the State Department (as in the Firestone case), they did provide an additional inhibition against "trading with the enemy."

What changed in the 1970s was not so much the decline of U.S. economic power as the changes in the domestic political landscape—that is, the Cold War ethic lost its irrefutability in the American political system as a result of the Vietnam War and détente. As a result, allies and private actors were more willing to challenge extraterritorial sanctions because of the decreased likelihood of reprisals by Congress or by U.S. consumers. The U.S. business community was also more willing to lobby against unilateral and extraterritorial sanctions because of the decreased stigma attached to East–West trade, and it found a more receptive audience in the U.S. Congress. In contrast to the early Cold War period, domestic pressures induced the executive branch to limit rather than expand jurisdictional claims because of the concern that repeated confrontations with allies might lead, not to legislated reprisals, but to efforts to limit its discretionary sanctions powers.

The resurgence of extraterritorial sanctions in the 1990s can also be attributed to domestic politics—that is, the role of ethnic lobbies, public concerns about terrorism, and a Congress that places less of a premium on alliance re-

lations with the end of the Cold War.[53] This increased activism on sanctions issues has placed pressures on the executive branch comparable to those in the
1950s and 1960s in seeking compromise formulas to assuage both legislators
and allies. Despite administration waivers, the laws had a deterrent impact on
many MNCs because the strength of the domestic coalitions behind the sanctions made credible the likelihood of penalties for proscribed behavior.

Third, the case studies indicate a need to qualify the view that MNCs have
become stateless actors for whom global economic rationality has replaced
national loyalty. For the most part, MNCs did view sanctions from a cosmopolitan rather than an ethnocentric perspective and opposed politicizing business with adversaries. Nonetheless, MNCs were generally more reluctant to
use their global networks to escape home state sanctions regulations than they
have been in relocating to minimize tax liabilities or shift production to more
favorable business climates.[54]

The reason lies in considerations of domestic political risk. If MNCs go
offshore to evade sanctions, they are still subject to U.S. law. The formal
penalty for defying the law, denying the affiliate access to the U.S. market,
"is a powerful incentive for good behavior on the part of corporate actors."[55]
Even without formal sanctions, MNCs may not veer too far from U.S. diplomatic preferences because they rely on the government for federal contracts
and for advancing their interests through negotiating market access or debt re-
structurings. Flouting intensely held public sentiments could create problems
with consumers, shareholders, and workers—providing a means through
which Washington could use the threat of adverse publicity to elicit compliance. As a result, MNCs often act more as risk minimizers than as global
profit maximizers, neither lobbying against or actively resisting public initiatives. This provides a means through which political actors can increase the
coincidence between corporate practices and their preferences.[56]

Finally, a strong case can be made that economic interdependence renders
extraterritorial sanctions both ineffective and costly. They are ineffective because those firms influenced by U.S. sanctions can usually be replaced by alternative suppliers less vulnerable to political risk in the U.S. market. They
are costly because they compromise U.S. leadership in multilateral institutions, such as alliances, nonproliferation supplier groups, and the World Trade
Organization (WTO). They also impose reciprocity costs (i.e., setting precedents the United States would oppose if practiced by others) and reputational
costs, principally on the U.S. business community whose reputation for reliability is called into question, both as a business partner and as a good corporate citizen of the host country.

These considerations usually dissuaded the executive branch (excluding
the early Reagan administration) from practicing extraterritorial coercion,

even at the height of American hegemony when the United States was purportedly better able to achieve its objectives unilaterally. Domestic political imperatives, however, often overrode interdependence concerns. This is because congressional sanctions proponents and their domestic constituencies dismissed the costs of coercion to alliance relations and multilateral institutions. When those societal pressures were most intense (anticommunist sentiment in the 1950s and 1960s; interest group pressures and public concerns about terrorism in the 1990s), the executive branch had to accommodate them. This posed a recurring dilemma for administrations from Truman through Clinton in trying to reconcile congressional and societal pressure to get tough with allies that "trade with the enemy" with the costs of extraterritorial coercion to alliance relationships and multilateral institutions.

NOTES

1. The quotation is from Gideon Rose, "Bully-Boy Foreign Policy," *New York Times*, 18 July 1996, A23.

2. Robert Gilpin, *U.S. Power and the Multinational Corporation: The Political Economy of Foreign Direct Investment* (New York: BasicBooks, 1975), 139.

3. See Robert O. Keohane and Joseph S. Nye, eds., *Transnational Relations and World Politics* (Cambridge, Mass.: Harvard University Press, 1971); and Richard W. Mansbach, Yale H. Ferguson, and Donald E. Lampert, *The Web of World Politics: Nonstate Actors in the Global System* (Englewood Cliffs, N.J.: Prentice Hall, 1976). For more recent work, see Thomas Risse-Kappen, ed., *Bringing Transnational Relations Back In: Non-State Actors, Domestic Structures, and International Institutions* (Cambridge, U.K.: Cambridge University Press, 1995).

4. See Charles P. Kindleberger, *American Business Abroad: Six Lectures on Direct Investment* (New Haven, Conn.: Yale University Press, 1969); and Raymond Vernon, *Storm over the Multinationals: The Real Issues* (Cambridge, Mass.: Harvard University Press, 1977).

5. This empirical argument has been made by some of the most enthusiastic proponents of the MNC and some of its severest critics. See Kenichi Ohmae, *The Borderless World: Power and Strategy in the Interlinked Economy* (New York: Harper Business, 1990); and David C. Korten, *When Corporations Rule the World* (West Hartford, Conn.: Kumarian Press, 1996).

6. Robert B. Reich, "Who Is Us?" *Harvard Business Review* 68 (January/February 1990): 53–64.

7. Vernon, *Storm over the Multinationals*, 105.

8. Korten, *When Corporations Rule the World*, 127. Also see Peter Willetts, "Transnational Actors and International Organizations in Global Politics," in *The Globalization of World Politics: An Introduction to International Relations*, eds. John Baylis and Steve Smith (Oxford, U.K.: Oxford University Press, 1997), 294.

9. Benjamin J. Cohen, *In Whose Interest? International Banking and American Foreign Policy* (New Haven, Conn.: Yale University Press, 1986), 19–26.

10. Cohen, *In Whose Interest?*, 73; and Cohen, "Balance of Payments Financing: The Evolution of a Regime," in *International Regimes*, ed. Stephen D. Krasner (Ithaca, N.Y.: Cornell University Press, 1984), 329.

11. Jack N. Behrman, *National Interests and the Multinational Enterprise: Tensions among North Atlantic Countries* (Englewood Cliffs, N.J.: Prentice Hall, 1970), 102.

12. Harold J. Berman and John R. Garson, "United States Export Controls—Past, Present, Future," *Columbia Law Review* 67 (May 1967): 851–853.

13. Howard V. Perlmutter, "The Tortuous Evolution of the Multinational Corporation," *Columbia Journal of World Business* 4 (January–February 1969): 11.

14. U.S. Department of State, Policy Planning Council, *U.S. Policy on Trade with the European Soviet Bloc* (26 July 1963): 46. Lyndon Baines Johnson Library, National Security Files (LBJ/NSF), Subject Files, East–West Trade, U.S. Policy on Trade with European Soviet Bloc 7/26/63, Box 310.

15. Behrman, *National Interests and the Multinational Enterprise*, 104.

16. Louis T. Wells, "The Multinational Business Enterprise: What Kind of International Organization?" in *Transnational Relations and World Politics*, eds. Keohane and Nye (Cambridge Mass.: Harvard University Press, 1971), 113.

17. *New York Times*, 21 May 1989, A1.

18. Perlmutter, "The Tortuous Evolution of the Multinational Corporation," 13.

19. Vernon, *Storm over the Multinationals*, 175.

20. See Stephen J. Kobrin, "Enforcing Export Embargoes through Multinational Corporations: Why Doesn't It Work Anymore?" *Business in the Contemporary World* 1 (winter 1989): 38; and Erik Lindell, "Foreign Policy Export Controls and American Multinational Corporations," *California Management Review* 28 (summer 1986): 38.

21. C. Fred Bergsten, Thomas Horst, and Theodore H. Moran, *American Multinationals and American Interests* (Washington, D.C.: Brookings Institution, 1976), 444.

22. Louis Turner, *Oil Companies in the International System*, 3d ed. (Winchester, Mass.: Allen and Unwin, 1983), 133–148, 229–230.

23. Perlmutter, "The Tortuous Evolution of the Multinational Corporation," 14.

24. Richard J. Barnet and Ronald E. Muller, *Global Reach: The Power of the Multinational Corporations* (New York: Touchstone, 1974), 16.

25. John F. H. Purcell, "The Perceptions and Interests of United States Business in Relation to the Political Crisis in Central America," in *Central America: International Dimensions of the Crisis*, ed. Richard E. Feinberg (New York: Homes and Meier, 1982), 112.

26. "The Ideological Battle at Chevron's Annual Meeting," *Business and Society Review* 59 (fall 1986): 41.

27. Testimony of George Vojta in U.S. Congress, House Committee on International Relations, *U.S. Private Investment in South Africa,* 95th Congress, 1st sess., 1978, 395.

28. J. Andrew Spindler, *The Politics of International Credit: Private Finance and Foreign Policy in Germany and Japan* (Washington, D.C.: Brookings Institution, 1984), 201.

29. Claude Singer, "The Political Morality of Lending to Nonfriendly Nations," *Banker's Magazine* 165 (November–December 1982), 21–22.

30. Kobrin, "Enforcing Export Embargoes through Multinational Corporations," 38.

31. Stephen C. Neff, *Friends But No Allies: Economic Liberalism and the Law of Nations* (New York: Columbia University Press, 1990), 212.

32. Statement by Douglas Rosenthal in *New York Times*, 17 August 1983, D1; for scholarly versions of this argument see Kobrin, "Enforcing Export Embargoes through

Multinational Corporations," and Kenneth W. Abbott, "Collective Goods, Mobile Resources, and Extraterritorial Trade Controls," *Law and Contemporary Problems* 50 (summer 1987): 121–127.

33. See Robert O. Keohane, "The Theory of Hegemonic Stability and Changes in International Economic Regimes, 1967–1977," in *Change in the International System*, eds. Ole R. Holsti, Randolph M. Siverson, and Alexander George (Boulder, Colo.: Westview, 1980), 131–162.

34. For studies that test hegemonic interpretations of U.S. sanctions, see Lisa Martin, *Coercive Cooperation: Explaining Multilateral Economic Sanctions* (Princeton, N.J.: Princeton University Press, 1992); and George E. Shambaugh IV, *States, Firms, and Power: Successful Sanctions in United States Foreign Policy* (Albany, N.Y.: SUNY Press, 1999).

35. Michael Mastanduno, *Economic Containment: CoCom and the Politics of East-West Trade* (Ithaca, N.Y.: Cornell University Press, 1992), 40–52.

36. "Extraterritorial Subsidiary Jurisdiction," *Law and Contemporary Problems* 50 (summer 1987): 72–89.

37. Gunnar Adler-Karlsson, *Western Economic Warfare, 1947–1967: A Case Study of Foreign Economic Policy* (Stockholm: Almqvist & Wiksell, 1968), 45–49.

38. Kobrin, "Enforcing Export Embargoes through Multinational Corporations," 31.

39. Kobrin, "Enforcing Export Embargoes through Multinational Corporations," 37–38.

40. Barry E. Carter, *International Economic Sanctions: Improving the Haphazard U.S. Legal Regime* (New York: Cambridge University Press, 1988), 83–85, 253.

41. Statement by David Rothkopf, cited in David E. Sanger, "Diplomacy's Erratic Hit Man: The Dollar," *New York Times*, 24 May 1998, sec. IV, 5.

42. Robert Gilpin, *The Political Economy of International Relations* (Princeton, N.J.: Princeton University Press, 1987), 73.

43. Bruce W. Jentleson, *Pipeline Politics: The Complex Political Economy of East-West Energy Trade* (Ithaca, N.Y.: Cornell University Press, 1986), 204–207.

44. *Congressional Quarterly Weekly Report*, 29 June 1985, 1302.

45. Kenneth A. Oye, introduction to *Eagle Resurgent? The Reagan Era in American Foreign Policy*, by Kenneth A. Oye, Robert J. Lieber, and Donald Rothchild (Boston: Little, Brown, 1987), 24.

46. Mastanduno, *Economic Containment*, 278–287.

47. See Richard N. Haass, ed., *Economic Sanctions and American Diplomacy* (New York: Council on Foreign Relations, 1998), 207.

48. David A. Baldwin, "Power Analysis and World Politics: New Trends versus Old Tendencies," *World Politics* 31 (January 1979): 193.

49. For a parallel argument on East–West trade, see Michael Mastanduno, "Trade as a Strategic Weapon: American and Alliance Export Control Policy in the Early Post-War Period," *International Organization* 42 (winter 1988): 148–149.

50. See Bruce Russett, "The Mysterious Case of Vanishing Hegemony or Is Mark Twain Really Dead?" *International Organization* 39 (spring 1985): 207–231; Susan Strange, "The Persistent Myth of Lost Hegemony," *International Organization* 41 (autumn 1987): 551–574.

51. Adler-Karlsson, *Western Economic Warfare*, 35.

52. Marshall Goldman, *Détente and Dollars: Doing Business with the Soviets* (New York: BasicBooks, 1975), 64–66.

53. See Kinka Gerke, "The Transatlantic Rift over Cuba: The Damage Is Done," *International Spectator* 32 (April–June 1997): 28.

54. See Vivien A. Schmidt, "The New World Order, Incorporated: The Rise of Business and the Decline of the Nation State," *Daedalus* 124 (spring 1995): 78–79.

55. Ethan B. Kapstein, "We Are Us: The Myth of the Multinational," *National Interest* 26 (winter 1991): 59.

56. Stephen D. Krasner, *Defending the National Interest: Raw Material Investments and U.S. Foreign Policy* (Princeton, N.J.: Princeton University Press, 1978), 75–82.

Part One

EXTRATERRITORIAL SANCTIONS FROM THE EARLY COLD WAR ERA THROUGH THE PIPELINE SANCTIONS

Chapter One

Extraterritorial Sanctions: Policy Rationales and Legal Controversies

During the early postwar period, American policymakers encouraged the overseas expansion of U.S. corporations in the expectation that the unfettered pursuit of their global interests would support important foreign policy goals. Toward this end, the United States played a leadership role in promoting and sustaining liberal international economic regimes designed to dismantle national barriers to trade and investment. Consequently, multinational corporations and banks became the world's dominant economic actors in transferring capital, technology, and goods and services across national boundaries. From the vantage point of the American objective of promoting an efficient and interdependent world economy, such an outcome was a considerable success.

Efficiency and interdependence, however, were not the only aims of U.S. economic statecraft. Since World War II, the United States became, in the words of one scholar, "the most prominent practitioner of peacetime restrictions on trade and other economic transactions."[1] These restrictive practices grew out of another leadership role the United States played after the Second World War—that is, containing the expansion of the Soviet Union and its allies. Therefore, while the United States was dismantling restrictions on trade with allies, it was erecting political barriers to trade with adversaries. Success in the former, however, created problems for the latter. America's principal allies and trading partners usually imposed less restrictive trade controls than did the United States. In theory, this made controls more porous, either through foreign firms transshipping technology purchased from the United States or by U.S. firms evading controls by relocating abroad.

Washington's solution to this dilemma was to apply its embargoes and export controls extraterritorially to cover the foreign subsidiaries of U.S. firms and U.S.-origin technology and know-how even after they left the U.S. boundaries. This chapter presents the policy rationales behind and the statutory basis for extending sanctions beyond the borders of the United States. It concludes with a discussion of the controversies between the United States and its allies over the legitimacy of U.S. efforts to apply its regulations to private activities in other sovereign jurisdictions.

EXTRATERRITORIAL SANCTIONS: POLICY AND LEGAL RATIONALES

The practice of extraterritorial sanctions grew out of U.S. differences with its allies in two areas: (1) the extensiveness of export controls against the Soviet Union and Eastern Europe, and (2) the comprehensive embargoes against the People's Republic of China and Castro's Cuba. Since the United States was unwilling or unable to coerce the compliance of its allies, extraterritorial sanctions were seen as a second-best solution. Extending jurisdiction would use MNCs to broaden the sanctions unilaterally by covering activities on the territory of allies that did not enact parallel restrictions.

Export Controls

Alliance differences over East–West trade can be traced back to late 1947 as the Truman administration moved from strategies of economic defense (i.e., restrictions on exports of direct military significance) to economic warfare (i.e., extending restrictions to all exports that would contribute to economic growth). The decision to broaden the scope of the controls was made at the 17 December 1947 meeting of the National Security Council (NSC), which recommended "the immediate termination, for an indefinite period, of shipment from the United States to the USSR . . . which would contribute to Soviet military potential."[2] On 1 March 1948, the Commerce Department implemented this new policy. U.S. exporters were required to obtain validated licenses for exports to all European destinations. The scope of the controls was expanded beyond items of direct military significance to anything that contributed to Soviet economic growth.[3] The purpose of the new controls was to "inflict the greatest economic injury to the USSR and its satellites."[4]

In order to implement this strategy, the Truman administration persuaded Congress to pass the Export Control Act in February 1949. It delegated to the executive branch sweeping powers to restrict exports for reasons of national security (limiting the military potential of the Soviet Union), foreign policy (to signal disapproval of or punish specific actions), or short supply. The national security controls included not only goods and technology of direct military significance, but anything that contributed to Soviet industrial growth, thereby freeing resources for the military. The Commerce Department was directed to establish a Commodity Control List, which identified by destination those items that required a validated license for export. Unauthorized exports were subject to heavy administrative and criminal penalties left entirely to the discretion of the executive branch. Ironically, the same government that sought to dismantle political barriers to international trade transformed "what had traditionally been a right to export [into] . . . a privilege, even in peacetime, to be granted by the government."[5]

The effectiveness of this policy required allied cooperation, particularly if it aimed to control exports that contributed to Soviet economic growth, for which the United States was not, as in the case of militarily significant technology, the sole or dominant supplier. As a result, the United States began negotiations with allies to coordinate a multilateral embargo. This resulted in the creation of CoCom, an intergovernmental group of fifteen countries, which included all members of the North Atlantic Treaty Organization (NATO) except Iceland, and Japan. Its purpose was to harmonize national controls on the export of technology that contributed to Soviet military potential.[6]

The United States succeeded in using CoCom to build a multilateral agreement to control items of direct military importance. That consensus fell short of U.S. preferences in two important areas. First, the Europeans construed the strategic embargo narrowly, resisting inclusion of nonstrategic goods banned by the United States because of the importance of East–West trade for their economies. Secretary of State Dean Acheson expressed disappointment at this because "industrial potential cannot be separated from war potential."[7] Second, the resources and attention devoted by allies to monitoring and enforcement were considerably less than what Washington deemed to be adequate. Intelligence reports indicated significant leakage of CoCom-controlled goods through European allies and neutrals.[8]

This posed a dilemma for U.S. economic statecraft. Without multilateral agreement on nonstrategic trade, economic warfare strategies would penalize U.S. exporters without imposing significant costs on the Soviet bloc. Without tough enforcement, even the strategic embargo would be weakened. The United States lacked the ability to resolve this dilemma through international institutions since CoCom was "an informal and voluntary arrangement," not a "treaty or agreement that obligates the participants internationally."[9] As a result, the United States could not expand the coverage of the CoCom embargo list without unanimous consent. Nor could it rely on CoCom to police the enforcement policies of its allies because it lacked any compliance mechanism other than voluntary cooperation. Exclusive reliance on multilateralism meant that the controls would be no stronger than their weakest link.

One unilateral option that was considered was coercion—that is, using America's position of economic dominance to link reconstruction aid to compliance with U.S. export control. This was advocated by many members of Congress and was the premise underlying the Mutual Defense Assistance Control Act of 1951 (the Battle Act), which linked financial aid to strategic trade. It was also supported by some members of the executive branch, most notably the Commerce Department and the Joint Chiefs of Staff.[10]

The coercive option was opposed by the State Department and ultimately rejected by the Truman administration. First, economic recovery was the primary focus of European containment, which, according to a State Department study, should take "precedence over efforts to weaken potential enemies in any case in which these purposes conflict."[11] Given the vital contribution of the Marshall Plan to this objective—and the importance of East–West trade for Western European economies—the actual implementation of linkage would have been self-defeating.[12]

Second, policymakers believed it was necessary to "avoid injecting an element of coercion into the negotiations" because they feared that this would create resentments that would disrupt alliance cohesion. This could hamper not only political and military cooperation, but also whatever level of cooperation on East–West trade was attainable through diplomacy. "If [allied] cooperation is given unwillingly," one State Department study noted, "enforcement of the controls will be negligible and inefficient."[13] Acheson reluctantly concluded that "In view of [the] much greater importance [of] East–West trade to Western Europe than [to] the US and [its] significance to [the] success of [the] ERP [European Recovery Program] it is essential to maintain at this time the long-established principle that US controls may have to be more restrictive than Western European [controls]."[14] As one historian concluded, "the political needs of the Alliance would prevail over export control aims."[15]

There were still limits to an exclusive reliance on multilateralism, particularly given the implications of the liberalized economic order on intra-Western trade. If the United States depended only on its allies' controls, then it could not prevent the transshipment of U.S. goods and technology imported by foreign firms whose home countries had narrower embargo lists or weaker enforcement. Nor could it prevent the relocation of U.S. industries offshore to escape accountability from the export control system. As a result, it would be more difficult to prevent the private interest of U.S. firms from increasing Soviet bloc economic capabilities.

The solution to this problem was to employ another unilateral option, namely the application of the regulations extraterritorially through what became known as reexport controls. Under the Export Control Act, all U.S. exporters were required to obtain written assurances from their foreign customers that they would not divert U.S.-origin items to prohibited destinations without U.S. authorization and that they would require similar obligations from any other purchaser of these goods. Those commitments applied not only to direct transshipment, but also to foreign-made goods that incorporated U.S.-origin parts, components, or technical data. While the United States could not attach criminal penalties to the activities of foreign firms, it could impose severe administrative penalties, such as blacklisting them from the U.S. market, "in effect telling foreign firms, we can deny you the opportunity to deal in U.S. products unless you play by our rules."[16] The United States thereby extended its jurisdiction abroad by requiring foreign firms to contractually submit to U.S. prohibitions on transactions that were legal in their home countries.

The reexport control system was designed as a unilateral alternative to coercion in broadening the strategic embargo. A State Department report argued that it was necessary to complement voluntary cooperation with allies with a licensing system in order "to assure that no shipment by the United States will result in greater availability to the Soviet Bloc of a strategic item."[17] As a result, private activities of American exporters and their European customers would be made to comport with U.S. strategy even if they took place outside U.S. territory. Or, as one Commerce Department official noted, export controls were to be utilized to "fight a cold war, and police the world, and using the American exporter as the medium by which you do that policing."[18]

Comprehensive Embargoes against China and Cuba

A second category of extraterritorial sanctions was the extension of the Chinese and Cuban embargoes to the foreign subsidiaries of U.S. firms. In both cases, the United States imposed comprehensive embargoes while its allies favored nonstrategic trade. Extraterritorial regulations were designed to prevent U.S. firms from frustrating the sanctions by moving offshore.

The statutory basis for extending sanctions to foreign subsidiaries was the Trading with the Enemy Act (TWEA). Enacted in 1917, TWEA granted the president virtually unlimited discretion to intervene in commercial or financial transactions during wars and, after President Roosevelt's "bank holiday" in 1933, national emergencies. Section 5(b) of TWEA applies its strictures to "any person or . . . property subject to the jurisdiction of the United States." During the Second World War, the Treasury Department interpreted this language as a grant of authority to extend its embargo against the Axis to subsidiaries in neutral countries if they are owned and controlled by U.S. citizens or corporations.[19] This jurisdictional claim went beyond the scope of the Export Control Act, where the legal nexus was goods and technology originating in the United States. Under TWEA, sanctions applied to any U.S.-controlled firm incorporated abroad even if it was dealing only in foreign-origin goods.[20]

The first Cold War application of this policy took place in response to China's entry into the Korean War. Until then, China had been subject to the same restrictions as the Soviet Union and Eastern Europe. This changed on 16 December 1950 when President Truman declared a national emergency and issued an executive order imposing sanctions against China and North Korea through TWEA. On the next day, Treasury issued the Foreign Assets Controls Regulations (FACRs), which prohibited U.S. firms located anywhere from trading with China without a license from the Office of Foreign Assets Control (OFAC) at Treasury, which administered the FACRs and subsequent TWEA controls. These licenses were routinely denied because Washington's aim was the complete economic and moral isolation of China from the West. As one OFAC director wrote, "it is not our policy to license Kleenex or anything else to be sold to Communist China."[21]

The United States was initially successful in persuading its allies to join the Chinese embargo in the early 1950s. The Europeans and Japanese initially resisted, but China's intervention in the Korean War persuaded them, in September 1952, to move toward U.S. preferences for economic warfare. The result was the creation of the China Committee (CHINCOM), a new institution to monitor the Chinese embargo. Even after the CoCom was liberalized in August 1954, there was no reduction of embargo lists for China and North Korea. As a result, CHINCOM controlled roughly two hundred items not embargoed to the Soviet Union and Eastern Europe, a list that became known as the "China Differential."[22]

The consensus behind the China Differential dissolved in the mid-1950s. Great Britain argued that it had lost its strategic meaning with the end of hostilities in Korea and its economic significance since nonstrategic goods banned by CHINCOM could be transshipped to China through the Soviet Union. The policy was also politically counterproductive because it forced China into greater dependence on the Soviet Union, delaying any tendencies toward a Sino–Soviet rift. Citing the importance of the China trade for its Asian colonies, Britain submitted numerous petitions for exemptions and called for a reduction of controls down to CoCom levels.[23] The United States still defended the China Differential, arguing that it delegitimized China, provided political reassurance to Asian allies, and added costs to China's industrial growth.[24] Washington was therefore unwilling to move as far in liberalizing the controls as its allies preferred. On 27 May 1957, London announced its unilateral withdrawal from CHINCOM and the rest of the allies followed suit shortly thereafter.[25] As a result, the United States was alone in continuing a strategy of economic warfare.

The second major case of extraterritorial sanctions was the Cuban embargo. The United States initiated its policy of economic pressure against Castro's Cuba on 6 July 1960, when the Eisenhower administration suspended Cuba's sugar quota in response to the nationalization of U.S.-owned oil refineries. On 19 October 1960, the United States banned the export of all goods to Cuba except food and medicine. On 3 February 1962, the sanctions were expanded to cover Cuban imports. Finally, on 8 July 1963, the Cuban embargo was placed under the authority of TWEA and the Treasury Department issued the Cuban Asset Control Regulations (CACRs).[26]

The purpose of the sanctions was economic warfare, targeting any transaction that contributed to Cuban economic growth. The resultant deprivation would stimulate political opposition to the Castro regime, precipitating its destabilization and eventual overthrow. Even if that aim could not be accomplished, sanctions would promote important secondary goals. Imposing harm on the Cuban economy would serve containment objectives by reducing the resources available to the Cuban government to promote revolution in Latin America. The Soviet Union would also have to bear a higher cost for subsidizing a client regime in the Western Hemisphere.[27]

An effective denial program, however, required multilateral coordination, even against a country as dependent on the U.S. economy as was prerevolutionary Cuba. As in the China embargo, the United States achieved only partial compliance with its preferences. It was most successful in Latin America. After the discovery of a Cuban arms cache in Venezuela, it persuaded the Organization of American States (OAS) in 1964 to sever diplomatic relations and ban all trade except food and medicine. Its NATO allies and Japan, however, limited their restrictions to strategic goods and continued to encourage civilian trade.[28]

U.S. policymakers consequently wanted to reach U.S. firms operating in nonparticipating countries. The Cuban regulations, however, did not explicitly cover foreign subsidiaries out of deference to allied sensitivities about extraterritorial sanctions. The impact of this exemption, however, was more form than substance. The law may not have formally covered subsidiaries, but it did apply to U.S. citizens who were directors, officers, or managers of the subsidiary if they had the ability to prevent a Cuban transaction.[29] Therefore, the CACRs tried to achieve the same extraterritorial ends through means less overtly offensive to the sovereignty of allied host countries.

The purpose of extraterritorial sanctions in both cases was to prevent U.S. firms from sidestepping U.S. regulations by operating in countries that encouraged trade with China and Cuba. One concern was the principle of equitable treatment of U.S. citizens—that is, the law should treat all U.S. companies in a nondiscriminatory manner whether they are operating at home or abroad. As one legal scholar explained it, there is a "desire to prevent one American from profiting from trade deemed to be against the national interest which another American is not allowed to engage in."[30] There was also the issue of diplomatic symbolism. If U.S. firms operating abroad were allowed to trade with China or Cuba, it would confer legitimacy to regimes that the United States sought to stigmatize as beyond the pale. It would also undercut containment in Asia and Latin America by demoralizing anticommunist allies and calling into question the U.S. commitment to come to their defense.[31]

Extraterritorial sanctions had instrumental as well as symbolic rationales. Foremost was the concern about transshipment. One former State Department lawyer testified that without extraterritorial jurisdiction, firms could do "the kind of shopping for a favorable legal climate that we have with flag of convenience shipping or offshore trusts."[32] This could seriously undercut the effectiveness of sanctions, particularly in the Cuban case, given that country's heavy reliance on U.S.-made goods before the revolution. Moreover, extending laws to subsidiaries provided a conduit through which the U.S. government could enhance the effectiveness of its unilateral measures since control over the behavior of subsidiaries might translate into control over the behavior of their foreign customers. As one observer noted, "If the U.S. can use its power over the headquarters of an MNC to control a subsidiary's trade, it may be able to extend its reach extraterritorially to ensure that actors within another state comply with American objectives."[33] As in the case of reexport controls, foreign subsidiary sanctions were seen as a way of enhancing the effectiveness of unilateral measures beyond what was attainable through multilateral diplomacy.

CONFLICTING INTERPRETATIONS
OF INTERNATIONAL RULES

The United States saw extraterritorial sanctions as means of preventing the global activities of American business from frustrating its export controls and embargoes. This practice was not legitimized through negotiations with allies. Rather, it was the result of the unilateral exercise of jurisdiction to which its allies, particularly in Europe and Canada, strongly objected. From their perspective, the United States had no right to apply its regulations to U.S.-owned firms incorporated in their territories or to U.S. goods and technology once they left U.S. borders. Hence, U.S.-sponsored rules governing extraterritorial jurisdiction were based on assertions of American power, not mutual consent.

This controversy over extraterritorial sanctions has its origin in competing bases for jurisdiction under international law. The Canadian and European positions are grounded in the *territorial principle*, which is the most fundamental basis for jurisdiction in public international law. It holds that a state is sovereign within its territory. Since sovereignty is exclusive, no state can act on the territory of another without explicit consent. Absent that consent, efforts to extend national laws extraterritorially represent a violation of the freedom of states to organize their affairs as they see fit.[34]

While the United States has been the principal practitioner of extraterritorial regulation since World War II, it had championed the territorial principle in the nineteenth and early twentieth centuries. The classic articulation of this position was Chief Justice John Marshall's opinion in *Schooner Exchange v. McFadden*:[35]

> The jurisdiction of the nation within its own territory is necessarily exclusive and absolute. It is susceptible to no limitation not imposed by itself. Any restriction upon it, deriving validity from an external source would imply a diminution of its sovereignty to the extent of the restriction. . . . All exceptions . . . must be traced up to the consent of the nation itself. They can flow from no other legitimate source.

This view was upheld by the Supreme Court as late as 1909 in the *American Banana* case, when it barred the Justice Department from applying the Sherman Anti-Trust Act to the United Fruit Company in Costa Rica and Panama, where restrictive business practices were not illegal. The majority opinion, written by Oliver Wendell Holmes, reaffirmed the exclusivity of territorial jurisdiction, stating that "the character of an act as lawful or unlawful must be determined wholly by the law of the country where the act is done."[36]

After the Second World War, American policymakers proclaimed a more expansive right to extend jurisdiction beyond U.S. borders, and U.S. courts have accepted this as legitimate. The primary reason for this was the change in America's position in the world. A strict territorial approach was the natural course for an emerging power like the United States when it was less concerned with enforcing the rules of the international system and more apprehensive that more powerful states might threaten its sovereignty. By the mid-twentieth century, the United States was the world's dominant power with an ambitious foreign policy agenda of restructuring the basic institutions of world politics. Expanding the reach of American laws would better enable policymakers to pursue that agenda.[37]

The need to claim extraterritorial jurisdiction was propelled by two other developments in the postwar world. The first was the emergence of the multinational corporation as the dominant corporate actor in the world economy. Prior to the emergence of the MNC, the territorial principle was compatible with effective regulation because trade was conducted by firms created under the law of a single state. Multinational corporations could escape that accountability since they operate in multiple jurisdictions.[38] The second factor was the growth of economic interdependence, in which states became more vulnerable to activities outside their boundaries. If host countries apply "parochial territorial zeal," blocking all extraterritorial jurisdiction, they can frustrate the ability of home states to implement effective public policies.[39]

In order to respond to these changes, American policymakers rely on two bases of jurisdiction that can rebut the presumption in favor of territoriality. The first is the *nationality principle*, which entitles states to regulate the actions of their nationals wherever they reside. This is the legal nexus used to reach foreign subsidiaries, which are assumed to retain their nationality since they are created by American capital and are subject to control by U.S. citizens. Therefore, the home government can assert jurisdiction through the nationality of the home office, local managers, or even shareholders, if they are able to block transactions disallowed by U.S. law. As explained in the *Restatement of the Foreign Relations Law of the United States*: "The enterprise itself cannot, by incorporating in a foreign state, escape all regulatory authority of the state of the parent corporation."[40]

The nationality principle is also used to justify reexport controls over U.S. goods and technology after they leave U.S. territory. The Export Control Act and its successors apply U.S. regulations to persons, goods, and technology "subject to the jurisdiction of the United States."[41] The Commerce Department construes the law to assign U.S. nationality to any property that originates in the United States. That nationality is retained even after the property crosses national boundaries and is transformed in the process of production. Foreign purchasers of U.S.-origin goods are bound by these rules because they have submitted voluntarily to U.S. export controls through the contracts they were required to sign by the U.S. exporter.[42] Therefore, U.S. jurisdiction with respect to the nationality of U.S. goods applies even when this conflicts with the policies and laws of the countries where those items are used.

Second, the United States often bases its claims of extraterritorial jurisdiction on the *effects doctrine*, under which jurisdiction can be claimed over "activity outside the state, but having or intended to have substantial effect within the state's territory."[43] The first expression of this doctrine in American jurisprudence was issued in 1945 by Judge Learned Hand in *United States v. Aluminum Co. of America*, which allowed the application of the Sherman Act to the participation of U.S. and Canadian aluminum companies in a cartel based in Switzerland. The ruling explicitly overturned territorial presumption underlying the *American Banana* case by concluding that "any state may impose liabilities, even on a person not within its allegiance, for conduct outside its borders that has consequences within its borders that it reprehends."[44] Since that time, the United States has championed an expansive interpretation of the effects doctrine to regulate overseas activity in areas, such as antitrust, securities regulations, foreign corrupt practices, and economic sanctions, and U.S. courts have never challenged its ability to do so.[45]

The European and Canadian governments object to these practices as violations of their sovereignty. Their position is grounded in the territorial principle, which allows sovereign states to decide for themselves how best to promote their national interests "without undue or unwarranted interference."[46] The extension of U.S. law into third countries effectively usurps this fundamental right, even when allies pursue the same policy. For example, a 1977 amendment to the Export Administration Act applied U.S. laws against corporate compliance with the Arab Boycott of Israel to the foreign subsidiaries of U.S. firms. Canada protested the reach of this law even though it enacted virtually identical legislation that same year.[47]

Allies explicitly challenge the validity of using bases of jurisdiction other than territoriality in applying embargoes and export controls. They reject the effects doctrine as an infringement of territorial sovereignty. While they acknowledge that interdependence may necessitate extending regulations across boundaries, this is only permissible if others consent through negotiated agreements.[48] According to a former British attorney general, the United States can exercise limited extraterritorial jurisdiction over foreign (including British) nationals on the high seas against oil tanker pollution or the international narcotics trade. The British government has seen such practices as unobjectionable because these are areas on which "there are shared views and common objectives" and the scope and limits of that jurisdiction are defined by formal treaties.[49] No comparable agreement has legitimized U.S. jurisdiction regarding sanctions or export controls. Moreover, for the effects doctrine to be a valid basis for jurisdiction, the private activities that one is trying to control must have a tangible effect inside the country exercising jurisdiction. Allied refusal to comply with U.S. economic restrictions has no effect in the United States other than on its "perceptions of national security and foreign policy interests."[50] Allied governments, however, define their security and diplomatic interests differently and those differences should be addressed through diplomacy, not the unilateral extension of American law.

Allies also challenge the validity of the nationality principle as a means of regulating foreign subsidiaries. They concede that public international law allows the United States to apply its laws to its nationals for acts outside its territory. Foreign subsidiaries, however, are not nationals of the home country; rather, they are legal creatures of the host country in which they are incorporated.[51] One Canadian government commission consequently concluded that "[i]nsofar as subsidiaries become instruments of policy of the home country rather than the host country, the capability of the latter to effect decisions— i.e., its political independence—is directly reduced."[52] Using the nationality of the home office to regulate subsidiaries licensed abroad is consequently labeled an encroachment on sovereignty.

Finally, the Europeans oppose the legal arguments behind U.S. reexport controls. First, the United States is alone in imputing nationality to goods and technology for the purpose of extending jurisdiction. Other countries take the position that once items leave U.S. borders, American law should give way to the law of the importing country.[53] If the controlled items are on the CoCom list, the United States should properly rely on the enforcement agencies of its allies. If the controlled items are only on the U.S. Commodity Control List, then reexport regulations violate the political independence of allies by using extraterritorial laws to impose "what it [the United States] has failed to achieve by agreement with the governments of the countries in which those businesses are operating."[54]

Second, Europeans reject the argument that their firms have consented to U.S. jurisdiction over imports from the United States through contracts with U.S. firms. These contracts, they argue, are neither private nor voluntary since Washington mandated them. Moreover, such contracts amount to a direct intrusion of U.S. law into European territory because their practical effect is that foreign companies are pressed into service of the trade policy of the United States rather than their home country.[55]

A partial exception to allied opposition to U.S. reexport controls is Canada. The Canadian government implements U.S. export controls on U.S.-origin goods within its territory in exchange for an open border between the two countries. Canada's willingness to apply U.S. laws, however, is part of a consensual agreement with the United States for which it receives a significant economic benefit—that is, immunity from U.S. export control regulations. Therefore, Canada's position is still within the territorial principle because its willingness to enforce U.S. regulations is the result of a bilateral agreement to which it consented, not unilateral American enforcement.[56]

In sum, American policymakers have seen extraterritorial regulations as a way to broaden private compliance with its sanctions and export controls in third countries beyond what was attainable through multilateral means. The United States has tried to elide the charge that it was violating the sovereignty of its allies by asserting jurisdiction through the nationality of the home office and of U.S.-origin goods and technology. Western allies have universally rejected U.S. legal arguments, characterizing them as infringements of their political independence to conduct whatever strategy of East–West trade they deemed appropriate. This set the stage for chronic disputes between the United States and its allies over theoretically irreconcilable principles.

NOTES

1. David Leyton-Brown, "Extraterritoriality in United States Trade Sanctions," in *The Utility of International Economic Sanctions*, ed. David Leyton-Brown (New York: St. Martin's, 1987), 255.

2. *Foreign Relations of the United States* (hereafter, *FRUS*), 1948, part 4, 512.

3. Philip J. Funigiello, *America-Soviet Trade in the Cold War* (Chapel Hill, N.C.: University of North Carolina Press, 1988), 36.

4. *FRUS*, 1948, part 4, 525.

5. Michael Mastanduno, "The United States Defiant: Export Controls in the Postwar Era," *Daedalus* 120 (fall 1991): 94.

6. Cecil Hunt, "Multilateral Cooperation in Export Controls—The Role of CoCom," *Toledo Law Review* 14 (summer 1983): 1285–1297.

7. *FRUS*, 1950, part 4, 174.

8. Funigiello, *American-Soviet Trade*, 45.

9. Hunt, "Multilateral Cooperation in Export Controls," 1287.

10. *FRUS*, 1950, part 4, 83–85, 171–72.

11. *FRUS*, 1948, part 4, 553.

12. *FRUS*, 1950, part 4, 118.

13. *FRUS*, 1950, part 4, 102.

14. *FRUS*, 1950, part 4, 94–95.

15. Robert A. Pollard, *Economic Security and the Origins of the Cold War, 1945–1950* (New York: Columbia University Press, 1985), 61.

16. Andreas F. Lowenfeld, *Trade Controls for Political Ends*, 2d ed. (San Francisco, Calif.: Matthew Bender, 1983), 67.

17. *FRUS*, 1950, vol. 4, 222.

18. Statement by William Swingle of the Commerce Department's Export Advisory Committee, cited in Funigiello, *American-Soviet Trade in the Cold War*, 43.

19. Department of State, *Digest of the Foreign Relations Law of the United States* (hereafter, *Digest*) (Washington, D.C.: Government Printing Office [GPO], September 1970), Publication 8547, vol. 14, 864.

20. Lowenfeld, *Trade Controls for Political Ends*, 91.

21. Stanley L. Sommerfield, "Treasury Regulations Affecting Trade with the Sino-Soviet Bloc and Cuba," *Business Lawyer* 19 (July 1964): 866.

22. Jing-Dong Yuan, "Between Economic Warfare and Strategic Embargo: U.S.–U.K. Conflict over Export Controls on the People's Republic of China, 1949–1957," *Issues and Studies* 30 (March 1994): 84.

23. Yuan, "Between Economic Warfare and Strategic Embargo," 87–88.

24. See Gordon H. Chang, *Friends and Enemies: The United States, China, and the Soviet Union, 1949–1972* (Palo Alto, Calif.: Stanford University Press, 1990), 106–108.

25. Yuan, "Between Economic Warfare and Strategic Embargo," 93.

26. Gary Clyde Hufbauer, Jeffrey J. Schott, and Kimberly Ann Elliott, *Economic Sanctions Reconsidered: Supplemental Case Histories*, 2d ed. (Washington, D.C.: International Institute of Economic Studies, 1990), 194–195.

27. David A. Baldwin, *Economic Statecraft* (Princeton, N.J.: Princeton University Press, 1985), 177.

28. Hufbauer, Schott, and Elliott, *Economic Sanctions Reconsidered*, 195.

29. *Digest,* vol. 14, 866.

30. Kingman Brewster, *Law and United States Business in Canada* (Montreal: Canadian-American Committee, 1960), 23.

31. *FRUS*, 1955–1957, vol. 10, 295n.

32. Testimony of Andreas Lowenfeld in U.S. Congress, House Committee on International Relations, Subcommittee on International Economic Policy and Trade, *Emergency Controls on International Economic Relations,* Hearings, 95th Cong., 1st sess., 1977, 5.

33. Kobrin, "Enforcing Export Embargoes through Multinational Corporations," 32–33.

34. A. D. Neale and M. L. Stephens, *International Business and National Jurisdiction* (Oxford, U.K.: Clarendon Press, 1988), 12.

35. Cited in "Constructing the State Extraterritorially: Jurisdictional Discourse, the National Interest, and Transnational Norms," *Harvard Law Review* 103 (April 1990): 1276.

36. Mark W. Janis, *An Introduction to International Law*, 2d ed. (Boston: Little, Brown, 1993), 323.

37. For an analysis of the historical evolution of the U.S. approach, see Gary Born, "A Reappraisal of the Extraterritorial Reach of U.S. Law," *Law and Policy in International Business* 24 (fall 1992): 21–29.

38. *Restatement of the Law (Third): The Foreign Relations Law of the United States*, vol. 1 (St. Paul, Minn.: American Law Institute, 1987), 273–274.

39. Edward Gordon, "Extraterritorial Application of United States Economic Laws: Britain Draws the Line," *International Lawyer* 14 (winter 1980): 166.

40. *Restatement of the Foreign Relations Law*, 271.

41. Joseph P. Griffin and Michael N. Calabrese, "Coping with Extraterritoriality Disputes," *Journal of World Law* 22 (June 1988): 7.

42. Griffin and Calabrese, "Coping with Extraterritoriality Disputes," 9.

43. *Restatement of the Foreign Relations Law*, 239.

44. Janis, *Introduction to International Law*, 327.

45. Born, "Reappraisal of the Extraterritorial Reach of U.S. Law," 71.

46. Allan E. Gotlieb, "Extraterritoriality: A Canadian Perspective," *Northwestern Journal of International Law and Business* 5 (fall 1983): 455.

47. A. L. C. de Mestral and T. Gruchalla-Wesierski, *Extraterritorial Application of Export Legislation: Canada and the U.S.A.* (Dordrecht, Netherlands: Martinus Nijhoff Publishers, 1990), 258.

48. Rosalyn Higgins, *Problems and Process: International Law and How We Use It* (Oxford, U.K.: Clarendon Press, 1994), 74.

49. Michael Havers, "Good Fences Make Good Neighbors: A Discussion of Problems Concerning the Exercise of Jurisdiction," *International Lawyer* 17 (fall 1983): 784.

50. Griffin and Calabrese, "Coping with Extraterritoriality Disputes," 16.

51. Griffin and Calabrese, "Coping with Extraterritoriality Disputes," 17.

52. Task Force on the Structure of Canadian Industry, *Foreign Ownership and the Structure of Canadian Industry*, report prepared by the Watkins Commission (hereafter Watkins Commission Report), January 1968, 311.

53. De Mestral and Gruchalla-Wesierski, *Extraterritorial Application of Export Legislation*, 34.

54. A. V. Lowe, "Export Controls: A European Viewpoint," *International Journal of Technology Management* 3 (1988): 80–81.

55. Griffin and Calabrese, "Coping with Extraterritorial Disputes," 18–19.

56. Watkins Commission Report, 314–316.

Chapter Two

Sanctions at Bay?
The Rise and Partial Decline
of Extraterritorial Sanctions

The United States sponsored international rules governing extraterritorial jurisdiction to prevent globalization from frustrating its economic statecraft. It equated this policy with the provision of a "public good" for the Western alliance. That is, stopping private actors in third countries from free riding on U.S. sanctions would increase Western security by limiting resources available to communist adversaries. To U.S. allies, that position conflated free riding with legitimate policy differences. They contended that sanctions should be limited to items of direct strategic importance and favored nonstrategic trade with China and Cuba and a narrower range of export controls vis-à-vis the European Soviet bloc. From their perspective, extraterritorial sanctions represented a paternalistic effort by Washington to substitute its judgments for their own, not the provision of common security interests.

Therefore, the U.S. effort to sustain rules governing extraterritorial jurisdiction did not represent a negotiated regime, in which states consent to procedures that prevent short-term self-interest from undercutting mutually agreed upon goals. Rather, it was an imposed regime—one "established deliberately by dominant actors who succeed in getting others to conform to the requirements of these arrangements through some combination of coercion, co-optation, and the manipulation of resources."[1] In other words, extraterritorial sanctions depended on acquiescence to the unilateral exercise of U.S. power.

The dominant model used to explain the strength of imposed regimes is the theory of hegemonic stability. It predicts that international regimes that lack consensus require an economically preponderant power that is willing and able to uphold the rules, either through the threat of economic punishment or the promise of compensation.[2] From this perspective, the United States was able to translate its dominant economic position in the 1950s and 1960s into the ability to dissuade allies from blocking corporate compliance with U.S. regulations on their territory. With the erosion of that predominance in the 1970s, host countries overtly challenged the legitimacy of extraterritorial sanctions against Cuba, and the United States was forced to adjust by amending the regulations to exempt foreign subsidiaries. The end result was the "erosion of the U.S. government's ability to use MNCs to implement policy extraterritorially when American objectives conflicted with those of host states."[3]

While the hegemonic model's predictions correspond to the general direction of policy from the 1950s to the 1970s, there are two factors that raise questions about its explanatory power. First, the United States was reluctant to enforce extraterritorial sanctions, even when it was economically dominant, because of the costs and risks to goals more important than broadening its sanctions. Reprisals against allies threatened the cohesion of the Western alliance and risked resentments that could have undermined cooperation in enforcing those export controls for which there was agreement. Targeting foreign firms would also have established the precedent of a secondary boycott, undermining U.S. leadership in the General Agreement on Tariffs and Trade (GATT) and its opposition to the Arab Boycott of Israel. The United States was therefore reluctant to translate differentials in resources into meaningful coercive power.

Second, domestic politics—both in the United States and in the host countries—played a more important role in determining the outcome of extraterritorial disputes than did the structural position of the United States in the world economy. During the period of American dominance, policymakers were reluctant to enforce their preferences because of the potential political fallout from a public dispute. At home, the fear was that reports of allied trade with communist adversaries would trigger a public and congressional furor. The end result could have been legislation that mandated reprisals against allies, eliminating the executive branch's discretion to balance sanctions against other diplomatic interests. Abroad, publicity could have aroused nationalist resentment, which would have made it politically impossible for host governments to compromise with U.S. preferences. As a result, the United States was less inclined to enforce its interpretation of jurisdiction than it was to insulate diplomatic relations from domestic fallout at home and abroad.

For the most part, allies recognized the same domestic constraints on their ability to fully vindicate their sovereignty. In theory, they could have used "tactical politicization"[4]—that is, publicizing the issue in order to inflame domestic opinion so that it would be politically impossible to back down. This kind of brinksmanship would also have inflamed domestic opinion in the United States, given the intensity of anticommunist sentiment, triggering a public or congressional reaction that would have harmed their economic interests. As a result, they subordinated principled resistance to compromise solutions.

What emboldened trading partners to use tactical politicization in the 1970s was not the decline of U.S. preponderance. Rather, changes in the domestic political environment reduced the likelihood of economic reprisals in the United States. In the détente environment following the Vietnam War, public opinion favored a more open policy toward Cuba and prominent members of Congress endorsed legislation to normalize trade and diplomatic relations. As a result, allies and foreign subsidiaries were more assertive in challenging the embargo because Cuban trade was less likely to trigger reprisals in the United States. Washington also concluded that the diplomatic costs of extraterritorial sanctions exceeded their strategic benefits. Since repeated conflicts with allies were likely to lead to congressional efforts to scale back the sanctions rather than efforts to punish allies, the administration decided to rein in the extraterritorial scope of its embargo regulations.

THE EARLY PATTERN (1950–1957): TOLERATING ALLIED DEFECTION WHILE KEEPING CONGRESS AT BAY

Conflicts between the United States and its allies over extraterritorial controls were relatively muted until the late 1950s. The principal reason for this was that Washington had for the most part persuaded its allies to conform to its preferred strategy of East–West trade. In 1950, the CoCom embargo was expanded to cover a wider range of items that contributed to Soviet bloc economic growth.[5] In 1952, the allies agreed to harsher sanctions on China and North Korea than those imposed on the European Soviet bloc.[6] Nonetheless, differences with allies over the extensiveness of the controls persisted. The U.S. response to those differences revealed diplomatic priorities that would continue through the late 1950s and 1960s—that is, the need to balance a reluctance to coerce its allies against assuaging a Congress that might legislate mandatory reprisals against them.

Some scholars have attributed U.S. success in persuading its allies to move in the direction of economic warfare to its hegemonic position in the early 1950s. This period represented the apex of its economic preponderance. The United States consequently used European dependence on U.S. economic and security assistance to prevail when allies dissented from its preferences.[7] This linkage was made explicit in 1951 when Congress passed the Battle Act, which directed the president to terminate aid to allies that sold strategic items to the Soviet bloc, as defined by the Commodity Control List of the U.S. Department of Commerce.[8]

This view has been challenged for exaggerating the importance of hegemonic coercion relative to other factors in explaining allied compliance. A more salient factor was the shared perception of a more imminent Soviet threat as a result of events, such as the Czech coup, the Berlin blockade, and the Korean War.[9] Moreover, while the allies moved closer to U.S. strategies in the early 1950s, their controls fell short of U.S. preferences for economic warfare. These differences were further magnified in 1954 after allied pressure led to an agreement to downsize CoCom controls after the end of the Korean War. Despite the widening gap between the United States and its allies, public officials were unwilling to coerce conformity with U.S. policy because of two other interests deemed vital at the time—European economic recovery and the cohesion of the Western alliance.

First, coercion would have forced Western Europe to choose between Marshall Plan aid and access to Eastern European markets and raw materials, both of which were seen as essential for economic recovery. Even the NSC document that called for targeting Soviet industrial growth did so with the caveat that this strategy must also "minimize the damage to the U.S. and the Western powers resulting from (a) probable Soviet retaliation, and (b) the inability of the East to continue exports of certain supplies to the West."[10] A 1950 State Department report argued against total economic warfare because "the contribution of East–West trade to the economic strength of the West is still important and that the political repercussions in Europe if that trade is lost are perhaps more important."[11]

Second, State Department officials feared that coercion could impair alliance unity. Overt arm-twisting would breed resentment on the part of America's partners. This could jeopardize efforts to build a stronger multilateral consensus on several issues, including strategic export controls. They consequently cautioned against "extensions of controls which would involve disproportionate expenditure of good will."[12]

The same priorities were evident in dealing with foreign subsidiaries in allied countries. In 1951, for example, a Polish offer to sell coal to Denmark was made contingent upon the delivery of spare parts for automobiles from the Danish subsidiaries of Ford and General Motors. Even though these items were on the U.S. Commodity Control List, the U.S. government granted a waiver to the subsidiaries. The State Department reasoned that Western Europe's shortage of coal increased Denmark's dependence on Poland and the United States was unable to make up the difference. Denial of the license would have scuttled the deal jeopardizing Danish economic recovery and its participation in CoCom.[13]

Implementing a strategy that balanced alliance cohesion with multilateral controls required discretion in applying the law. A persistent concern was that Congress might remove that discretion in response to what it saw as the administration's reluctance to take more forceful measures. As a result, successive administrations sought to placate Congress by adopting symbolic measures even if their actual impact was negligible. For example, the FACRs implemented an extraterritorial asset freeze despite the fact that China had few assets abroad and the action created some problems in terms of both policy and law. Acheson dismissed these concerns, stating that "this action is important only because if it is not taken, people will get kicked around on the Hill. It will have little or no real effect."[14]

The same reasoning was evident in Truman's acceptance of the Battle Act. The legislation preserved executive discretion since it only mandated sanctions against allies that traded goods on the CoCom list—that is, those goods already controlled multilaterally. If the item was controlled unilaterally, the president had a national security waiver.[15] Even though the law interfered with what the administration saw as an executive branch prerogative, it was embraced to deter passage of the more severe Kem Amendment, which would have mandated sanctions with no waiver provision.[16]

Nonetheless, the executive branch had serious reservations regarding congressional involvement in East–West trade. The Truman and Eisenhower administrations saw coercion as subversive of both the Marshall Plan and CoCom. As a result, they interpreted the requirements of the law loosely and routinely used the national interest waiver. At the end of 1956, the State Department reported twenty-nine cases of allied exports from the Battle Act list by seven different countries and issued waivers in each case.[17] In fact, the Battle Act was only invoked once—against Ceylon for the sale of rubber to China, which was largely irrelevant because Ceylon was not a recipient of U.S. aid.[18]

While the executive branch was successful in maintaining its relative freedom from congressional interference, there was nonetheless a pervasive concern that some event might prompt Congress to take control of that issue and remove the discretion over retaliation against allies. These considerations would persist as allies moved further away from U.S. strategies of East–West trade in the late 1950s.

THE FOREIGN ASSETS CONTROL REGULATIONS (FACRS) AND EXTRATERRITORIAL SANCTIONS AGAINST CHINA

Conflicts between the United States and its allies over extraterritorial sanctions increased in the late 1950s after the abolition of the China Differential. There were sharp disagreements within Eisenhower's cabinet on how to respond to the collapse of the multilateral embargo against China. On one end of the debate, the Defense Department and Joint Chiefs of Staff called for the use of coercion to deter allied trade with China.[19] On the other side were free traders, such as Clarence Randall of the Council on Foreign Economic Policy (CFEP), who advocated a reduction of the China controls to the multilateral consensus. Unilateral economic warfare only handicapped American business without imposing additional costs on Beijing.[20]

The Eisenhower administration rejected both options and continued the comprehensive embargo unilaterally. It eschewed coercion for much the same reason that the Truman administration had routinely waived the Battle Act—that is, it would impose costs on the alliance disproportionate to any prospective gains.[21] Even though this meant that China could obtain embargoed goods from other sources, the NSC was unwilling to follow Randall's advice for reasons of international prestige and domestic politics. First, a full-scale embargo was necessary to stigmatize China—or as Secretary of State John Foster Dulles put it, to "penalize her for her aggression, and make her repent of her ways."[22] It was also a symbol of U.S. commitment to allies in Asia and its removal would have "far-reaching political and psychological repercussions, which would seriously undermine our position in the Far East."[23] Second, there was a need to insulate economic statecraft from legislative interference. Public and congressional antipathy toward China was particularly strong because of the impact of the "China Lobby" and the fact that American soldiers had recently fought against Chinese soldiers on the Korean Peninsula. A State Department official speculated that downgrading the China embargo could "affect public and Congressional opinion so as to impair the flexible administration of the Battle Act."[24]

Hence, considerations of international credibility and domestic politics dictated the need to maintain a comprehensive embargo against China. These same factors also provided the rationale for extending the embargo to the subsidiaries of U.S. firms in countries that favored civilian trade with China. Yet, this policy collided directly with what allies saw as their sovereign prerogatives and led to a number of disputes, particularly with Canada, in the late 1950s and early 1960s.

Ford–Canada and the Eisenhower–Diefenbaker Accords

In December 1957, a Canadian trader charged that the Canadian subsidiary of the Ford Motor Company backed out of a deal to sell one thousand trucks to China on instructions from the U.S. parent because of its liability under the U.S. Trading with the Enemy Act. The charge was heavily publicized in the Canadian press and sparked a nationalist outcry in the House of Commons. This pushed Prime Minister John Diefenbaker to challenge Washington on this issue.[25]

The dispute set the stage for the first overt diplomatic clash over whether U.S. embargoes covered the foreign operations of American multinationals. In response to protests from the Canadian embassy, the director of OFAC replied that since U.S. citizens owned sufficient stock to block the sale, it was asserting jurisdiction over the parent corporation, not the subsidiary.[26] The Canadian government rejected this reasoning because the effect of U.S. policy was the imposition of U.S. law on Canadian soil. This violated Canada's political independence because Ottawa favored nonstrategic trade with China. Moreover, since all of Canada's automobile industry was U.S.-controlled, U.S. claims of jurisdiction effectively denied the China market to Canadian automobile exports.[27]

Eisenhower and Diefenbaker addressed the dispute at their Ottawa summit on 9 July 1958. In what became known as the Eisenhower–Diefenbaker Accord, the U.S. agreed that Canada's economy should not be disadvantaged by the application of U.S. embargoes. To defuse future conflicts, both countries agreed to a consultation procedure when a subsidiary wanted to pursue a transaction banned by U.S. law. In such cases, Canada would formally approach the United States, which would favorably consider an exemption for the parent company. The subsidiary could then complete the transaction without subjecting its headquarters to legal liability.[28]

The agreement represented a compromise of principle by both countries to avoid a diplomatic rift that could have been widened by domestic politics on both sides of the border. Washington chose not to apply diplomatic and economic pressure to enforce its jurisdictional claims because the issue had become an incendiary one in Canadian politics. No government in Ottawa was likely to compromise with Washington if confronted publicly. In fact, Dulles even speculated that the Chinese tenders were really "phantom orders" designed to sow discord between the United States and its allies.[29] As a result, the United States replaced an absolute ban on foreign subsidiary trade with an agreement to license such transactions to defuse political conflict.

A number of officials went further, questioning the utility of maintaining extraterritorial sanctions. A CFEP proposal, supported by some officials at State, argued that the diplomatic controversies were not worth the relatively small amount of trade involved. It recommended extending the Eisenhower–Diefenbaker procedure to other allies to minimize the risk of future confrontations.[30]

The NSC rejected this option. One official argued that it would "constitute an incentive for US corporations to establish in friendly countries new subsidiaries for the expressed purpose of trading with Communist China."[31] Policymakers were also concerned with the domestic repercussions. Exempting foreign subsidiaries would enrage influential members of Congress who might respond by removing executive discretion over trade controls. Eisenhower was sympathetic to the CFEP proposal. He characterized unilateral controls over nonstrategic goods as "damned silly practices" and opposed their extension extraterritorially. He was nonetheless dissuaded from accepting it.[32] Therefore, while domestic politics in Canada made coercion a prohibitively costly option, domestic politics in the United States dictated that the regulations be kept on the books even though they guaranteed the recurrence of jurisdictional disputes with allies.

The outcome was also a compromise for Canada. Diefenbaker publicly declared that it restored Canada's sovereignty over subsidiaries of U.S. firms.[33] The accord, however, implicitly accepted the principle of extraterritoriality. There was no general waiver from the FACRs, only an agreement to consult. Ottawa would still have to plead its case for an exemption for the parent so it would not be prosecuted for its subsidiary's trade with China.[34] In addition, the issuance of licenses was not automatic. Dulles informed Diefenbaker that they would be granted only if the export had an "appreciable effect on the Canadian economy" and no Canadian-owned firms could do the job.[35] In other words, the right of subsidiaries to trade with China would not be determined solely by the sovereign judgments of Canada; U.S. permission was still necessary.

Moreover, the impetus to challenge the United States came not from the Diefenbaker government, but from the media, interest groups, and opposition parties. Prior to the Ford–Canada case, Canada's Department of Trade and Commerce (DTC) was aware of several cases where subsidiaries had been prevented by their parents from trading with China.[36] Ottawa, however, never pushed the issue. In part, this was because it would lead to "long and difficult negotiations" with Washington. The intensity of anticommunism in U.S. domestic politics also inhibited a strategy of diplomatic pressure. As long as there was no possibility of change in congressional or public attitudes, subsidiaries would be deterred from challenging the U.S. embargo.[37] As a result, DTC concluded that there was little it could do beyond advising Canadian firms "not to misuse opportunities by introducing U.S.-controlled companies when arranging business contracts"[38]—in other words, to work around what was regrettably accepted as a fait accompli.

What made the Ford–Canada case different, according to a DTC memorandum, was the "publicity which has been attached to the refusal of the order."[39] In other words, it was domestic politics in Canada that shifted Ottawa's position from private protest to public challenge. The fact that the outcome represented something less than a complete vindication of Canadian sovereignty indicates that the principal objective was not to end U.S. extraterritorial practices. Like their American counterparts, Canadian diplomats saw the accord as a way to insulate diplomatic relations from domestic political fallout on both sides of the border.

Implementing the Eisenhower–Diefenbaker Accord

The consultation procedure established in the Eisenhower–Diefenbaker Accord was successful in defusing potentially disruptive bilateral conflicts over foreign subsidiary sanctions. In most cases, the Canadian embassy persuaded State to prevail on Treasury to issue licenses to the parent corporations. It was less successful in actually promoting trade between U.S.-controlled subsidiaries and China. This was due primarily to political risk in the U.S. market, a factor that also influenced some Canadian firms that were heavily involved in the United States.

In the late 1950s, Canada used the consultation process to obtain licenses for two transactions—export of bleached pulp by Rayonier and steam locomotives by Fairbanks-Morse.[40] In both cases, it argued that the exemptions were consistent with the bilateral understanding—that is, the exports were 100 percent Canadian content, they were from industries that had experienced layoffs, and there were no Canadian-controlled firms that could have filled the orders. In the former case, the license was issued quickly.[41] In the latter case, State was initially reluctant to recommend approval because it contended that steam locomotives were crucial to China's industrial growth given its dependence on coal rather than oil.[42] Canada responded that these determinations should be made in Ottawa, not Washington. If its judgment was overridden, "it would be clear that the United States was trying to impose its own policy on Canadian firms and that the understanding would be valueless."[43] The United States relented and issued the license.

In neither case, however, did the sales materialize. The exemptions both followed the second Taiwan Straits crisis and the political risks in the U.S. market convinced the parent corporations to prevent the subsidiaries from following through on their China sales.[44] In fact, the U.S. parent sacked the Canadian manager of Fairbanks-Morse who had pressured the company to apply for the exemption.[45]

Another controversy emerged in 1961 when Standard Oil of New Jersey instructed its Vancouver subsidiary, Imperial Oil, not to provide bunkering oil to ships carrying wheat to China. This was a case in which the parent had approached OFAC for an exemption and was informed that the regulations covered the bunkering of ships owned or chartered by China. At the 1961 Ottawa Summit with President John F. Kennedy, Diefenbaker asserted that the U.S. action violated his understanding with Eisenhower given the importance of the grain deal and the absence of alternative companies that could provide the oil. Kennedy replied that if Canada formally requested an exemption, the United States would take no action to frustrate the transaction. Diefenbaker retorted that this was unacceptable since it implied consent to the extraterritorial jurisdiction. If word got out, it would be a "politically inflammatory issue" that might stimulate a negative reaction against U.S. investment. Given its concern about the political repercussions in Canada, the United States waived the regulations without a formal request.[46]

This consideration of Canadian sentiment did not extend to transactions that did not conform to the criteria spelled out by Dulles. For example, after Canada's 1961 grain deal with China, a number of U.S. subsidiaries were informed by Treasury that barter deals with China for the milling of grain designated for China violated the FACRs.[47] When the State Department was approached by the Canadian embassy, it insisted on evidence of the impact of the denial on the Canadian economy and the absence of other firms who could perform the job. Since Canadian-controlled firms could have filled the orders, State did not intercede with Treasury, as it had in the Imperial Oil case. As a DTC study had predicted, the U.S. government, even with the consultation process, was still in the "position of judging the merits of a transaction that is permissible under Canadian law."[48]

Yet even when the United States waived the restrictions, most subsidiaries were inhibited from pursuing business with China because the perceived risks in the U.S. market were disproportionate to the advantages of export deals. For example, shortly after the Ford–Canada case, a Canadian subsidiary of Chrysler received a $6 million order from China for twelve thousand Dodge passenger cars. The case clearly fell under the Eisenhower–Diefenbaker guidelines—the recession in Canada forced the firm to lay off thirty-five hundred workers and no Canadian-owned firm could have filled the order. The U.S. parent, however, never submitted a license application because the proposed deal coincided with the Sino-American crisis over the Taiwan Straits.[49] For similar reasons, several U.S.-owned firms informed DTC that they were prevented from quoting prices to Chinese buyers by their home offices.[50]

These risks even influenced some Canadian-controlled firms that were heavily dependent on the U.S. market. The most publicized case was Alcan's refusal to consider a $1 million order from China for two thousand tons of aluminum after Canada had removed aluminum from its list of strategic controls.[51] The sale would have been important for the company. It was producing at 65 percent of capacity and had just laid off 650 workers. Since it was the only Canadian firm that could have filled the order, the export was effectively lost to Canada.[52] The case was also heavily reported in the Canadian press and triggered an uproar in Parliament with charges that U.S. law had blocked the sale. While Alcan was not a U.S. subsidiary, its president and six of the fifteen members of its board of directors were U.S. citizens. Hence, it was technically within reach of the FACRs.[53]

U.S. law, however, did not block the sale. Treasury informed the Canadian embassy that it would exempt the U.S. directors and shareholders from liability.[54] Rather, it was the fear of what might happen to Alcan's position in the U.S. market, which represented 40 percent of its sales. As the company president informed DTC, "if competitors were to learn of a shipment to Communist China, they would publicize it throughout the United States and this would jeopardize [Alcan's] U.S. market which is [its] largest one."[55] He went on to argue that the decision was not politically motivated and was based "entirely on commercial considerations"[56]—which were heavily influenced by political risk in the U.S. market!

In sum, the consultation procedure succeeded in defusing bilateral conflicts through the waiver of U.S. jurisdiction. It did not translate into a significant increase in foreign subsidiary trade with China because of corporate fears of alienating the U.S. government and the perceived risks in the American market. This was acknowledged in a 1961 State Department briefing paper that advised President Kennedy that the strategic costs of deferring to Canadian economic nationalism through the waiver process were minimal because "no business has resulted from this relaxation over the past three years."[57]

MULTINATIONAL CORPORATIONS
AND THE CUBAN EMBARGO

The United States also sought to enlist overseas corporate cooperation with its economic denial program against Castro's Cuba. This was considered important because the United States succeeded only in obtaining OAS cooperation with its strategy of economic isolation. Western Europe, Canada, and Japan agreed only to a strategic embargo. Nonstrategic trade was governed by commercial rather than political considerations. These commercial considerations led to a revival of allied interest in trade with Cuba in 1963–1964 because an increase in the price of sugar provided it with hard currency to import Western goods.[58] This development also opened the door to the possibility of trade by U.S. subsidiaries incorporated in allied countries.

As a result, the Johnson administration initiated a high-level policy review of the Cuban denial program in early 1964. It was agreed that current trends had to be reversed or the economic denial program would be seriously compromised. Assistant Secretary of State for Inter-American Affairs Thomas Mann warned that "persuasion alone will not be an effective means of denying Castro access to free world markets" and there was a need to "devise more effective means to deny Castro access to items produced in the Free World which his economy desperately needs."[59] This implied consideration of more forceful pressure against allies. Serious coercion, however, was ruled out for much the same reason that previous administrations had shied away from applying the Battle Act and FACRs. As a result, the United States adopted the same conflict-avoidance strategy as it did in the China case, seeking discreet compromises over foreign subsidiary sanctions and rejecting proposals for the systematic blacklisting of foreign firms that traded with Cuba.

The CACRs and Foreign Subsidiary Trade

The Johnson administration believed that extending CACRs to foreign sub-sidiaries was a key part of a strengthened embargo. Prior to its revolution, Cuba's economy was heavily dependent on trade and investment by U.S. firms. As one historian noted, "virtually all the machinery, equipment, and supplies used in Cuban industry, agriculture, mining, transportation, commu-nications, and utilities—more than 70 percent of Cuban total imports—had come from the United States."[60] Extending sanctions to U.S.-owned firms anywhere would deny the Cuban economy access to spare parts for U.S equipment.

Unlike the FACRs, however, the CACRs did not formally extend sanctions extraterritorially. Foreign subsidiaries were theoretically free to trade non-strategic goods as long as there was no U.S.-origin content and the parent company was not involved.[61] The exemption was designed to assuage third country hostility over the infringement of sovereignty. Nonetheless, the United States used two devices to reach foreign subsidiaries in a way that was less offensive to allied sensitivities. First, "moral suasion" was applied to the home office to pressure it to police the behavior of affiliates. The appeal was at times cast in terms of corporate patriotism, but also implied threats of ad-verse publicity or difficulties in securing federal contracts.[62] Second, while subsidiaries were exempted from liability, U.S. citizens who served as direc-tors, officers, or managers were not.[63] Treasury interpreted the regulations to require U.S. citizens to take all available steps to block a Cuban sale or face criminal penalties. It reasoned that this would remove the objections of allies who "might have some basis for contending that we ought not to control en-tities incorporated under Canadian law, they would not similarly object to our control over U.S. citizens."[64]

This distinction was unacceptable to Canada and other U.S. allies. Ottawa agreed to ban the export of strategic goods to Cuba and the transshipment of U.S.-origin items.[65] That consent did not extend to nonstrategic Canadian goods. In fact, Ottawa expected all Canadian firms, including foreign sub-sidiaries, to "maximize development of market opportunities in [Cuba]."[66] From a commercial perspective, exempting foreign subsidiary trade with Cuba was attractive for precisely the reason the United States wanted to pre-vent it: "[W]e hold a particular advantage in supplying commodities with United States specifications required because the major part of the economy is still operating on United States or United States–style equipment."[67] Canada's initial reading of the CACRs indicated that the United States would not interfere with the pursuit of these interests.

As a result, Canada's interest in increasing Cuban opportunities for all Canadian-based firms ran up against Treasury's construction of its authority, leading to a pattern of conflict resolution similar to that for the Chinese embargo. From 1964 to 1967, OFAC denied or held up the issuance of waivers for at least eight transactions between Canadian subsidiaries of U.S. firms and Cuba.[68] Canada protested each of these denials. One Department of External Affairs (DEA) study asserted that Canada "never agreed . . . that nationality of one or more of the directors of a [Canadian] company should place any impediment on a particular transaction by that country." Acquiescing to this would set a dangerous precedent because the "activities of the great majority of all corporations in [Canada] . . . would be subject to restrictions imposed by USA law."[69] It consequently informed the State Department that Treasury's actions "could largely nullify the exemption for U.S. subsidiaries which is otherwise provided in the CACRs."[70]

In almost every case, State prevailed on Treasury to grant an exemption for "overriding foreign policy reasons."[71] The only exception was a 1966 Canadian wheat deal with the Soviet Union, a substantial portion of which was diverted to Cuba. State saw this as overstepping the bounds of allied trade with Cuba and used the threat of liability under the CACRs to dissuade three U.S.-controlled firms from milling Canadian wheat destined for Cuba.[72] There were also domestic political reasons for taking a harder line. The Johnson administration had been attacked for its passivity vis-à-vis a similar deal in 1964 not only by Kenneth Keating (R-N.Y.), the Senate's chief policy entrepreneur on this issue, but also by Democratic allies, such as Senator Paul Douglas (D-Ill.), who accused the Canadians of "trading on our indulgences."[73] As a result, the administration publicly denounced the deal and U.S. subsidiaries declined a Russian invitation to bid on milling contracts. Canada issued a protest, asserting that "[a]ny directive from abroad which might interfere with the normal exercise of commercial judgment by Canadian companies would be in conflict with . . . good corporate citizenship."[74] No business was lost to Canada, however, as Canadian-owned companies filled the orders.

As with the FACRs, the outcome represented a compromise on both sides to protect diplomatic relations from domestic politics. Canada's ideal solution was unconditional exemption for U.S. directors and managers of Canadian subsidiaries. A DTC study observed that while Canada had been successful in getting waivers, it was still "subject to individual licenses by U.S. authorities . . . [without] any assurance that the U.S. in all cases would be prepared to grant the required license."[75]

Ottawa was unwilling to force the issue through tactical politicization. Canadian officials did at times point to nationalist sensibilities in bargaining with the United States, as in the Imperial Oil case.[76] They nonetheless preferred discreet consultations to publicity, as when the minister of trade and commerce informed one subsidiary that approached it to "see to it that the case does not break loose."[77] An open clash would unleash a public reaction at home that would make compromise impossible. This would guarantee an escalation of the conflict because, as a DEA memorandum noted, "Cuba is an emotional issue which has aroused very strong feelings in the United States, and this factor has a bearing on our policy regarding Cuba."[78] Canadian diplomats, therefore, preferred to keep consultations private and confidential—even if that meant compromise—in order to insulate other aspects of U.S.-Canadian relations from domestic political controversy.

The same was true on the U.S. side as State pressed Treasury for exemptions in almost every case where Canada made a representation. In early 1965, Treasury demanded a review of the policy because in its view, State had equated "overriding foreign policy interests" with "the mere existence of Canadian protests." Treasury's preference was to administer the regulations impartially, either limiting exemptions to situations in which "unusual factual distinctions exist" or abandoning the policy altogether.[79] In the spring of 1965, the Justice Department presided over an interdepartmental review of the policy, which decided to preserve the status quo.[80] As a result, extraterritorial sanctions remained on the books, but exemptions were issued once the diplomatic temperature was raised.

State's position was based on a logic of conflict management similar to that for the FACRs. It did not want to abandon the policy because that would encourage U.S. firms to move abroad and would be seen "as a signal abroad that we were reorienting our policy toward Castro."[81] At the same time, it was reluctant to use serious economic pressure for the same reason that Canada was unwilling to use tactical politicization. On the Canadian side, nationalist resentment would not only complicate diplomacy, it would confirm the view of economic nationalists that U.S. firms in Canada work for U.S. political rather than Canadian economic interests.[82] Discretion was also necessary on the U.S. side because openly airing differences with Canada would create public expectations that were unlikely to be satisfied given the constraints under which both countries were operating. This could only inflame public and congressional opinion in ways that might lead to legislation that impaired diplomatic flexibility.[83]

Despite the almost routine issuance of waivers, very little trade developed between Canadian subsidiaries of U.S. firms and Cuba. Even the issuance of licenses often did not lead to increased foreign subsidiary trade with Cuba. In one case, the home office interceded to prevent the deal from being consummated. In another, the parent corporation assured Washington that its subsidiaries would seek no more Cuban trade after the licensed deal was completed.[84] As in the China case, the reason for corporate reticence about "trading with the enemy" lay in private calculations of risk vis-à-vis an administration strongly committed to the sanctions and an anticommunist public for whom Castro's regime was a pariah state, particularly after the Cuban Missile Crisis. In discounting the costs of the waivers, Rusk concluded that there are "many other cases that never come to the attention of the Government of Canada because the firms are dissuaded from pursuing the matter by U.S. officials whom they might contact for guidance."[85]

Foreign Multinationals

Successful economic warfare against Cuba meant controlling not only the foreign subsidiaries of U.S. firms, but foreign corporations as well. Policymakers were aware that NATO allies did not equate Cuban trade with the export of revolution. Hence, the Johnson administration established two priorities in securing multilateral cooperation with the denial program. First, it pressed allies not to export equipment and machinery for agriculture and transportation, which were seen as potential bottlenecks to Cuban economic growth.[86] Second, it targeted government-guaranteed credits, which increased Cuba's ability to import critical commodities, potentially providing it with "the margin between a wallowing economy and one showing satisfactory growth."[87]

The first major allied challenge to these priorities was a $12.2 million sale of buses and spare parts to Cuba by British Leyland Motors Corporation in January 1964. U.S. officials denounced the deal, citing its strategic importance to Cuba's economy. The British government defended the transaction, arguing that controls on Cuba should seek to limit its military capability, not its industrial growth. Since buses were not on the CoCom list, Cuba should be treated no differently from the European Soviet bloc.[88] Leyland's chairman was less diplomatic, ridiculing U.S. assertions as to the deal's strategic implications by stating that, "You would look damned silly going to war in a bus."[89]

From an economic warfare perspective, the deal crossed the two lines the United States drew for its allies. It was the first major export of new machinery and spare parts by a Western firm to Cuba and helped rescue a public transport system that policymakers believed was on the verge of collapse. It was also accompanied by a five-year government-guaranteed credit. Rusk feared that this would have a "severe erosive effect on our position," particularly with France, which reversed its policy of denying government guarantees after Leyland beat out its French competitor, Berliet, for the bus contract.[90]

The United States consequently applied strong diplomatic pressure on Britain to rescind the deal. The most overt example of this was a decision to bring Britain up for a vote of censure in NATO. The issue was also raised at a February 1964 summit between President Johnson and Prime Minister Alec Douglas-Home.[91] Britain refused to block the sale but agreed to suspend government-guaranteed credits—an informal understanding that lasted until late 1966.[92]

The Leyland deal also prompted a review of the Cuban embargo at the 19 February 1964 meeting of the NSC. The NSC study began by presenting the problem: "It has become clear that the United States Government must either change its methods of restricting free world trade with Cuba or accept the probability of a significant increase in this trade, with all its consequences. Our present tactics of relying essentially on diplomatic persuasion . . . have not prevented major breaches in our efforts to isolate Cuba."[93] Since diplomacy had been unsuccessful, there was a need to consider more aggressive ways of obtaining allied compliance.

One option was to link aid to conformity with the embargo.[94] Congress had taken steps in this direction through an amendment to the Foreign Assistance Act that directed the president to terminate military and economic aid to states that failed to take steps to prevent cargo-carrying ships from calling on Cuban ports. In early 1964, the administration used this provision to terminate small aid programs to Britain, France, and Yugoslavia.[95]

Nonetheless, the administration rejected an expansion of this approach because of the risks to diplomatic relations. For example, Spain and Morocco had also failed to restrict shipping to Cuba. The administration waived sanctions against both countries so as not to jeopardize access to strategic facilities, even though it conceded that the waivers would be harmful to the multilateral effort, particularly Spain's decision to buy Cuban sugar at preferential prices.[96] Moreover, publicly announcing such a policy of linkage might heighten public and congressional expectations for a tougher and more consistent policy. One State Department report noted that "free world commercial relations with Castro has become in part symbols to the American public expectations of the U.S. resolve not to co-exist with Castro."[97] Since the results of a linkage strategy were likely to fall short of public expectations, the ensuing frustration could lead to "legislation that might allow the Executive little discretion in dealing with U.S. allies."[98]

A second option was to target foreign firms rather than their governments.[99] The Kennedy administration had already blacklisted ships that called on Cuban ports from carrying U.S. government-financed cargoes. It considered expanding this policy to cover all foreign firms and the entire U.S. market. This could be done by identifying foreign firms that dealt with Cuba as Special Designated Nationals (SDNs) of the Cuban government. All persons subject to U.S. jurisdiction would be forbidden from entering into any unlicensed transactions with the blacklisted firms. One official noted that applying such measures to a firm such as Leyland would have forced it "to choose between selling buses in Cuba and selling Triumph automobiles in the United States."[100]

This strategy was also rejected even though the NSC review predicted that many firms would forego Cuban trade because of the importance of the U.S. market. The costs of such an approach were deemed to be too high because of its likely effects on the liberal trading order. As the study noted, a secondary boycott "could set a dangerous precedent that might at some later time work to the disadvantage of the United States, and threaten the long-range integrity of GATT."[101] First, it would weaken U.S. arguments regarding the illegality of secondary boycotts, such as the Arab League's boycott of Israel. Second, it could undermine trade liberalization either by provoking retaliatory action by trading partners or by jeopardizing the Kennedy Round of multilateral trade negotiations at GATT. As a result, the U.S. leadership role in the liberal trading order precluded serious use of secondary boycotts to coerce compliance with the Cuban embargo.

The administration did employ a number of intermediate steps to discourage foreign business with Cuba. First, it informally used eligibility for government contracts as an inducement to stay away from Cuba. It did persuade some firms with large defense contracts—such as Fiat (Italy) and Vickers (U.K.)—to forego Cuban trade, and it denied a $3.3 million Interior Department contract to English Electric (U.K.) for exporting telephone equipment to Cuba.[102] Second, it solicited the assistance of the U.S. business community to discourage their foreign partners from pursuing Cuban opportunities, sometimes using the threat of dropping them as customers.[103] These overtures produced limited results. A few firms, such as France's Le Nickel, stopped buying Cuban nickel so as not to jeopardize mining ventures with U.S. firms elsewhere.[104] A more common result was the inability to find strong U.S. connections, as with the French firms, Berliet and Brissoneau, which signed contracts to export trucks and locomotives to Cuba shortly after the Leyland deal.[105]

In sum, U.S. policy did not move far beyond diplomatic exhortation because of the costs and risks of coercion. One State Department official characterized it as a "response to both domestic pressures to 'do something' about Cuba and foreign pressures not to do too much."[106] As a result, the United States expended considerable diplomatic effort to broaden the embargo without the leverage to back it up. Predictably, it had only limited success in persuading its allies to join the denial program. It was temporarily successful in persuading them to limit export credits, but this agreement lasted only until late 1966—in large measure because of the potential of such credits in winning contracts from other competitors. As long as sugar prices remained high and Cuba maintained its reputation as a reliable debtor, Western countries treated nonstrategic trade with Cuba no differently from trade with any other Latin American country. As Jorge Dominguez concluded, Cuba's trade with the West "depend[ed] upon Cuba's ability to pay, not on U.S.-imposed political restrictions."[107]

PARTIAL CHALLENGES TO THE SYSTEM IN THE 1960S

The ability of the United States to use American multinationals as instruments of its sanctions depended on two factors—host country acquiescence to extraterritorial control and corporate willingness to cooperate with U.S. policy. Neither of these was fully overturned in the 1960s. Nonetheless, the decade saw increasing examples of resistance to U.S. policy that were harbingers of more serious challenges in the 1970s.

Host Country Policies

Two controversies in the 1960s illustrate some of the difficulties the United States confronted in applying its controls to foreign subsidiaries. The first began in 1961, when Britain approved a sale by Vickers of six Viscount civilian aircraft to China. London justified the transaction on diplomatic as well as commercial grounds. The Chinese had turned to a British supplier because of their disillusionment with the Ilyushin aircraft they had received from the Soviet Union. Approving the deal would not only drive a wedge between China and the Soviet Union; it would also moderate Chinese policy by "drawing the Chinese Communists into wider contacts with the West."[108]

The United States disagreed with the premises underlying British policy. It was still practicing economic warfare against China; civilian imports would free resources that could be diverted to the military. Moreover, it predicted that Sino-Soviet friction was more likely to come from Beijing's frustration with its economic relationship with Moscow, and that providing a Western alternative made it less likely that economic dissatisfaction would spill over into political friction.[109] Therefore, the United States opposed the sale, which was China's first purchase of aircraft from a Western ally.

In trying to block the sale, the United States supplemented diplomatic persuasion with extraterritorial controls. The legal nexus used to assert jurisdiction was the Viscount's navigational system, which was manufactured by Standard Telegraph & Cable, a U.K. subsidiary of American Telegraph & Telephone Company (AT&T). London protested, arguing that the navigational equipment was specified in the contract. If U.S. law forced its renegotiation, this would be a "public admission that U.S. jurisdiction extends to U.S. subsidiaries registered in the U.K."[110] Washington refused to yield. London was forced to adapt by renegotiating the contract and finding a British-owned electronics company to replace the U.S. equipment at considerable cost.[111]

At one level, the United States succeeded in forcing the issue and getting Britain to accept U.S. jurisdiction even when that required renegotiating a contract. At another level, it was unable to alter British policy because extending jurisdiction to the subsidiary delayed but did not block what the

United States considered to be a strategic export. Moreover, the principal casualty in the affair was the U.S. firm, which not only lost the sale, but also was seen by the British government and by Vickers as an unreliable supplier.

A more significant challenge to the legitimacy of extraterritorial sanctions came from the French government in the *Fruehauf v. Masardy* case. In October 1964, the French subsidiary of Fruehauf won a bid from Berliet, France's largest truck manufacturer, to build two hundred truck trailers to be shipped to an unknown destination. Fruehauf–France did not discover that the ultimate destination was China until after it had purchased the materials and started work on the project.[112] When Treasury learned of the deal, it informed Fruehauf's Detroit headquarters that it fell under the Trading with the Enemy Act since two-thirds of the stockholders and five of the eight members of the board of directors were U.S. citizens.[113] Under instructions from Treasury, the parent corporation ordered the subsidiary to annul the contract and try to keep losses to a minimum. The subsidiary complied even though the trailers were built entirely in France without any U.S.-origin content.[114]

Fruehauf–France was unable to execute this directive. First, Berliet refused to accept an amicable dissolution of the deal and sued for $1 million in damages for breach of contract. Second, the French manager and the minority French directors resigned and sued the U.S. directors in French commercial court for a temporary administrator to manage the firm and execute the contract. The legal basis for their claim was the French concept of *abus de droit*—that is, the French courts have the right to overrule corporate management should it make decisions for personal gain contrary to the interests of the corporation. The plaintiffs contended that this principle applied to the actions of the U.S. directors because they risked bankruptcy by alienating the company's largest customer (Berliet) and making it liable to civil action.[115]

On 16 February 1965 the Commercial Court granted the requested relief. On 22 May, the Court of Appeals affirmed this decision and appointed a temporary administrator to oversee the performance of the contract. The court's decision found that the U.S. directors had abused their rights. In order to avoid personal liability under TWEA, they took actions "that would ruin the financial equilibrium and the moral credit of Fruehauf–France, S.A., and provoke its disappearance and the unemployment of more than 600 workers."[116] Extraterritorial regulations could not override the French law of contract. Treasury consequently considered the license application to be moot because the French court removed the control from the U.S. company—or, to use the language of TWEA, Fruehauf–France was no longer a "person subject to the jurisdiction of the United States."[117]

While the French courts determined the outcome, the French government strongly weighed in against the U.S. action. President Charles De Gaulle had been pursuing a foreign policy independent of the United States, a major part of which was his 1964 decision to recognize the People's Republic of China. After the initial Treasury decision, Paris issued a strongly worded diplomatic protest, asserting that French subsidiaries were fully subject to French law and could not be bound by U.S. regulations or the parent companies acting under its directives. Moreover the French *Avocat General* appeared before the court representing the French public in the outcome of the private litigation.[118]

The *Fruehauf v. Masardy* case was the strongest challenge to U.S. extraterritorial sanctions until the 1970s as the United States had to accept an outcome imposed by French jurisdiction. It was not, however, an unequivocal repudiation of extraterritorial regulation. It demonstrated to U.S. policymakers that the French legal system would not allow foreign directives to compel firms to violate the French law through abrogating contracts.[119] This did not necessarily extend to French policy of encouraging trade with China for which Paris could not "assert an obligation . . . to disregard U.S. controls."[120] Moreover, a year earlier, the United States blocked a French subsidiary of IBM from selling computers to the French government until it agreed not to use them for its nuclear weapons program. Paris sharply objected to the extension of U.S. law onto French territory. It did not block those controls since IBM was under no legal obligation to sell to the French government.[121]

Nor did the *Fruehauf* case set a precedent for other allied host countries. In 1968, Treasury prevented Clayson, a Belgian company, 65 percent of which was owned by a U.S. firm, Sperry-Rand, from selling $1.2 million in agricultural equipment to Cuba. Brussels protested this as interference in its domestic economic affairs, particularly since this was a depressed sector of the economy in which the government was encouraging exports to avoid layoffs. Sperry, however, complied with U.S. directives, noting, "It is corporate policy to conduct all of its international affairs in full conformity with the policies of the United States government." Brussels chose not to force the issue, citing the "necessity to strike a balance between the loss of employment involved in this and the fact that workers in our country have benefited from foreign capital."[122]

Corporate Policies

A second base on which the U.S. government relied in extending its sanctions was corporate cooperation—both in adhering to and enforcing the sanctions beyond the requirements of the law and in passively acquiescing to restrictive trade legislation. By the mid-1960s, private economic actors took a dimmer view of this role as something that disabled them vis-à-vis foreign competitors.

First, the United States was initially able to persuade U.S.-based MNCs to police their foreign subsidiaries, often beyond what was formally covered in the regulations. For example, U.S. oil companies agreed to deny China access to oil from their Asian affiliates and U.S. steel companies were persuaded to embargo steel to Cuba before they were legally required to do so.[123] U.S. firms also exerted pressure on foreign customers to stay away from trade with Cuba and China. A State Department official noted that they were "exceedingly cooperative" in "inform[ing] partners that if they did a deal with Cuba, they would be dropped as suppliers." Several U.S. firms also kept State apprised of unexpectedly large orders from third parties of items known to be needed by Cuba and withheld those sales if concerns were expressed about the risk of transshipment.[124]

By the mid-1960s, many U.S. firms increasingly questioned this relationship. Foreign subsidiaries, such as AT&T and Fruehauf, had to pay for the strategy through lost sales and a reputation as unreliable suppliers. Moreover, their claim for equal treatment with national firms was undercut when they were used as conduits for U.S. foreign policy at the expense of host country economic interests. Consequently, U.S.-based MNCs increasingly opposed extraterritorial controls.[125]

This also meant that MNCs were less likely to forego their private economic interests when not bound to do so by U.S. law. For example, in 1968, the State Department was alarmed at a Venezuelan decision to allow Soviet oil tankers to haul Venezuelan crude oil to Europe for sale to independent refiners on their return trip from shipping oil to Cuba. Among the companies taking advantage of this opportunity was the Venezuelan subsidiary of Standard Oil of New Jersey. Although its action was not covered by TWEA, the State Department sought to discourage it through moral suasion, arguing that the relationship "helps the Russians reduce their heavy financial burden in keeping Castro afloat." The company did not comply. Doing so would have created an advantage for its principal rival in Venezuela, Shell, because the Russians were offering lower rates, which were necessary to remain competitive in capturing European markets.[126]

Second, the U.S. business community initially offered little resistance to sanctions legislation, including unilateral measures that exceeded those of U.S. allies. Even though U.S. firms were handicapped by such measures, they either shared the Cold War frame of reference of public officials or recognized that domestic anticommunism made East–West trade too risky in terms of the U.S. market.[127]

This also began to change by the mid-1960s. According to one study, the turning point was President Kennedy's 1963 wheat sale to the Soviet Union, which broke the domestic taboo on East–West trade. Shortly thereafter, major corporate trade associations called for the elimination of unilateral measures that prevented U.S. businesses from competing with foreign businesses on a level playing field.[128] Extraterritorial sanctions were seen as part of the same general problem. One CEO testified that they were an "outmoded and inappropriate" policy that "only seems to antagonize friendly countries."[129]

None of this directly constrained the executive branch. Congress did not legislate any new restrictions on the wide executive latitude over wielding economic sanctions. Nor did MNCs defy U.S. jurisdiction unless—as in the *Fruehauf* case—they were compelled to do so by host country law. It did, however, indicate an evolution of corporate perceptions of interest that would make it more difficult for the United States to use MNCs as instruments of economic sanctions in the future.

THE RETREAT FROM
EXTRATERRITORIAL SANCTIONS IN THE 1970S

During the 1950s and 1960s, the United States was usually able to curb foreign subsidiary trade with China and Cuba. While domestic politics in the United States and abroad often forced diplomats to seek compromise, allies implicitly resigned themselves to U.S. jurisdiction by requesting waivers from Washington rather than legally forcing the issue. The only exception was the French response in the *Fruehauf* case, which was less an outright repudiation of all extraterritorial controls than a response to a forced contractual abrogation that threatened the viability of the firm. American MNCs also cooperated voluntarily in policing affiliate behavior. As late as 1972, *Business Latin America* reported that U.S. firms "have shown little appetite for trading with Cuba because to do so might harm the public image and sales of the parent firm."[130]

By the mid-1970s, these policies were challenged more aggressively by host countries. That period saw the steady erosion of U.S. efforts to isolate Castro, not only with NATO allies, but with the Latin American republics that agreed to OAS sanctions in 1964. Politically, Cuba was seen as less of a revolutionary threat, and establishing relations with Castro was seen as a means of bolstering one's nationalist credentials vis-à-vis the United States. Economically, Cuba had become a more attractive trading partner since higher sugar prices increased its ability to pay for imports in hard currency.[131]

As governments in Latin America, Canada, and Europe encouraged expanded Cuban trade, foreign subsidiaries were placed in a difficult dilemma. Economic self-interest dictated pursuit of trade with Cuba, both for the value of the transaction and to demonstrate to host governments that they were "good corporate citizens," not agents of U.S. foreign policy. On the other hand, trade with Cuba was still contrary to both U.S. policy and law.

In contrast to previous decades, host governments unequivocally repudiated U.S. claims of jurisdiction and were more willing to use tactical politicization to challenge U.S. practices. Despite the fact that the United States wanted to retain foreign subsidiary sanctions as a bargaining chip in prospective negotiations with Cuba, it concluded that the costs in terms of chronic conflicts with allies exceeded the benefits. In September 1975, foreign subsidiary sanctions were removed from the CACRs.

The principal reason for the more aggressive and successful challenge to U.S. policy had less to do with the decline of American economic preponderance than it did with the decline of anticommunism as a frame of reference in U.S. domestic politics. In prior decades, there were limits as to how far allies and corporations were willing to go in pursuing their economic interests because they feared congressional reprisals or adverse repercussions in the U.S. market. This was no longer the case in the climate of détente that followed the Vietnam War. Public opinion polls showed a significant majority favored a more open policy with Cuba.[132] Prominent members of Congress from both parties endorsed the normalization of trade and diplomatic relations and introduced legislation to that effect.[133] Not only did this remove many of the inhibitions facing allies and corporations, it prodded the United States to rein in the reach of its sanctions in order to prevent Congress from removing the embargo program altogether.

Argentina and the U.S. Automakers

The first public challenge to U.S.-sponsored rules governing extraterritorial sanctions came from Argentina. In May 1973, the new government of Juan Peron defected from the OAS sanctions and reestablished diplomatic relations with Cuba. In December, it negotiated a six-year $1.2 billion supplier credit for the Cuban purchase of Argentine industrial goods. The Cubans were particularly interested in goods manufactured by U.S. subsidiaries given their reliance on U.S.-made goods before the revolution. As a result, they approached subsidiaries of General Motors, Ford, and Chrysler to purchase forty-two thousand passenger cars and spare parts.[134]

The offer placed the U.S. automakers in a difficult position between the CACRs and Argentina's policy of encouraging Cuban trade. Moreover, Buenos Aires was determined to force the issue. Washington asserted that the CACRs banned any unlicensed transaction with Cuba. Argentina denied that the United States had any right to control firms incorporated on its soil and threatened to nationalize the firms if the United States tried to obstruct the transaction.[135]

This posed a dilemma for the United States. Secretary of State Henry Kissinger noted the threat to the denial policy. If the United States accepted

Argentina's argument, it would "encourage OAS members to increase their efforts to end multilateral sanctions against Cuba" and "make other governments less willing to accept continued U.S. control of American companies operating in their territory." This would have repercussions for other embargoes, such as those against North Korea and North Vietnam.[136]

Diplomatic considerations, however, prevailed over enforcing the embargo and licenses were issued to the automakers. The Nixon administration viewed Peron as a source of stability in the region and as a barrier to the domestic left despite his opening to Cuba. Kissinger recommended that a confrontation should be avoided in order to develop a "closer working relationship with Argentina."[137] There was also concern that enforcement could put the U.S. automakers out of business and "place substantial U.S. investment in Argentina ($1.3 billion) in a precarious position."[138] This involved risks beyond Argentina given the rise of economic nationalism throughout Latin America and its suspicion of foreign corporations. Public pressure could delegitimize U.S. business elsewhere in the hemisphere by reinforcing the notion that U.S. investors were instruments of Washington.

Kissinger, however, was not yet prepared to abandon the denial program or its extraterritorial dimensions. To stem any further erosion of the sanctions, he recommended that the United States should "reaffirm our Cuban policy at every opportunity and . . . [keep] the pressure on U.S. companies and other governments to hold the present line with us."[139] When the exemption was announced on 18 April 1974, State Department officials were careful to note that it was an exception that should not be construed as a precedent either in terms of Cuban policy or the CACRs.[140]

Buenos Aires, however, was not content to allow Washington to save face and asserted an unconditional right to shield companies incorporated on its soil from foreign laws. When Treasury Secretary George Shultz announced that the issue was under review, Argentina's economic minister retorted: "[T]his is a decision not subject to negotiation or discussion with anyone."[141] In other words, Argentina served notice that it rejected extraterritorial presumptions and this undercut the credibility of the U.S. contention that this was an exceptional case.

Another illustration of change was the attitude of the U.S. automakers. *Business Latin America* noted that the resolution of the conflict would have implications for American MNCs throughout Latin America because it would "contribute to the nagging question of where the allegiance of foreign-owned corporations belongs."[142] In the past, that allegiance lay primarily with the United States, either because they shared its anticommunist perspectives or feared retaliation in the home market. By the mid-1970s, those calculations changed as host country nationalism increased and the post-Vietnam environment in the United States made East–West trade less risky in the U.S. market. The automakers were consequently less concerned with repercussions from Washington or Main Street than they were with Argentine incentives (meeting export quotas was necessary to get permission to expand in the domestic market) and threats (i.e., nationalization). Hence, when General Motors filed a petition for a waiver to Treasury, it unequivocally rejected the U.S. presumption of jurisdiction by asserting that "GM subsidiaries in Argentina operate under the laws and policies of that country."[143]

Conflicts with Canada: MLW Worthington and Litton Industries

The Argentine case was followed by two public disputes with Canada over foreign subsidiary sanctions. The first took place in early 1974 when MLW Worthington, a 52 percent–owned subsidiary of Studebaker Corporation of New Jersey, agreed to sell thirty diesel locomotives to Cuba for $18 million. The parent corporation applied for an exemption from OFAC because of its controlling share of the company and the fact that two of the nine directors of the subsidiary were U.S. citizens.[144] After a lengthy delay, Ottawa sent a formal protest to the State Department, asserting that it had assisted in the negotiation and financing of a transaction by a corporation organized under Canadian law.[145]

Unlike comparable cases from the 1960s, State did not intercede with Treasury to grant relief to the parent corporation and the U.S. directors. At the time, the United States was discreetly exploring the normalization of relations with Cuba and wanted to use the offer of removing extraterritorial sanctions as a bargaining chip in exchange for a comparable Cuban concession. If host states were able to negate foreign subsidiary controls on their own, that bargaining chip would be removed.[146]

Ottawa decided to press its case publicly, particularly after it was reported in the Canadian press and debated in the House of Commons. Government ministers demanded that the sale take place. That position was backed by the implied threat of ending federal orders from and subsidies to MLW and other U.S.-controlled firms because their susceptibility to U.S. directives called into question their corporate good citizenship.[147] This threatened a key aim of U.S. economic diplomacy toward Canada—that is, the principle of "national treatment," in which U.S. firms in Canada are entitled to all the opportunities available to Canadian-owned firms.

On 8 March, MLW voted to proceed with the sale. The two U.S. directors voted against the deal to shield themselves from possible prosecution under the CACRs. The chairman of MLW publicly claimed that a waiver from Washington was wholly unnecessary because "the U.S. government isn't in a position to approve or disapprove the sale."[148] Despite the public rebuke to official policy, Washington chose to ignore the transaction rather than precipitate a confrontation with Canada.

The second dispute took place in December 1974 when Cole, a Canadian subsidiary of Litton Industries, agreed to sell $500,000 in office furniture to Cuba. The parent company ordered the subsidiary to cancel the sale after a preliminary inquiry with OFAC, which indicated that the license application would be rejected.[149] Litton was motivated by political risk in the United States as the transaction was a very small part of its $3 billion annual sales, including substantial defense contracts. The subsidiary, however, was clearly interested in the sale, which it saw as a first step in a continuing economic relationship.[150]

These calculations of political risk changed after the issue was made public. The minister of the Department of Industry, Trade, and Commerce declared that Litton should not have interfered and denounced U.S. policy as "commercial colonialism" and "intolerable interference in our internal affairs."[151] The case also led to the passage of the Combines Investigation Act, which made it illegal for Canadian-incorporated firms to comply with foreign directives that adversely affect Canada's economy.[152] As a result, future extraterritorial disputes would become conflicts of law, not merely conflicts between U.S. law and Canadian policy. On 13 February 1975, the State Department announced that the exemption to Litton would be granted, citing the need for flexibility in order to avoid conflict with allies. It continued to deny that this had any bearing on the overall embargo policy.[153]

The Removal of Extraterritorial Sanctions

These public repudiations of foreign subsidiary sanctions coincided with a high-level NSC review of the Cuban denial program. Its purpose was to frame a response to growing Latin American defections from OAS sanctions. As a result, Kissinger and Undersecretary of State for Inter-American Affairs William Rogers concluded that the multilateral embargo "was no more than marginally effective at best," and that ended the rationale for extending U.S. law into third countries.[154]

Moreover, extraterritorial sanctions were seen as costly, not only to diplomatic relations but also to the position of American business abroad. In Latin America, they further delegitimized the position of U.S. investors in an environment of economic nationalism, provoking restrictive legislation or threats of expropriation as in Argentina. In Canada, the U.S. embassy warned that they were "tailor-made for Canadian nationalists who want to place greater restrictions on foreign investments."[155] A State Department study concluded that the foreign subsidiary sanctions should be removed because the "future political cost of enforcement can be expected to exceed any lingering benefit to U.S. policy in denying Cuba this particular form of trade."[156]

These changed priorities were evident in the way the administration handled subsequent conflicts. Shortly after the Litton case, a Mexican affiliate of Chrysler filed a license application to participate in a trade fair in Havana because of pressure from the Mexican government to increase exports. The United States had a stronger legal claim to deny the license than in the Argentine and Canadian cases since the U.S. content was over 20 percent, meaning that the regulations could follow the goods rather than the firm. Nonetheless, the State Department supported the waiver because "failure to approve the Cuban application could lead to a serious tangle with the Mexican Government and damage the position of U.S. investment in Mexico."[157]

Nonetheless, Kissinger wanted to maintain the initiative in changing the policy. At the time, the United States was exploring the possibility of a détente with Cuba through secret negotiations. Removing the extraterritorial sanctions was to be used as a "gesture of good will" which would, in Kissinger's words, "put the onus on [Castro] to take the next conciliatory gesture toward us."[158]

There was a need to move quickly on this issue because other actors might reverse the policy on their own. First, the United States recognized that more conflicts over foreign subsidiary sanctions were on the horizon and the United States would have no choice but to issue exemptions. The State Department therefore recommended "acting before individual exemptions thoroughly erode the current policy." That way, the United States could "control the timing of the OAS consideration of the Cuban problem so as to be able to shape the process by which it is resolved."[159]

Second, the policy could be reversed legislatively, removing a bargaining chip and dealing the administration a humiliating defeat. The State Department recognized that support for sanctions "has markedly declined in the Congress and among the American public" because of "a widespread perception that Castroism is no longer an external threat and that the policy of isolation cannot be sustained in a world of détente."[160] In contrast to previous decades, the fear was that repeated disputes with allies would lead Congress to eliminate the sanctions altogether, preventing the executive branch from fine-tuning them to a new international environment. As Rogers concluded, "If the Executive does not take the initiative, Congress, which has already grabbed it, will keep it."[161]

The solution was for the United States to support the OAS decision in San José on 29 July to end the multilateral sanctions and support the right of each member state to adopt diplomatic or economic relations with Cuba "in accordance with its national policy and interests."[162] Kissinger reasoned that the end of the OAS embargo removed "our legal and political justification for continued efforts to punish other countries which trade with Cuba."[163] On 8 October 1975, Treasury revised the regulations to exempt foreign subsidiaries. The new regulations did not represent a complete abdication of jurisdiction. The parent corporations still had to apply for licenses and approval would only be granted if certain conditions were met—that is, the goods must be nonstrategic, the U.S. content must be less than 20 percent, and the subsidiary must be acting independently of the parent company. While these criteria were occasionally used by Treasury to deny licenses, there was, nonetheless, "a decreased effort by the United States to formally regulate subsidiaries."[164]

The late 1970s saw an international and domestic political environment less hospitable to extraterritorial sanctions. Abroad, economic nationalism in Latin America made such exertions costly in terms of the climate for American investment, and key allies, such as Canada and Great Britain, enacted legislation that criminalized compliance with foreign directives. At home, business was more assertive in lobbying to reform restrictive trade practices and Congress was trying to rein in some of the president's emergency powers, including his virtually unlimited right to impose economic sanctions. The Ford and Carter administrations accommodated themselves to these changes and limited the extraterritorial reach of sanctions. That would continue until the early 1980s when the Reagan administration sought to implement the most punitive strategies of East–West trade since the economic warfare policies of the early 1950s. The attempt to coerce its allies to cooperate with this strategy through extraterritorial sanctions would lead to one of the worst crises in the history of the Atlantic alliance.

NOTES

1. Oran Young, *International Cooperation* (Ithaca, N.Y.: Cornell University Press, 1989), 88.

2. Oran Young, *International Cooperation*, 201.

3. Kobrin, "Enforcing Export Embargoes through Multinational Corporations," 31.

4. David Leyton-Brown, "The Multinational Enterprise and Conflict in Canadian-American Relations," *International Organization* 28 (autumn 1974): 745.

5. Jentleson, *Pipeline Politics*, 67.

6. John R. Garson, "The American Trade Embargo against China," in *China Trade Prospects and U.S. Policy*, ed. Alexander Eckstein (New York: Praeger, 1971), 17–18.

7. Adler-Karlsson, *Western Economic Warfare*, 205.

8. Berman and Garson, "United States Export Controls," 811.

9. Mastanduno, *Economic Containment*, 89.

10. *FRUS*, 1948, vol. 4, 525.

11. *FRUS*, 1950, vol. 4, 167.

12. NSC 152/3, 18 June 1954 (Declassified Documents Reference System [DDRS] 1983-592), 7.

13. *FRUS*, 1951, vol. 1, 1169–1176.

14. NSC, "Summary: 75th Meeting of the NSC," 15 December 1950 (DDRS 1995-3527), 6.

15. Berman and Garson, "United States Export Controls," 836–837.

16. Garson, "The American Trade Embargo against China," 21–23.

17. Martin, *Coercive Cooperation*, 187.

18. Berman and Garson, "United States Export Controls," 832.

19. Memorandum, Adm. Arthur Radford to the Secretary of Defense, 10 June 1957 (DDRS 1981-471A).

20. *FRUS*, 1955–1957, vol. 10, 492.

21. Chang, *Friends and Enemies*, 115.

22. Paul M. Evans, "Caging the Dragon: Post-War Economic Sanctions Toward the People's Republic of China," in *The Utility of International Economic Sanctions*, ed. Leyton-Brown, 68.

23. Position of the Department of Commerce in CFEP, "Report on Political Regulation of Trade with Communist China," 13 August 1957 (DDRS 1982-29).

24. *FRUS*, 1955–1957, vol. 10, 287.

25. David Robert Leyton-Brown, *Governments of Developed Countries as Hosts to Multinational Enterprise: The Canadian, British, and French Policy Experience* (Ph.D. diss., Harvard University, Department of Government, August 1973), 94 95.

26. Washington (Robertson) to Department of External Affairs (DEA), 2 April 1958 (National Archives of Canada [NAC], Record Group [RG] 25, vol. 7607, File 11280-1-40, pt. 1.1).

27. Lowenfeld, *Trade Controls for Political Ends*, 101.

28. Leyton-Brown, "Extraterritoriality in United States Trade Sanctions," 264–265.

29. *FRUS*, 1958–1960, vol. 4, 755.

30. *FRUS*, 1958–1960, vol. 4, 720–725.

31. "Summary of 15 January 1959 NSC Meeting," 3.

32. See *FRUS*, 1958–1960, vol. 4, 706, 755–757.

33. *New York Times*, 12 July 1958, 1.

34. Kobrin, "Enforcing Export Controls through Multinational Corporations," 34.

35. Appendix to "United States Foreign Assets Controls," February 1961 (NAC, RG 25, File 11280-1-40).

36. Grey, "United States Control of Commercial Activities of Canadian Companies," Economic Division, 25 April 1958; Harvey, DTC to DEA, 2 April 1958, and Small to Collins, "Canadian Cars to Communist China," 24 January 1958 (all in NAC, RG 25, File 11280-1-40, vol. 1.1).

37. See Smith to Harvey, 3 February 1954 (NAC, RG 20, File 7637, vol. 2); R. B. Bryce, "U.S. Foreign Assets Controls: Effect on Canadian Assets," Cabinet Conclusions, 2 July 1958 (NAC, RG 2, vol. 1898).

38. Harvey, "Trade with China," 25 June 1957 (NAC, RG 25, File 11280-1-40, 1.1).

39. Harvey to Undersecretary of State for External Affairs, 2 April 1958 (NAC, RG 25, File 11280, vol. 1.1).

40. Leyton-Brown, *Governments of Developed Countries as Hosts to Multinational Enterprise*, 98–100.

41. Jones (Canadian Embassy, Washington) to English (DTC), "Trade with China— U.S. FAC Exemption for Rayonier Incorporated," 30 July 1958 (NAC, RG 20, File 7637, vol. 4).

42. Jones (Canadian Embassy, Washington) to U.S. Area Trade Officer, "U.S. FAC Exemption for Fairbanks Morse & Co.," 6 May 1959 (NAC, RG 20, File 7637, vol. 4).

43. N.A.R. Memorandum for the Prime Minister, "U.S. FACRs—Exemption for Fairbanks, More & Company," 6 May 1959 (NAC, RG 25, File 11280-1-40, vol. 1.2).

44. DTC, "United States Foreign Assets Controls," 19 December 1958 (NAC, RG 20, File 7637, vol. 4), appendix, 2.

45. Leyton-Brown, *Governments of Developed Countries as Hosts to Multinational Enterprise*, 100.

46. *FRUS*, 1961–1963, vol. 13, 1143–1144.

47. Department of External Affairs, "FACRs," 3 March 1961 (NAC, RG 25, File 11280-1-40, vol. 2.1).

48. Department of Trade and Commerce, "United States Foreign Assets Control," 19 December 1958 (NAC, RG 20, File 7637, vol. 4), appendix, 2.

49. Thorne, "Export of Chrysler Engines to Communist China," 8 September 1958; Thorne to Hopper, 29 August 1958; "Export of Dodge Passenger Car Engines and Spares to the Chinese Mainland," minutes of meeting held in Mr. English's office, 27 August 1958 (NAC, RG 20, File 7637, vol. 3).

50. Tedford to Harvey, 5 May 1958 (NAC, RG 20 File 7637, vol. 3); Department of External Affairs, "Foreign Asset Control Regulations," 3 March 1961 (NAC, RG 25, File 11280-1-40, vol. 2.1); Jones, "Discussion of FACs," 29 October 1958 (NAC, RG 20, File 7637, vol. 4).

51. *Toronto Globe and Mail*, 22 January 1959, 1.

52. Kobrin, "Enforcing Export Controls through Multinational Corporations," 34.

53. Isaiah A. Litvak, Christopher D. Maule, and Richard D. Robinson, *Dual Loyalty: Canadian-U.S. Business Arrangements* (Toronto and New York: McGraw-Hill, 1971), 25.

54. Harvey, "Refusal of Alcan to Supply Aluminum to China," 28 January 1959 (NAC, RG 20, File 7637, vol. 4), 1.

55. Jones, "FAC—Trade with China—Aluminum for Communist China," 26 November 1958 (NAC, RG 20, File 7637, vol. 4).

56. Harvey, "Refusal of Alcan to Supply Aluminum to China," 2.

57. Addendum to "China Policy" (John F. Kennedy Presidential Library, Personal Office Files [JFK/POF], Canada, Security, JFK Trip to Ottawa 5/61B), 4.

58. Jorge I. Dominguez, *To Make a World Safe for Revolution: Cuba's Foreign Policy* (Cambridge, Mass.: Harvard University Press, 1989), 187.

59. Thomas C. Mann, "Memo Re: Cuba," 7 February 1964 (DDRS 1996-101), 1.

60. Louis A. Perez Jr., *Cuba and the United States: Ties of Singular Intimacy* (Athens: University of Georgia Press, 1990), 250.

61. Michael P. Malloy, *Economic Sanctions and U.S. Trade* (Boston: Little, Brown, 1990), 509.

62. James Corcoran, "The Trading with the Enemy Act and the Controlled Canadian Corporation," *McGill Law Journal* 14 (1968): 181.

63. De Mestral and Gruchalla-Wesierski, *Extraterritorial Application of Export Legislation*, 213.

64. Charles A. Sullivan (Treasury) to G. Griffith Johnson (State), 29 December 1964 (LBJ/NSF, National Security Action Memoranda, NSAM 326).

65. Morris H. Morley, *Imperial State and Revolution: The United States and Cuba, 1952–1986* (Cambridge: Cambridge University Press, 1987), 191.

66. Annex, "Flour for Cuba," attached to Memorandum to the Minister, "Prevention of Canadian Flour Companies from Trading with Cuba," 13 July 1966 (Department of External Affairs [DEA], File 37-16-1, vol. 3).

67. D. W. Fulford (Charge D'Affaires, Havana) to Undersecretary of State for External Affairs, 18 March 1964 (DEA, File 37-16-1, vol. 1), 2.

68. See appendix to J. G. H. Halstead, Memorandum to the Minister, "Trade with Cuba—CACRs," 14 January 1975 (DEA 37-16-1, vol. 10); and "Examples of Problems Resulting from Applications of Foreign and Cuba Assets Control Regulations on Foreign Subsidiaries of U.S. Companies," attachment to Solomon to Katzenbach, 19 November 1968 (U.S. National Archives and Records Service, Diplomatic Branch, Central Foreign Policy Files [NARS/D/CFP], 1967–1969, Box 1398, STR 9-1 Chicom).

69. DEA to Canadian Embassy (Washington), 4 August 1967 (DEA, File 37-16-1, vol. 4).

70. "Application of CACRs to Canadian Companies," 1.

71. Memorandum for the Minister, "Prevention of Canadian Four Companies Trading with Cuba," 13 July 1966 (DEA, File 37-16-1, vol. 4), 1–2.

72. Morley, *Imperial State and Revolution*, 220.

73. *New York Times*, 1 September 1964, 1.

74. Annex, "Flour for Cuba" (n. 66), 2.

75. "Application of CACRs to Canadian Companies," 14 July 1964 (RG 20, 7-544-2, vol. 1), 2.

76. Canadian cabinet ministers warned their U.S. counterparts that they were "sitting on top of a volcano" and that "the U.S. should avoid any type of action that could trigger the Canadian reaction he [Prime Minister Diefenbaker] had outlined." See Draft of Minutes, Joint Canadian-United States Committee on Trade and Economic Affairs, 13–14 March 1961, Washington D.C. (NAC, RG 25. File 11280-1-40, pt. 2.2).

77. Reported in American Embassy, Ottawa (Butterworth) to State, 21 April 1967 (NARS/D/CFP, 1967-1969, Box 1400, STR 9-Cuba).

78. Department of External Affairs, "Canadian Policy on Cuba," 23 March 1966 (DEA, File 37-16-1, vol. 3).

79. Sullivan to Johnson (n. 64), 2.

80. Whiteman, *Digest*, vol. 14, 865–866.

81. *FRUS*, 1964–1968, vol. 9, 468.

82. A State Department memo noted that "the internal Canadian political situation . . . restricts our response to general expressions of concern about the Cuban threat in the hemisphere." See "Canadian Trade with Cuba," briefing paper for visit of Canadian Prime Minister Pearson, 21–22 January 1964, 17 January 1964 (DDRS 1995-71), 2.

83. Congress actually introduced legislation that would have mandated aid cutoffs to all countries that failed to stop their ships from calling on Cuban ports. See *Congressional Record:* House, 25 May 1965, 11534-35.

84. See "Examples of Problems" (n. 68), 3; and Chase to Bundy, 11 March 1964 and 7 August 1964 (LBJ/NSF, Country File, Cuba, U.S. Policy, vol. II, Box 29).

85. Rusk to Ottawa, 13 September 1967 (NARS/D/CFP, 1967–1969, Box 1398, STR9-CUBA).

86. Morley, *Imperial State and Revolution*, 218.

87. "Memorandum on Some Basic Issues in the Cuban Problem Requiring Policy Decision," attached to U. Alexis Johnson to McGeorge Bundy, 19 February 1964 (LBJ/NSF, Country File, Cuba, U.S. Policy, vol. II, Box 29), 14.

88. George Lambie, "Anglo-Cuban Commercial Relations in the 1960s: A Case Study of the Leyland Motor Company Contracts with Cuba," in *The Fractured Blockade: West European–Cuban Relations during the Revolution*, eds. Alistair Hennessy and George Lambie (London: MacMillan, 1993), 172.

89. *New York Times*, 9 January 1964, 6.

90. Rusk to London (Bruce), 25 January 1964 and Bohlen (Paris) to Rusk, 11 February 1964 (LBJ/NSF, Country File, Cuba, U.S. Policy, vol. II, Box 28).

91. Morley, *Imperial State and Revolution*, 230–231.

92. Morley, *Imperial State and Revolution*, 232.

93. "Memorandum on Some Basic Issues," 13.

94. "Memorandum on Some Basic Issues," 4.

95. Lambie, "Anglo-Cuban Commercial Relations in the 1960s," 174–176.

96. "Further Measures Which Might Be Taken against Free World Economic Ties with Cuba," 12 November 1964 (LBJ/NSF, Country File, Cuba, U.S. Policy, vol. II, Box 29), 28.

97. "U.S. Policy Toward Cuba, April to Nov. 1964," 22 March 1964 (LBJ/NSF, Country File, Cuba, U.S. Policy, vol. II, Box 29), 15.

98. "Memorandum on Some Basic Issues," 16.

99. "Memorandum on Some Basic Issues," 13.

100. Thomas C. Mann, "Memorandum Re: Cuba," 7 February 1964 (DDRS 1996-101), 2.

101. "Memorandum on Some Basic Issues," 21.

102. Mann to Rusk, 3 November 1964 (NARS/D/CFP, 1964, Box 1431, Cuba–U.K.).

103. "Memorandum on Some Basic Issues," 24; Morley, *Imperial State and Revolution*, 313.

104. Lambie, "DeGaulle's France and the Cuban Revolution" in *The Fractured Blockade*, eds. Hennessy and Lambie, 222.

105. Chase to Bundy, 25 April 1964 and 28 April 1964 (DDRS 1989-410, 411).

106. U. Alexis Johnson (State), Memorandum, 19 February 1964 (DDRS 1996-102), 3.

107. Dominguez, *To Make a World Safe for Revolution*, 189–190.

108. Calvin Mehlert (London) to State, "UK–Communist China Trade and Trade Missions, 1961," 9 October 1961 (NARS/D, 441.9341/10-961), 3.

109. Department of State, "Comments on the Feasibility of Modifying U.S. Economic Relations with Communist China," 28 February 1962 (DDRS 1980-396B).

110. Department of State Cable, 12 February 1962 (DDRS 1984-247).

111. Behrman, *National Interests and the Multinational Enterprise*, 109–110.

112. Leyton-Brown, *Governments of Developed Countries as Hosts to Multinational Enterprise*, 348.

113. Kobrin, "Enforcing Export Embargoes through Multinational Corporations," 35.

114. Lowenfeld, *Trade Controls for Political Ends*, 97.

115. William Laurence Craig, "Application of the Trading with the Enemy Act to Foreign Corporations Owned by Americans: Reflections on *Fruehauf v. Massardy*," *Harvard Law Review* 83 (January 1970): 582.

116. *International Legal Materials* (Washington, D.C.: American Society of International Law, 1966), 476.

117. Lowenfeld, *Trade Controls for Political Ends*, 99–100.

118. Craig, "Application of the Trading with the Enemy Act," 581.

119. After *Fruehauf*, licenses were routinely issued in cases when the U.S. subsidiary was bound by contract to disregard U.S. law since it was no longer under the control of

U.S. persons. See the response to a similar case in Italy (Eaton Industries) shortly after the *Fruehauf* case in *FRUS*, 1964–1968, vol. 9, 519–520.

120. *FRUS*, 1964–1968, 524.

121. Leyton-Brown, *Governments of Developed Countries as Hosts to Multinational Enterprise*, 261.

122. *New York Times*, 7 February 1968, 3.

123. On the China case, see Luke T. Lee and John B. McCobb, "United States Trade Embargo On China, 1949–1970: Legal Status and Future Prospects," *New York University Journal of Law and Politics* 4 (spring 1971): 4; on the Cuban case, see Mann to Nichols, 23 June 1960 (DDI 1994-125).

124. Morley, *Imperial State and Revolution*, 190, 211, 313.

125. Behrman, *National Interests and the Multinational Enterprise*, 107n.

126. Rusk to American Embassy (Caracas), 24 July 1968 (DDRS 1980 391D), 3.

127. Mastanduno, "Trade as a Strategic Weapon," 128.

128. Adler-Karlsson, *Western Economic Warfare*, 105–106.

129. Testimony of John T. Connor, CEO, Allied Chemical Corp., in U.S. Congress, Senate Committee on Banking and Currency, Subcommittee on International Trade, *Export Expansion and Regulation*, Hearings, 91st Cong., 1st sess., 1969, 183–184.

130. *Business Latin America*, 20 April 1972, 122.

131. Rosemary H. Werret, *Cuba at the Turning Point: How the Economy Works, Changes in the Offing, New Opportunities for MNCs* (New York: Business International Corp., 1977), 29.

132. A 1973 Harris Poll found that the public favored normalization by a margin of 51 percent to 33 percent. See *Harris Survey Yearbook of Public Opinion*, 1973 (New York: Louis Harris Associates, Inc., 1976), 259.

133. Philip Brenner, *The Limits and Possibilities of Congress* (New York: St. Martin's, 1983), 72-76.

134. *Business Latin America*, 16 January 1974, 21.

135. *New York Times*, 18 April 1974, 5.

136. Kissinger to Nixon, "Argentina and Our Cuban Denial Policy," 30 December 1973 (Department of State, Freedom of Information Act [DOS/FOIA]), 1.

137. Kissinger to Nixon, 30 December 1973, 2; also see Morley, *Imperial State and Revolution*, 275.

138. Kissinger to Nixon, 30 December 1973 (n. 136), 2.

139. Kissinger to Nixon, 30 December 1973, 3.

140. *Department of State Bulletin*, 20 May 1974, 544.

141. Hill (Buenos Aires) to Kissinger, 7 March 1974 (DOS/FOIA).

142. *Business Latin America*, 12 December 1973, 393.

143. Thomas N. Gladwin and Ingo Walter, *Multinationals under Fire: Lessons in the Management of Conflict* (New York: Wiley, 1980), 242.

144. Kobrin, "Enforcing Export Embargoes through Multinational Corporations," 35.

145. *International Canada*, March 1974, 46.

146. See Peter Kornbluh and James G. Blight, "Dialogue with Castro: A Hidden History," *New York Review of Books*, 6 October 1994, 45–49.

147. *Business International*, 10 May 1974, 151.

148. *Wall Street Journal*, 11 March 1974, 6.

149. Kobrin, "Enforcing Export Embargoes through Multinational Corporations," 36.

150. *New York Times*, 24 December 1974, 3.

151. *International Canada*, December 1974, 230–231.

152. David Leyton-Brown, "Extraterritoriality in Canadian-American Relations," *International Journal* 36 (winter 1980–1981): 191.

153. *New York Times*, 15 February 1975, 11.

154. "Background—Cuba Policy," 7 February 1975 (Ford Library, Kissinger/Scowcroft Files [Ford/KSF], Latin America–Cuba), 1; also see Kornbluh and Blight, "Dialogue with Castro," 45n.

155. Porter (Ottawa) to State, 27 December 1974, (DOS/FOIA), 3.

156. Ingersoll to Ford, "Cuba Policy—Our Constraints on U.S. Subsidiaries," 25 February 1975 (Ford/KSF, Cuba—Economic, Social Sanctions, 1975), 2.

157. "Cuba Policy: License Application to U.S. Subsidiary in Mexico," 21 February 1975; American Embassy Mexico City (Jova) to Kissinger, 28 January 1975; and State Department, Memorandum of Conversation, "Licenses for Participation of Chrysler de Mexico in Cuban Trade Fair," 20 February 1975 (DOS/FOIA).

158. Kornbluh and Blight, "Dialogue with Castro," 48.

159. "Background—Cuba Policy," 5; "Cuba Policy," briefing paper, 15 August 1974 (Ford/KSF, Latin America-General), 3.

160. "Background—Cuba Policy," 1–2.

161. Kornbluh and Blight, "Dialogue with Castro," 47 n.15.

162. *International Legal Materials*, 1975, 1354.

163. Kissinger to Ford, "Lifting Third Country Constraints on Trade with Cuba," 12 August 1975 (DOS/FOIA), 1.

164. Robert B. Thompson, "United States Jurisdiction over Foreign Subsidiaries: Corporate and International Law Aspects," *Law & Policy in International Business* 14 (1983): 334.

Chapter Three

Sanctions Defiant: The Reagan Administration, Extraterritorial Sanctions, and the Lessons of the Pipeline Case

The Reagan administration entered office committed to enlarging the capacity of the United States to control the international environment. Ironically, the evolution of Reagan administration foreign policy may appear in retrospect, as a textbook example of how the international environment shapes foreign policy.

—Kenneth A. Oye[1]

Cap [Weinberger] loves those sanctions. He thinks the allies are like the air traffic controllers. But we can't fire the allies. We need them.

—George P. Shultz[2]

After taking office in 1981, the Reagan administration saw its central foreign policy mission as the reassertion of American power to confront the Soviet Union. Its "grand strategy" was to maximize the strains on its adversary's economic and political system to the point where it would either have to retreat from the Cold War competition or face an intensified economic crisis at home. This new agenda required a rejection of the conventional wisdom of the 1970s—that is, that the unilateral exercise of American power was increasingly constrained in a more interdependent and pluralistic world. To succeed in its ambitions, the United States would have to act in defiance of these constraints.

One area in which the Reagan administration sought to break through the presumed constraints of the 1970s was its strategy of East–West trade. While there were differences within the Reagan cabinet, influential bureaucratic actors in the Defense Department, CIA, and NSC favored a return to the economic warfare strategies of the 1950s as part of a grand strategy to exhaust the Soviet Union. The Reagan administration had two opportunities to wage economic warfare after the declaration of martial law in Poland in December

1981. The first arose when Poland was unable to repay U.S. government-guaranteed agricultural loans. Influential members of the administration wanted to declare Poland in default, a decision that would have forced other creditors to do likewise because of the cross-default clauses in their contracts. This option, however, would have posed unacceptable risks to the international financial system and the multilateral cooperation that was needed to manage the debt crisis. As a result, the administration adapted to the constraints of the international system and eschewed financial sanctions, rolling over Poland's overdue payments.

The second test was the application of sanctions against the European-Soviet natural gas pipeline. When NATO allies refused to abandon plans to continue the project despite the repression in Poland, the sanctions were applied extraterritorially to the foreign subsidiaries of American firms and their European licensees. The Europeans responded by denouncing this action as an infringement of their sovereignty and by invoking legislation that blocked corporate compliance with foreign directives. The United States initially escalated the conflict by imposing penalties on U.S. and European companies that complied with host country law rather than U.S. sanctions. In the end, the Reagan administration was forced to back down in exchange for a face-saving compromise.

To many observers, this outcome reinforced the lessons drawn from the 1970s and served as the frame of reference for a conventional wisdom regarding the futility of extraterritorial sanctions. It held that the ability of the U.S. government to use the foreign operations of U.S. firms as instruments of foreign policy had been eroded by the growth of the MNC and the decline of U.S. economic preponderance. In addition, the growth of international economic interdependence increased the costs and risks of unilateral sanctions, both to the rules of multilateral institutions and to the reputation and profits of American business. As a result, domestic political constraints on unilateral economic sanctions increased as corporations and their trade associations became more aggressive in challenging unilateral measures and Congress became receptive to their efforts.

U.S. ECONOMIC STATECRAFT IN THE 1980S

A More Constrained Environment: The Domestic and International Context

The Reagan administration sought to return U.S. strategies of East–West trade back to the economic warfare approach of the early Cold War era. In so doing, it faced a more constrained environment than did its predecessors from that period, both in applying its sanctions generally and in enlisting the voluntary cooperation of American multinationals.

First, the 1970s saw an expansion of the trend toward the globalization of American business. American MNCs were more aggressive in establishing foreign direct investments as opportunities in industrialized and developing countries increased relative to those in the U.S. market. The change in banking was even more dramatic as the recycling of OPEC's petrodollars expanded the participation of U.S. private financial institutions in the Eurocurrency market. This meant that private commercial banks operating offshore replaced public institutions as the primary conduits for the international transfer of capital.[3] Since an increasing proportion of U.S. commercial and financial activity took place outside the territorial boundaries of the United States, policymakers could no longer assume that American MNCs were instruments of foreign policy that could be commanded to follow state preferences.

This problem was compounded by changes in corporate perceptions of interest away from an ethnocentric identification with U.S. Cold War aims. Some firms had become more economically dependent upon host countries and sought to legitimize their stakes by cultivating a reputation there as good corporate citizens. Others wanted to maintain their freedom to pursue their global economic interests, even with those radical or communist regimes who were pragmatic in their business dealings. Given this change in corporate mind-set, voluntary cooperation with U.S. foreign policy initiatives was less likely than it was in the 1950s and 1960s.[4]

Second, the domestic political environment was less conducive to the use of sanctions. During the height of the Cold War, U.S. firms were inhibited from lobbying against sanctions or even engaging in legally permissible trade with communist countries because of the intensity of anticommunist sentiment in the American political system. As a result, most deferred to Cold War economic statecraft even when it worked against their private interests.[5] These inhibitions were less compelling during the détente era of the 1970s. U.S. firms became increasingly interested in East–West trade and more concerned about the impact of U.S. regulations on their reliability as a trading partner. They consequently lobbied Congress to modify the Export Administration Act to remove those regulations that made it more difficult to compete internationally, such as extraterritorial sanctions or controls on goods available elsewhere.[6]

Congress also tried to limit the president's export control and emergency economic powers. During the early Cold War era, Congress had delegated to the president nearly unlimited discretion to interrupt foreign economic transactions. By the mid-1970s, many members of Congress saw that as an anachronism of the early Cold War. They were more inclined to agree with corporate trade associations that controlling goods freely traded by allies hurt U.S. business without adding costs on the Soviet Union and that extensive re-export controls damaged U.S. companies' reputation for reliability. These changes in perspective led to some modifications of the law. In 1969, the Export Control Act, renamed the Export Administration Act, eliminated mandatory controls on exports that contributed to Soviet bloc economic as opposed to military potential.[7] The 1979 act set up consultation and reporting requirements when controlled items were available from allies.[8] In 1980, Congress introduced legislation to terminate the grain embargo after the Soviet invasion of Afghanistan and later passed a bill making it more difficult for any administration to use this weapon in the future.[9] While none of these bills tied the hands of the president, they did send a signal designed to deter sanctions and export controls that were too costly to domestic economic interests. Failure to heed that signal could have triggered more restrictive legislative encroachments on executive autonomy over economic statecraft.

Congress was also concerned that the president's emergency powers under TWEA had become an unlimited grant of authority without congressional oversight. In fact, the national emergency declared by President Truman during the Korean War was never terminated. It served as the basis not only for subsequent economic sanctions, but for other unrelated actions, such as the Johnson administration's 1968 decision to place controls on U.S. direct foreign investment or the Nixon administration's 1971 decision to impose a 10 percent import surcharge.[10] By the mid-1970s, a majority in Congress concluded that such a sweeping delegation of authority was unjustified in an era of superpower détente and was dangerous given the abuses of power that occurred during the Vietnam War.

In 1976, Congress passed the National Emergency Act, which terminated authority presidents had claimed from past emergencies and established legislative oversight of future declarations. It also passed the International Emergency Economic Powers Act (IEEPA) to "revise and delimit the President's authority to regulate international economic transactions." In order to impose sanctions under IEEPA, the president must report an "unusual and extraordinary threat to the national security, foreign policy or economy of the United States which has its origin wholly or partly outside the U.S."[11] TWEA was to be limited to wartime, though the sanctions imposed under its authority (i.e., the embargoes against Cuba, Vietnam, North Korea, and Cambodia) were grandfathered.[12] The bill was designed as an economic version of the War Powers Resolution by establishing stronger congressional accountability over the use of peacetime economic sanctions.

This is not to argue that Congress abandoned the right to place overseas corporate activity under its laws. IEEPA may have increased congressional oversight, but retained virtually the same extraterritorial powers as existed under TWEA.[13] A 1977 amendment to the Export Administration Act extended U.S. export controls to foreign subsidiaries selling non-U.S.-origin goods despite a Senate report that indicated that such measures "were not un-likely to go unchallenged by the governments of the countries in which the subsidiaries are located."[14] Congress was also not averse to adding an extra-territorial dimension to legislation designed to impose its agenda on the exec-utive branch, such as the Foreign Corrupt Practices Act or the amendment to the Export Administration Act banning corporate collaboration with the Arab Boycott of Israel.[15] For the most part, however, the congressional role had changed from a source of pressure on administrations to get tough with allies who "traded with the enemy" into more of a restraining influence on unilat-eral sanctions and export controls that sacrificed national economic interests.

Finally, the international environment had become less hospitable to extra-territorial sanctions. Western allies were generally skeptical about economic sanctions and did not follow the U.S. lead in linking economics to diplomacy for Cold War, human rights, or nonproliferation policies. On East–West trade, they maintained a strategic embargo under CoCom, but resisted controls on nonstrategic trade. As a result, the United States failed to get allied support for linking economic relations to Soviet behavior. In 1978, for example, the Carter administration cut technology sales to the Soviet Union in response to Soviet dissident trials. British, West German, and Japanese firms almost im-mediately replaced those contracts.[16] After the Soviet invasion of Afghanistan, the allies were willing to tighten the rules for the strategic em-bargo—that is, the "no exceptions" policy on exemptions from the CoCom list. That cooperation did not extend to the grain embargo or controls on what were viewed as civilian rather than strategic technology.[17]

To some extent, the Europeans were motivated by commercial considera-tions, but there were political rationales as well. The United States came to see détente as a failure because of Soviet interventions in the Third World. The Europeans saw détente in Europe as successful in stabilizing the region and increasing economic and cultural contacts. While they deplored Soviet activities in the Third World, they did not see a threat to their vital interests. As a result, they sought to insulate East–West cooperation in areas of con-vergent interests (i.e., stabilizing Europe, East–West trade, arms control) from competition in areas of divergent (and less important) interests. Moreover, separating commerce from geopolitics would provide political dividends be-cause it would encourage an evolution to less conflictual East–West relations by increasing interdependence and strengthening the hands of those Soviet officials who had a vested interest in détente.[18]

Given this perspective, allied governments were more resistant to extrater-ritorial controls. By the mid-1970s, they objected more vociferously to the ap-plication of sanctions to the local subsidiaries of American firms and their po-sition was strongly supported by popular sentiment at home. Some countries enacted legislation that blocked the extension of foreign law onto their territory. In 1975, Canada passed the Combines Investigations Act, which made it illegal for a Canadian firm to obey foreign laws or directives that harm the Canadian economy.[19] In 1980, Great Britain passed the Protection of Trading Interests Act (PTIA) in response to extraterritorial antitrust actions against the uranium cartel.[20] As a result, the United States could expect much stronger allied resistance to its extraterritorial controls than it did in the 1950s and 1960s.

A More Ambitious Agenda: Economic Warfare as Grand Strategy

The Reagan administration was determined to press the outer limits of these constraints in forging more restrictive strategies of East–West trade. There was a bureaucratic consensus that the détente strategy of the 1970s—namely, using economic inducements to moderate Soviet behavior—had failed and that there was a need to move from "carrots" to "sticks." There were, however, deep divisions over "grand strategy" and the kinds of "sticks" that would best support it.

The Defense Department's case for economic warfare was advocated by Secretary Caspar Weinberger and Assistant Secretary Richard Perle. It was also supported by the director of Central Intelligence, William Casey, and influential members of the NSC, such as National Security Adviser William Clark and its Russian specialist, Richard Pipes. They concluded that the Soviet economy was in dire straits due not only to the inefficiencies of its central planning system, but also to excessive military spending and imperial overextension. The United States ought to impose on the Soviet Union what one NSC official called a "full court press," maximizing pressure on the Soviet system to "force our principal adversary . . . to bear the brunt of its economic shortcomings."[21] The administration's military buildup and its support of insurgencies against Soviet clients in the Third World were among the strategies that were designed to force upon Moscow painful choices between Cold War competition and internal economic reform. In other words, the aim was not to influence Soviet behavior through bargaining; it was to limit the resources available to it in order either to force it to turn inward or face economic crisis and destabilization.[22]

Economic warfare was a logical outgrowth of this strategy and was justified in both defensive and offensive terms.[23] First, since Moscow's expansionist aims were seen as immutable, anything that contributed to the Soviet Union's economic growth freed resources for its military. Second, denial of credit and civilian technology to the Soviet bloc would complement an arms race and support for anti-Soviet rebellions in adding to the pressures on the Soviet economy. Therefore, the United States had to expand the multilateral consensus to cover not only strategic items, but anything that aided the Soviet economy.

The hard-liners knew that the Europeans did not share this perspective and recognized that failure to gain their cooperation would eviscerate the strategy. Of particular concern was the Soviet–West European project to jointly develop the Urengoi natural gas fields in Siberia. The fields were to be developed by European firms, in collaboration with U.S. corporate partners, and supported by European government credits. Defense's opposition was motivated in part by vulnerability concerns: the deal would create an unacceptable level of allied dependence on Soviet energy sources which could be used as political influence in times of crisis.[24] More importantly, the project threatened the economic warfare component of the grand strategy. It would provide Moscow with the civilian technology that its economic system had neglected and alleviate the hard currency shortages by providing subsidized credits and a projected $8 to $10 billion in foreign exchange from energy exports. Weinberger and Perle advocated the use of unilateral pressure on allies to abandon the deal with veiled threats of rethinking commitments if they failed to comply.[25]

The case for a more pragmatic approach was made by the Department of State and supported by the secretaries of Commerce and Treasury. To Secretary of State Alexander Haig (and his successor, George Shultz), the purpose of a tougher foreign policy was not to debilitate the Soviet Union, but to negotiate from a position of strength.[26] On East–West trade, State opposed economic warfare. It argued that the Soviet economy was less dependent on trade with the West than claimed by the Defense Department. It also viewed unilateral economic warfare as futile and counterproductive. If the United States sought to control goods readily available from allies, it would have an adverse impact on the competitiveness of American business and the U.S. balance of payments.[27]

Finally, State opposed economic warfare because of the premium it placed on alliance cohesion. It supported tighter restrictions on East–West trade in areas in which there was multilateral agreement, such as militarily significant technology. No such consensus existed for economic warfare. Any attempt to coerce allied agreement would produce a bitter confrontation that would impede cooperation elsewhere. Quiet diplomacy was State's preferred option, even in cases in which it was dubious of East–West deals, such as the pipeline project.[28] These priorities were largely consistent with State Department policy in previous administrations—that is, using diplomacy to broaden the consensus underlying the strategic embargo, but subordinating pressure for a tougher embargo to the need for multilateralism.

Until the Polish crisis in December 1981, President Reagan generally sided with State's position. An NSC paper produced in March, entitled "The Prudent Approach," advocated tightening strategic controls within the framework of a multilateral consensus.[29] This was the tack adopted at the Ottawa Summit in July 1981, the first major negotiations with the Group of Seven (G-7) allies on East–West trade. In the final communiqué, the allies agreed to noncommittal language that East–West trade should be "compatible with our political and security objectives."[30] They also established contingency plans for the imposition of sanctions should the Red Army invade Poland. Finally, they agreed to a high-level review of the CoCom embargo in January 1982, the first such review since 1957. One U.S. official noted the modest achievements in terms of the constraints of multilateralism—it was "not a question of what we wanted but of what could be achieved."[31]

The same moderation was evident in the initial approach to the pipeline deal. At Ottawa, the Reagan administration made clear its concerns about the vulnerability issue, but took no steps to impede the project. The United States accepted the pipeline as a fait accompli and focused more on agreements to limit European vulnerability—such as a NATO study of what constituted a safe level of dependence, backup energy supplies, and the long-term development of alternative supplies.[32] President Reagan also sided with Haig over Weinberger in declining to bar U.S. firms from participating in the project. In fact, only four days before the declaration of martial law, Commerce approved a license for Caterpillar Tractor to sell pipelayers to the Soviet Union for natural gas development.[33]

In sum, prior to the Polish crisis, bureaucratic debates over East–West trade were generally resolved in favor of those who wanted to strengthen policy within a multilateral consensus. As a result, no effort was made to coerce allies, and U.S. firms were allowed to participate in the pipeline project. All of this would change dramatically on 13 December 1981, when the Polish military declared martial law.

SANCTIONS DETERRED: THE POLISH DEBT CRISIS

Poland's declaration of martial law and suppression of the Solidarity trade union movement provided the catalyst for a renewed bureaucratic debate over economic warfare. Defense and its allies at the NSC and CIA argued for placing the Soviet system under greater strain by redoubling economic pressures against it. Such strategies would require a collision with allies, who condemned the repression but refused to move from diplomatic protest to economic sanctions. While the State Department still preferred diplomacy and consensus building, Defense called for unilateral measures to coerce allied compliance.

Among the first economic instruments considered were financial sanctions. A potential source of vulnerability was Poland's difficulty in servicing its $26 billion debt, $71 million of which was due to U.S. banks for Commodity Credit Corporation (CCC) loans guaranteed by the U.S. government. Weinberger and Perle called for a declaration of default—an action that could have required all other creditors to follow suit because of cross-default clauses in their contracts. This option was attractive from an economic warfare perspective because it would have forced the Soviet Union to assume Poland's debts and would have dried up new Western credits to the East. It was, however, an option not taken because of the risks it posed to the international financial system.

The origins of Poland's heavy indebtedness can be traced to two developments in the 1970s. First, the banks had an incentive to increase lending because of excess liquidity—a direct result of the enormous petrodollar deposits from oil-producing countries after the 1973 OPEC price increases. From their perspective, Poland was a good credit risk. It had abundant natural resources, particularly coal, and a good repayment record. Moreover, the banks assumed that if there were problems, the Soviet Union would serve as a lender of last resort rather than let one of its satellites go under.[34] Second, European governments encouraged private lending to Eastern Europe in support of their strategy of détente. As a result, they reduced the risk of such lending through loan guarantees and export credit insurance. From 1970 until 1981, Poland's hard currency debt increased from $1 billion to $26 billion. During the same period, the debt burden for Eastern Europe as a whole increased from $17 billion to $66 billion.[35]

U.S. policymakers were more reticent about private lending to the East, even during the early détente era. They did not want to subsidize Soviet military spending and were concerned that overextended banks might become conduits for Soviet influence. As a result, they tried to negotiate multilateral policies to curtail export financing as early as 1974.[36] These concerns did not dissuade Washington from extending CCC loans for Polish imports of American grain. Nor did Washington discourage U.S. banks from participating in Eastern bloc lending. By 1981, private U.S. bank exposure in Poland was roughly $1.3 billion.[37]

By 1979, it was clear that the premises underlying the lending were no longer valid. The Polish economy had stopped growing and was unable to generate the export earnings needed to service its debt on schedule. Moreover, the Solidarity trade union movement had launched widespread industrial strikes against decreased wages and subsidies. The Polish government was unable to reconcile competing pressures from foreign banks and Polish workers. On 5 March 1981, it announced a moratorium on debt repayments and initiated negotiations with public and private creditors to reschedule its debt.[38]

   The Reagan administration adopted a relatively benign approach to
Poland's repayment problems. It avoided actions that might have destabilized
the Polish economy in order to protect the Solidarity trade union movement
and the opening toward greater pluralism. As a result, it cooperated with allies in supporting liberal terms for the renegotiation of official debt at the
Paris Club in late April.[39] This set the stage for the rescheduling of private
loans later that year. The priority was not economic warfare, but maintaining
economic stability so as to avert Soviet intervention. As one State Department
official noted, "The purpose was to ease their payments problems in lieu of
official aid. In essence, this was political relief."[40]

   Once martial law was declared, Defense saw an opportunity for a major
change in the direction of economic warfare. When the Polish government
was unable to make timely payment on $71.3 million due from its $1.6 billion in loans guaranteed by the CCC, Weinberger argued that the United
States should formally declare Poland's debt in default. This would, in turn,
force all commercial banks to follow suit because of cross-default clauses in
their loan contracts.[41]

   Weinberger and Perle reasoned that default would confront the Soviets
with two unpalatable choices—assuming the Polish debt or letting Poland and
its creditors fend for themselves. The first option would add to Moscow's financial burdens and divert hard currency away from military-industrial production. The second option would give creditors the right to accelerate their
loans and demand immediate repayment. Since Polish compliance with this
demand was impossible, it would trigger the freezing of Poland's foreign assets and the drying up of virtually all new lending not just to Poland, but to
the rest of Eastern Europe, which would be seen as a much greater credit risk.
Either outcome would undercut other East–West economic relationships that
developed under détente given their dependence on Western credits.[42] In effect, unilateral measures would coerce the compliance of allies as private
commercial banks became instruments of economic warfare.

   The Departments of State and Treasury opposed the default option. Default
was characterized as a blunt and inflexible instrument, difficult to reverse if
the situation in Poland improved. It would also absolve the Polish government of any obligation to repay its loans and there would be few assets to
seize in retaliation.[43] By contrast, keeping Poland's debt on the books would
create, in the words of one State Department official, "pressure on them to divert a part of their very scarce foreign exchange to the repayment of debt."[44]
This, in turn, could provide the West with leverage to link debt relief to the
removal of martial law.

   State and Treasury won the bureaucratic argument. On 29 January 1982,
the administration ordered the CCC to reimburse U.S. banks for the $71.3

million that Poland was unable to service. It did so through an emergency waiver to get around the statutory requirement that default must be declared prior to reimbursement. By the end of the year, the CCC had assumed $344 million owed to U.S. creditors without insisting on any quid pro quo from Warsaw.[45] At the same time, the United States erected a number of impediments to Poland's access to foreign capital, such as blocking Poland's application for membership in the IMF, suspending the 1982 negotiations on rescheduling official debt, and freezing all new official credits. Each of these measures closed avenues that would have alleviated Poland's debt problem, and their removal was linked to the end of martial law.[46]

The decision to forego the default option was harshly criticized by many Cold War conservatives for elevating the private interests of U.S. banks over the need to punish and reverse communist tyranny.[47] Indeed, the policy did comport with the interests of both U.S. and foreign bankers in protecting their assets. Creditors rarely declare sovereign governments in default because that would jeopardize the prospects for repayment. This was of particular concern in the Polish case because banks would have had to write off $7.4 billion in unguaranteed private loans to Poland, $1.3 billion of which were owed to U.S. banks.[48] Poland had few foreign assets that could be seized to offset liabilities. U.S. banks were also concerned that the European Community (EC) would negotiate a separate deal on repayment whereby European creditors would be repaid while they would be left out.[49] They had a strong preference for rescheduling the debt — deferring or rolling over the payment of principal while continuing to collect interest and requiring internal economic reforms to make Poland more creditworthy. In this strategy, many bankers equated their private interests with martial law since it enabled the Polish government to suppress domestic opposition to many of the reforms they had been pressing on it to better service its debt — namely, currency devaluation, a six-day work week, and the reduction of wages and food subsidies. Some bankers privately and publicly expressed sympathy with these developments, the most controversial of which was Thomas Theobald, the CEO of Citibank, who said, "[W]ho knows what political system works? The only test we care about is: can they pay their bills?"[50]

More was at stake, however, than the private interests of the banks. The Reagan administration was constrained from using default as a political weapon because of the risks to the international financial system. The central fear was that the repercussions of a Polish default could not be contained. As Benjamin Cohen noted, it could have led to a kind of domino effect — "a scramble by banks to reduce their exposure in Eastern Europe, which might have led to a chain reaction of defaults throughout the region."[51] This, in turn, could have spread to Latin America, where U.S. banks were considerably more exposed.

Moreover, financial sanctions could have created a major disruption in the alliance since the Europeans, particularly the West Germans, were more exposed in Eastern Europe than their U.S. counterparts. A strategy that placed the financial institutions of America's closest allies at risk might have succeeded in coercing their compliance in the short run. In the long run, it could have imperiled European cooperation in dealing with other international financial crises, particularly in Latin America.[52] As a result, the Reagan administration rejected unilateral options because of their likely impact on multilateral cooperation in an area where the United States was unable to achieve its objectives alone.

SANCTIONS DEFIANT AND CONSTRAINED: THE PIPELINE SANCTIONS

In the debate over financial sanctions, the Reagan administration adapted to the constraints of interdependence. In imposing sanctions on the pipeline project, it defied those constraints. When diplomacy failed to persuade allies to back away from the deal, the United States sought to force the issue by applying the sanctions extraterritorially.

On 29 December 1981, the Reagan administration used the Export Administration Act to impose new foreign policy controls on the Soviet Union, citing its responsibility for the repression in Poland. The executive order extended the controls to cover energy transmission and refining equipment sold by U.S. firms for use in the pipeline project. It retroactively withdrew those licenses already granted, forcing U.S. firms, such as Caterpillar Tractor, Dresser Industries, and General Electric (GE), to cancel contracts.[53] The most significant of the forced cancellations was GE's contract to sell rotors and nozzles to be used in turbines and compressors manufactured by European firms, such as AEG-Kanis (Germany), John Brown Engineering (U.K.), and Nuovo Pignone (Italy). At the time of the sanctions, GE was the only firm that manufactured this technology.[54] These new controls represented a departure from the earlier policy of criticizing the pipeline but not trying to reverse it. As Haig noted, they were a direct challenge to "the continued ability of the Europeans to build the pipeline."[55] The allies objected to U.S. policy, but did not see a threat to their sovereignty since the regulations were limited to items originating in the United States.

Unilateral sanctions were followed by diplomatic efforts to persuade the Europeans that repression in Poland had refuted the logic of détente and that they ought to abandon the pipeline deal. Two lines of argument were presented. First, U.S. diplomats reiterated their concern that Western Europe would become overly dependent on imports of Soviet energy resources. Second, they contended that the hard currency the Soviets earned from the pipeline would free resources for military-industrial production. These considerations should be more compelling because the Polish repression, combined with the Afghanistan invasion and the military buildup, indicated that détente had failed and the Soviet threat was more urgent. Hence, the allies ought to join Washington in adopting a zero-sum approach to East–West trade, equating anything that contributed to Soviet economic growth with a security threat to the West.[56]

The Europeans were not persuaded by U.S. arguments regarding the failure of détente and the dangers of the pipeline deal. While they condemned the Soviet Union for the repression in Poland, they did not see this as a cause for disavowing détente. As reprehensible as the crackdown was in moral terms, it was not viewed as a new threat to European security. Therefore, the Reagan administration could not point to Poland the same way its predecessors pointed to the Soviet bloc behavior in the early Cold War period to persuade them that the threat was so imminent that they should practice economic warfare. To the Europeans, regional stability and any possibility of liberalization in Poland were more likely to come from continued engagement rather than isolation.[57]

The Europeans disputed the zero-sum premises underlying U.S. policy. First, they dismissed the vulnerability argument; imports of Soviet natural gas would enhance their economic security by diversifying sources of supply away from the volatile regions of the Persian Gulf and North Africa. They would not be vulnerable to Soviet coercion because (1) their level of dependence on Soviet natural gas would only amount to 6 percent of their energy consumption, and (2) the Soviet Union would be deterred from cutting off supplies because it would not risk the loss of items vital to its economy—that is, hard currency and civilian technology.[58] Second, the EC did not see the prospect of Soviet hard currency earnings from the vantage point of economic warfare. Increased Soviet exports meant the Soviet bloc would be better able to service its debts to Western (mostly European) creditors. Therefore, they preferred to view East–West trade in terms of mutual gains from interdependence rather than in terms of relative vulnerabilities.[59]

The allies consequently saw no reason not to pursue their commercial interests. The pipeline contracts were important for profits and employment in a number of key industries that had been hurt badly during the recession of the early 1980s.[60] Moreover, the Europeans regarded as hypocritical U.S. arguments about shared sacrifice for the sake of the alliance because of the Reagan administration's decision to make good on a campaign promise to rescind the Carter administration's grain embargo. From their perspective, the United States lacked credibility because it was promoting free trade in areas of greatest interest to itself (agricultural goods) while calling for tighter restrictions on civilian technology trade, which was of greatest economic significance to Western Europe.[61]

Given these differences, negotiations produced only modest results. On 4 January 1982, the EC responded to U.S. demands by condemning the Soviet Union for its responsibility for the Polish crackdown. It did not impose parallel sanctions, though it promised that it would not exploit those imposed by the United States.[62] A NATO ministerial meeting later that month produced an accord tying future official credit to developments in Poland and postponing debt rescheduling. On trade, however, there was no more than an agreement to "examine possibilities for further action."[63] A similarly ambiguous result emerged from the CoCom meeting in Paris. The U.S. representatives tried to broaden the strategic embargo list, but the Europeans resisted any controls that targeted the Soviet economy rather than its military capability.[64]

In early 1982, the Reagan cabinet was still divided over how far the United States should go in pressing its allies. Proponents of economic warfare called for an intensification of U.S. efforts. A 1982 CIA study indicated that the Soviet economy was in dire straits and that energy production was a clear source of vulnerability.[65] NSC Director William Clark publicly stated that "the U.S. should declare economic and technological war on the USSR."[66] That war, however, could not be won if allies followed through with the pipeline project and other East–West deals. As a result, the hard-liners recommended serious consideration of coercive options, including the threat of extending the sanctions extraterritorially. As one Reagan administration official put it, "Germany will have to choose between the Alliance and Ostpolitik. It can no longer have it both ways."[67]

State opposed this strategy, contending that extraterritorial sanctions would create a rift in the alliance whose costs would exceed those of European-Soviet trade. Its preference was to rely on diplomacy to strengthen restrictions within attainable limits. The bargain visualized by Haig as the best means of defusing the crisis was to forego extraterritorial sanctions if the Europeans would abandon government subsidized credits and established quantitative limits on the volume of imported natural gas. Undersecretary of State James Buckley led a high-level delegation to European capitals to negotiate such an arrangement.[68]

The last chance for compromise was at the G-7 Summit in Versailles in early June. While the United States called for the cancellation of the pipeline deal, it was isolated on this issue. The final communiqué represented an ambiguous agreement that called for "commercial prudence in limiting export credits" without any binding commitments. Even the pretense of agreement disappeared a few weeks later when French President François Mitterrand declared that he was not bound by the summit to cut the amount of official credits extended to Moscow.[69]

The hard-liners used Mitterrand's statement to persuade President Reagan to abandon diplomacy in favor of coercion. On 18 June 1982, the administration extended the December 1981 controls to the foreign subsidiaries and licensees of American firms. As one Commerce Department official explained it, "[T]he impact on the pipeline project could be greater if exports by U.S. subsidiaries and exports of foreign equipment based on previously supplied U.S. technology could be stopped."[70] In other words, the aim was to use U.S. law to force the participation of European firms in an embargo their governments opposed. The decision also led to Haig's resignation since it was adopted at an NSC meeting that he was unable to attend because he was at a New York meeting with Soviet Foreign Minister Andrei Gromyko.[71]

The most novel and controversial aspects of the new sanctions were their extraterritorial reach and retroactive application, both of which were necessary to prevent European firms from honoring their contracts. First, Commerce utilized a 1977 amendment to the Export Administration Act, which enabled it to extend foreign policy controls to "persons subject to the jurisdiction of the United States." As a result, its scope exceeded traditional export controls by reaching foreign subsidiaries, even if their products had no U.S. content. In so doing, the United States tried to enjoin the French subsidiary of Dresser Industries, which had signed a contract with the French firm, Creusot-Loire, to sell gas compressors for delivery to the Soviet Union. Dresser-France had been unaffected by the December sanctions because its manufacturing had taken place wholly in France without any U.S. parts or technology.[72]

Second, unlike previous controls, the June sanctions applied not only to new contracts entered into by foreign subsidiaries and licensees; they also covered contracts signed prior to the imposition of the December sanctions. In other words, they forced subsidiaries and licensees to abrogate contracts that were legal at the time in which they were consummated, even if by doing so they were forced to pay damages for breach of contract.[73] Commerce justified the retroactive controls through the legal argument that reexport controls are subject to regulations at the time of reexport, not at the time of the initial contract. Therefore, foreign licensees had consented to U.S. law through their contracts with U.S. firms and that jurisdiction remained even when U.S. regulations changed from those existing at the time of the initial deal.[74]

The central target of this decision was the French state-owned enterprise, Alsthom-Atlantique, which had received a license from GE to produce the rotors and blades prior to the Polish crisis. Once the United States imposed unilateral sanctions in December, GE was barred from exporting these items to its European customers for use in turbines destined for the pipeline project. As a result, these firms turned to Alsthom-Atlantique as the only European source for this equipment.[75] Only by applying the sanctions retroactively could the United States argue that Alsthom-Atlantique's production of GE rotors was subject to U.S. law and its European purchasers were within the ambit of U.S. export controls.

European governments condemned the new sanctions. On 22 June, EC foreign ministers registered a formal protest, asserting that the extraterritorial and retroactive provisions of the sanctions violated international law. Public and official anger was further fueled by the Reagan administration's decision, in the middle of the crisis, to sign a new long-term grain agreement with the Soviet Union. Referring to that deal, German Chancellor Helmut Kohl remarked, "One should not demand of the other what one would not like to have demanded of oneself."[76] The opposition in Europe even included British Prime Minister Margaret Thatcher, Reagan's strongest ally in NATO, who condemned as illegal the U.S. effort to prevent the fulfillment of "existing contracts that do not, in any event, fall under its jurisdiction."[77]

The EC presented its legal case in a formal note sent to the State Department on 12 August. It asserted that the June sanctions violated the territorial principle because they tried to "regulate companies not of U.S. nationality in respect to their conduct outside the United States." The intended result of this policy was that "European companies are pressed into service to carry out U.S. trade policy toward the USSR . . . if they are not to lose their export privileges in the United States and face other penalties."[78] In other words, the pipeline sanctions interfered with their sovereign right to pursue strategies of East–West trade that differed from that of the United States.

The note went on to argue that U.S. jurisdictional claims could not be supported by any accepted construction of international law. The nationality principle was inapplicable because the nationality of a subsidiary is based on the place of incorporation, not the location of the home office. Asserting jurisdiction over foreign firms through the nationality of U.S.-origin goods or technology was also rejected because "there are no known rules of international law for using goods or technology situated abroad as a basis for establishing jurisdiction over persons controlling them." Two other potential bases for jurisdiction were considered and rejected. First, the protective principle may be used to extend jurisdiction when national security is at stake. The United States, however, could not make such a claim since it had imposed the pipeline sanctions under its foreign policy rather than national security controls. Second, the effects doctrine could justify intervention when an act abroad has an effect on public policy that is "direct, foreseeable and substantial." This might cover acts mutually agreed to be criminal, such as counterfeiting or espionage. The export of energy technology, however, represented a policy difference between allies for which the effects doctrine was inapplicable.[79]

The Europeans put their legal theory into practice by taking actions to block the extension of U.S. jurisdiction. On 23 August, the British government invoked the Protection of Trading Interests Act, ordering subsidiaries and licensees to ignore U.S. regulations and perform their contracts. The French government issued a direct requisition order, compelling Dresser-France to honor its contract or face criminal penalties. The West German and Italian governments did not invoke blocking legislation, but put strong pressure on their firms to go forward with their pipeline contracts.[80]

The blocking orders placed subsidiaries and licensees in an irreconcilable conflict of jurisdictions. As an attorney for Dresser noted, "Dresser-France is being told by the French government to honor its contract or else. Dresser-France is being told by the U.S. not to honor its contract or else."[81] In the United States, *or else* meant a temporary denial order (TDO) from the Commerce Department, which would blacklist them from U.S. exports, a potentially devastating penalty. In Europe, it meant liability for breach of contract and, in those countries that issued blocking orders, criminal prosecution. Prior to the issuance of blocking orders, some firms (e.g., Dresser) were prepared to follow the U.S. lead. Once the orders were issued, they asserted they had no choice but to comply with the laws of the territorial state.[82] As a result, they openly violated the embargo in late August as the first shipments of pipeline equipment left their European ports for the Soviet Union.

The Commerce Department promptly issued TDOs against six companies—Dresser-France and its French partner, Creusot-Loire, and four European firms (John Brown Engineering, AEG-Kanis, Mannesmann, and Nuovo Pignone) which had exported turbines using GE-designed rotors from Alsthom-Atlantique.[83] These sanctions, however, could not prevent firms based in Europe from honoring their contracts because of the European blocking orders. Dresser asserted that its French subsidiary had no choice but to comply with the directives of the host country. It did try to vacate the sanctions in the United States through both administrative petitions and court challenges using a foreign sovereign compulsion argument—that is, that Dresser-France should not be punished for matters beyond its control since adhering to U.S. law would subject its employees to criminal and civil penalties in France. This had no effect in mitigating the sanctions because the argument was rejected by the Commerce Department and by a federal district court when Dresser sought injunctive relief in a public hearing.[84]

Even where specific blocking orders were absent, host country courts rejected U.S. jurisdiction as a basis for opting out of binding contracts. For example, Sensor, a Dutch subsidiary of a U.S. firm, had a contract with a French firm to sell twenty-four hundred seismometers for use in the pipeline. After the June sanctions, Sensor informed its French importer that it could not fulfill its contract.[85] The French firm immediately sued Sensor at the District Court of the Hague, which ordered performance of the contract. The ruling explicitly denied U.S. claims of jurisdiction by rejecting the applicability of both the nationality principle and the effects doctrine. Since Sensor was incorporated in the Netherlands, the Dutch law of contracts superseded U.S. sanctions regulations.[86]

The crisis was ultimately resolved because of Secretary of State George Shultz's efforts to find a face-saving retreat from an untenable situation. As an economist, Shultz opposed most economic sanctions and had referred to their use during the Carter administration as "light-switch diplomacy."[87] Shultz was no less skeptical of Reagan's pipeline sanctions. He recognized that extraterritoriality and retroactivity were "fighting words" to the Europeans from which they would not back down. Persisting in the application of such sanctions, he reasoned, only complicated negotiations on potential areas of agreement, such as subsidized credits and high technology. As a result, he convened an informal NATO ministers meeting in Canada in October that sought to establish principles for a series of studies of East–West trade that would enable the United States to stand down from its sanctions.[88]

On 13 November, the United States and its allies concluded an agreement to defuse the crisis. In exchange for the removal of the sanctions, the NATO allies agreed to hold off on new gas contracts pending a study of European energy vulnerability by the International Energy Agency. They also agreed to participate in studies on export controls and high technology trade. President Reagan announced the agreement as a victory in forging a stronger consensus on strategic trade controls. The EC, however, refused to be bound by the findings and recommendations of the studies and continued to resist U.S. pressure to define oil and gas technology as a strategic good. France went even further, disavowing the agreement altogether because it did not want to appear to have made a concession in exchange for exercising what it saw as its sovereign right.[89] In sum, the United States received very little besides diplomatic cover in its forced retreat from a failed strategy of coercion.

THE LESSONS OF THE PIPELINE SANCTIONS

The experience with sanctions during the Polish crisis reinforced many of the lessons of the 1970s drawn by policymakers, international lawyers, and scholars, each of which was in evidence during this episode. Each of the factors that were used to explain the futility of extraterritorial sanctions influenced both the decision to forgo financial sanctions and the inability to assert extraterritorial jurisdiction to thwart the pipeline project. They were also cited by scholars and policy analysts as the reasons why extraterritorial sanctions were futile and counterproductive, causing the United States to rein in the territorial scope of its subsequent sanctions.

Hegemonic Decline

The hegemonic model posits that the United States will be less able to secure multilateral compliance with its sanctions as its position in the world economy declines. The Polish sanctions were viewed as confirmation of this logic. The Reagan administration used extraterritorial sanctions as a means of coercing allies to accept economic warfare. In seeking to return alliance policy to the strategies of the early 1950s, it employed coercion with fewer reservations than any of its predecessors, even at the height of American predominance. Yet its leverage to effectively wield carrots and sticks had receded. The Europeans were not so dependent on U.S economic resources that coercion could have kept them in line. Nor did the United States have the economic resources to compensate the Europeans by providing energy alternatives to Soviet natural gas.[90]

Coercion predictably failed. EC governments rejected economic warfare as contrary to their economic and diplomatic interests and denounced extraterritorial sanctions as violations of their sovereign rights under international law. Given the limits on American leverage, the Reagan administration could not prevent the states in whose territory the transactions were taking place from blocking compliance with U.S. law. As Stephen Kobrin concluded, the outcome confirmed the pattern established by the Argentine and Canadian cases in the 1970s—"unambiguous host country rejection of extraterritorial application of American policy in practice and in principle."[91]

Critics of extraterritorial sanctions noted that they were not only futile, but counterproductive as well. By creating resentment, they frayed multilateral institutions dealing with problems that the United States could not solve unilaterally. In fact, the need for allied cooperation to deal with the debt crisis in Latin America as well as Eastern Europe was one of the key factors that deterred the Reagan administration from declaring Poland in default.

The pipeline sanctions, by contrast, placed greater strains on the alliance than they did on the Soviet Union. As one German official noted, the diplomatic fallout from the crisis stimulated a "mood of defiance inimical to the achievement of legitimate goals in the East–West context."[92] A former director of the State Department's Office of East–West Trade concurred, arguing that export control cooperation is better served by the "give and take of negotiation that will sometimes require compromise" rather than "relentless pressure to persuade the other CoCom countries that U.S. judgments are superior to theirs."[93] The potential costs of the latter approach were revealed in the EC note protesting the pipeline sanctions. It not only condemned the unprecedented assertion of the right to regulate subsidiaries and force the abrogation of contracts. It also challenged the legality of the entire reexport control system when it rejected the extension of jurisdiction based on the nationality of goods and the use of submission clauses in which "the freedom of contract is misused in order to circumvent the limits imposed on national jurisdiction by international law."[94] In other words, practices to which the Europeans had reluctantly acceded came under greater scrutiny because of an overreaching U.S. policy.

A corollary to the case against extraterritorial coercion is the argument for bargaining to strengthen controls within the existing consensus. This view was acknowledged by Shultz, who argued that the proper response to extraterritorial problems was not to extend U.S. law unilaterally, but to "resolve the policy differences that underlie many of these conflicts of jurisdiction."[95] In other words, U.S. economic statecraft should focus on strengthening controls in areas where there is multilateral agreement and avoid coercing its allies in areas where that agreement is absent. During the Cold War, the former represented national security controls within CoCom; the latter represented controls over nonstrategic trade to signal disapproval of Soviet behavior or to wage economic warfare.[96] To extrapolate to post–Cold War sanctions, such as those against Iran, efforts should be directed at convergent interests, such as controls over nuclear or missile-related technology exports, and away from divergent aims, such as energy-related trade and investment.

Multinational Corporations

Business-government relations during the Polish crisis suggested a second constraint on the use of coercive economic statecraft—namely, the globalization of American business. This constrained the ability of policymakers to wield economic instruments by (1) locating an increasing share of manufacturing and financial activity outside the boundaries of the United States, and (2) contributing to corporate perceptions of interest that made voluntary private cooperation with public initiatives less likely.

The pipeline episode demonstrated the role of the MNC in contributing to the diffusion of technologies that the United States defined as strategic and its allies did not. This was the conclusion of a 1981 study by the Office of Technology Assessment (OTA). In the 1960s, the United States was the sole source for the very kind of oil and gas equipment that was embargoed by the Reagan administration in the early 1980s. Over time, however, an export originating in the United States "lost its American identity over the years through licensed production and wholly-owned subsidiaries overseas and the employment of U.S. commerce and expertise worldwide." As a result, globalization "significantly reduce[d] the number of areas where the U.S. is the sole source of supply."[97]

The Reagan administration used extraterritorial controls as a means to compensate for this loss of control. American MNCs resisted this practice. Virtually every corporate trade association denounced it as contrary to international law and harmful to American business. As one scholar noted: "The MNC and the host government are natural allies bonded by a mutual interest in maintaining sales and contracts. The MNC strives to maintain its independence vis-à-vis U.S. national controls and the host government pressures it to do so. The power of the U.S. government to harness trade for diplomatic purpose is shrunken accordingly."[98]

During the pipeline case, Dresser Industries put this logic into practice, as it instructed its French subsidiary to honor its Soviet contract rather than comply with U.S. law. In defending its decision, a Dresser spokesperson asserted that "our French subsidiary is a French company that must obey the laws of that country."[99] In effect, it sided with the European legal argument that nationality is determined by the place of incorporation, not the location of the home office—a sharp contrast with the policy of corporate headquarters during the *Fruehauf* case in 1965. Kobrin concludes that this confirms the trend illustrated by the Argentine and Canadian cases in the 1970s whereby "management took the position that their subsidiaries were local firms subject to local law."[100]

The attitudes and policies of U.S. banks during the Polish debt crisis also revealed a shift away from an ethnocentric identification with U.S. Cold War aims. The bankers' primary interest was in protecting their assets in Poland and the rest of Eastern Europe. As a result, they strongly lobbied the administration against default. Many responded with equanimity to Poland's declaration of martial law because they believed that repressive regimes were better able to impose the financial discipline necessary to service its debt. In fact, after martial law, the banks negotiated a rescheduling of Poland's private debt at a time when NATO governments refused to enter into negotiations over Poland's official debt.[101] Some observers inferred from this episode a general trend in which private financial institutions were less responsive to U.S. diplomatic interests. One survey of American bankers noted "a general unwillingness to cooperate with *any* attempt by the U.S. government to instruct them on where and when to lend internationally."[102] This change in outlook suggests that public officials will have greater difficulty in securing the voluntary cooperation of private financial institutions with its strategies of economic statecraft.

Interdependence

International economic interdependence was a third factor that constrained extraterritorial sanctions. During the postwar period, the expansion of international trade, investment, and finance enmeshed the U.S. economy with those of its allies and its adversaries. As Stephen Neff noted, this process has "linked the countries of the world so effectively through material ties, as to make the imposition of sanctions an unacceptably costly or risky business for the sanctioner himself."[103] As a result, certain coercive options were foreclosed because of their risks to liberal international economic regimes and to national economic interests.

During the Polish crisis, the one area in which interdependence deterred the use of coercion was the decision to forego financial sanctions. To the proponents of economic warfare, default was a theoretically attractive option because it could unilaterally force private and official creditors to comply with economic strategies that they opposed. However, given the large exposure of Western banks in Eastern Europe and the need for European cooperation in dealing with the Latin American debt crisis, the option was rejected as prohibitively risky. Comparable considerations of financial interdependence influenced British and Argentine economic statecraft during the Falklands War. British banks were Argentina's largest creditors, but London was unwilling to declare Argentina's debts to be in default because of the potential repercussions on the London-based Eurocurrency system. Argentina also kept up its loan payments to its British creditors (albeit in escrow accounts) because of its desire to avoid default and maintain its reputation as a reliable debtor. As one scholar noted, the common interests and aversions created by financial interdependence "ensured that only human, not financial, blood was spilled."[104]

Interdependence arguments were also used by the bureaucratic opponents of the pipeline sanctions in advocating their rescission and greater restraint in exercising extraterritorial jurisdiction. Economic warfare advocates dismissed such considerations. According to Shultz, Weinberger's response to international law arguments was, "I don't want to hear about legalities."[105] Implicit in this statement is a crude version of the realist critique of legalism—that is, that international laws are little more than conveniences that can be discarded when they conflict with national interests.[106] From this perspective, legal niceties, such as contract sanctity and territorial jurisdiction, should give way to grand strategy.

In conditions of interdependence, however, a cavalier disregard of international rules can be costly. It can undercut one's reputation for reliability in future transactions. It can also lead to reciprocal violation of the rules by others that could adversely affect one's long-term self-interest.[107] Critics of extraterritorial sanctions argued that considerations of reputation and reciprocity should serve as deterrents to the exercise of economic instruments of questionable legality.

The reputational costs of unilateral sanctions fall directly on U.S. businesses involved in foreign trade and investment and indirectly on the U.S.

economy. First, the frequent use of foreign policy controls makes foreign customers wary of the unpredictability of their relationships with U.S. firms. Caterpillar Tractor's executive vice president, for example, testified that from 1970 through 1978, that company supplied 85 percent of the pipelaying and earth-moving machinery imported by the Soviet Union while its chief Japanese competitor, Komatsu, supplied only 15 percent. By the early 1980s, Caterpillar's reliability was called into question because of the Carter administration's 1978 controls on oil and natural gas equipment and the Reagan administration's proclivity toward unilateral controls. As a result, by 1981, the market shares of Caterpillar and Komatsu were reversed with the latter controlling 85 percent of the Soviet market.[108] When the Soviet Union wanted to import five hundred pipelayers after the pipeline sanctions (which by then had been decontrolled), Caterpillar was not even invited to bid because repeated use of foreign policy controls had made it an unreliable supplier.[109] This is what George Shultz warned about in his 1979 article on unilateral sanctions: "Major commercial relationships cannot be turned on and off like a light-switch . . . [because] there emerges an interdependence that necessitates confidence in the continued good faith on both sides."[110]

This problem was exacerbated by the retroactive provisions of the June sanctions that ordered U.S. firms to abrogate existing contracts. Shultz analogized the episode to the Nixon administration's soybean embargo against Japan, which was implemented while he served as Treasury secretary. The action achieved its short-run goal of bringing down domestic food prices. In the long run, it hurt the U.S. economy because it created a reputation for unreliability that caused Japan to shift its imports from the United States to Brazil.[111] A 1983 OTA study found that the retroactive provisions of the pipeline sanctions had a comparable effect on the reputation of U.S. technology firms.[112] As a result, U.S. firms were not only excluded from Soviet contracts; European manufacturers either shifted away from U.S. suppliers or designed out U.S. technology to avoid the risk that transactions might be interrupted by unpredictable export controls.

Even without retroactivity, extraterritorial sanctions undermine the reputation of U.S. firms in seeking equal treatment with national firms when they establish direct investments abroad. The logic was spelled out in testimony before Congress by George Ball who, as a State Department official in the 1960s, had defended such practices against Cuba, but had since become one of the principal critics of the use of economic sanctions:[113]

> For our Government to reach its long arm into foreign countries and try to force local subsidiaries to disobey the policies of the countries where they are domiciled undercuts the vitality—even the existence—of the whole multinational system. A

fundamental assumption of that system is that foreign-owned subsidiaries be good corporate citizens of the countries where they are operating. On that basis, they are granted national treatment, which means they are accorded the same treatment as any domestically owned corporation. That treatment is clearly challenged when our Government orders an American parent company to sabotage a project favored by the host country.

This could also legitimize discrimination against U.S. enterprises seeking to purchase local firms because of the host country's concern that a U.S.-owned firm would be more responsive to U.S. foreign policy than to the host country's economic interests.

Another reason why interdependence raises the costs of extraterritorial sanctions is concern about reciprocity—that is, avoiding actions contrary to the rules of the liberal trade and investment system that might set precedents for others. The United States has historically played a leadership role in creating and maintaining a liberal trading order. To play such a leadership role, it had to act within the framework of the rules it was promoting. As a result, the Johnson administration considered but ultimately rejected a secondary boycott against allied firms that traded with Cuba because it would undermine American leadership within GATT and its opposition to the Arab League's use of this practice against Israel. Several legal scholars have argued that the pipeline sanctions undermined this role because, like the Arab Boycott, they blacklisted companies on foreign soil with no connection to U.S. persons or technology.[114] More recently, several commentators have argued against the secondary boycott provisions of the Helms-Burton law and ILSA, both of which have been criticized for violating U.S. obligations under the WTO and the North American Free Trade Agreement (NAFTA).[115]

Another reciprocity argument against extraterritorial jurisdiction is that it tries to regulate U.S. investors abroad in a way that the United States would find unacceptable if practiced by other governments vis-à-vis foreign investors in the United States. The potential problem with this discrepancy was illustrated by the former head of the Justice Department's Foreign Commerce Section by the following hypothetical scenario:[116]

What if American Motors Corp., a U.S. affiliate of the French enterprise Renault and an arguable "corporate national of France," was ordered by the French government not to export 10,000 cars to Chile which it was contractually required to sell and as to which export financing had been obtained from the U.S. government's Export-Import bank. Would the U.S. government acquiesce to the French order? Would the American Motors Corp. be liable for damages in a breach of contract action brought in a U.S. court by the Chilean purchasers? Would the UAW accept the loss of, say, 500 jobs because the purchase order could not be filled due to the operation of French law?

Such an assertion of foreign jurisdiction would have violated both U.S. public policy and legal practice. This view was affirmed in a 1982 Supreme Court decision, *Sumimoto Shoji America, Inc. v. Avagliano*, which held that a wholly owned subsidiary of a Japanese firm incorporated in the United States is a U.S. person subject to U.S. law. As a result, it must adhere to U.S. civil rights law even if it required actions contrary to corporate practices in Japan.[117] One international lawyer cited this case in noting the double standard in the American position: "[W]e tend to feel that if incorporated here, you are one of ours, and incorporated over there but owned by us, you are still one of ours."[118] Since this is a position other countries are unlikely to accept, a likely cost of extraterritorial sanctions is either reciprocal action by others or an unwillingness to afford American foreign investors national treatment.

Domestic Politics

A final purported constraint on the imposition of economic sanctions lies in American domestic politics. Interest group models suggest that the possibility of societal frustration of public policy is greatest when the costs of that policy are concentrated on specific sectors while the benefits are diffused throughout the society.[119] Economic sanctions and export controls fit this model. While public officials claim that they promote broader national interests and values, they are "paid for by the industries most deeply affected." Even firms that are not directly affected may express concern that U.S. actions would diminish foreign confidence in American business as a whole.[120] Therefore, the interest group model predicts serious constraints on the use of economic leverage, either from corporate lobbying of Congress or presidential reluctance to utilize certain sanctions instruments that would impose costs on politically significant constituencies.

Interest group constraints on the implementation of economic sanctions appeared to have been augmented by changes in the world economy and the American political system. First, as U.S. firms became less technologically dominant and allied firms were increasingly able to "free ride" on unilateral sanctions, the competitive disadvantages facing U.S. business had been magnified. As a result, U.S. corporations and their trade associations became more aggressive in challenging unilateral practices that sacrificed the profits and reputation of American business without imposing serious costs on adversaries.

Second, the domestic political environment was more conducive to corporate challenges to prevailing U.S. government practices. The decline in the intensity of anticommunist sentiment emboldened corporate interest groups to oppose unilateral policies that imposed costs on U.S. businesses relative to foreign competitors. Congress was more receptive to these pressures, both for economic reasons and because of the post-Vietnam concern that too much power had been ceded to the executive branch. The Reagan administration sought to reverse these trends by pointing to a heightened Soviet threat, but was at best partially successful. Neither corporate nor congressional behavior returned to the pattern of the early Cold War era.

This was evident in the corporate lobbying campaigns that followed the pipeline sanctions and the subsequent legislative battle over the reauthorization of the Export Administration Act. Corporate opposition to both the December and June sanctions was nearly universal. Representatives of the affected firms, such as Caterpillar Tractor and GE, complained of lost sales to foreign competitors as the result of the unilateral sanctions imposed in December. Nor did the American business community see extraterritorial controls as a means of forcing foreign competitors to play by the same rules. Several corporate officials cited the Fruehauf–France case and imbroglios with Canada and Argentina in the 1970s as evidence of the futility of such measures. Richard Lesher, the president of the U.S. Chamber of Commerce, sent a personal letter to President Reagan warning that extraterritorial sanctions would "only aggravate further our already poor reputation for commercial reliability."[121]

The congressional reaction to the pipeline sanctions also confirmed the change in its attitude toward unilateral controls from the 1950s through the 1970s—that is, from pressing the State Department to get tougher with allies whose controls fell short of U.S. standards to protesting unilateral controls which penalized U.S. business. Given the severity of the recession in 1982 and the economic problems confronting U.S. manufacturing firms, the decision to expand the sanctions aroused strong congressional criticism. The House Committee on Foreign Affairs voted 22 to 12 to lift the pipeline sanctions. Half of the committee's Republicans voted with the majority and they were joined on the floor by Republican Minority Leader Robert Michel, whose Illinois district included the headquarters for Caterpillar Tractor, one of the firms hardest hit by the sanctions.[122] While the House as a whole fell three votes short of passing the bill, its action was more of a means of signaling the administration than in legislatively reversing the sanctions. Had the bill passed, the Senate was unlikely to follow suit. Even if it did, a presidential veto would almost certainly have been sustained. Nonetheless, the closeness of the vote and the defection of a number of prominent members of the president's own party were designed to send a message to the administration. If ignored, the administration would likely see further legislative encroachments on executive branch authority when the Export Administration Act came up for renewal in 1983.[123]

The battle to limit presidential discretion over export controls was joined almost immediately after the rescission of the pipeline sanctions because the authorization granted under the Export Administration Act of 1979 expired on 30 September 1983. Corporate lobbyists mobilized an intense campaign to narrow presidential discretion over foreign policy controls in three areas. First, they sought to eliminate the ability to extend foreign policy controls extraterritorially because that "affected the ability of foreign subsidiaries to operate in accordance with the laws and policies of other nations where they are incorporated."[124] Second, they pushed for a contract sanctity exemption because the forced abrogations placed a "triple burden" on American business as "unreliable suppliers, unreliable investors, and unreliable licensors."[125] Finally, they wanted a foreign availability provision to make it more difficult to control items traded by allies because such measures surrendered Eastern markets to non-U.S. companies.[126]

These private efforts were most successful in the House. Its revision of the Export Administration Act, sponsored by Representative Don Bonker (D-Wash.), reflected corporate preferences on contract sanctity and extraterritoriality, as well as on liberalized licensing requirements for technology exports to CoCom members.[127] The Senate bill was less responsive to corporate entreaties and placed fewer restrictions on executive branch prerogatives. Its only significant revision of the 1979 act was granting greater immunity to existing contracts—a provision that mirrored the legislation passed on agricultural export contracts after the Carter administration's grain embargo. The bill was a compromise between Jake Garn (R-Utah), the Senate's leading "hawk" on export controls, and John Heinz (R-Penn.), one of its leading moderates. It was also supported by the administration, both because it was a moderate alternative to the Bonker Bill and because contract sanctity provisions comported with Shultz's concerns about "light-switch diplomacy." Given the differences between the House and Senate versions, the final bill did not pass until 1985 when the House conferees agreed to the Senate bill without substantial changes.[128]

At one level, the corporate lobbying campaign was unsuccessful. Despite its effort to limit the scope of foreign policy controls, the 1985 amendments imposed no meaningful change in executive branch powers. On foreign availability, there were more reporting and consultation requirements, but no binding obligations. Even the contract sanctity provision—the only major change in the law—could be overridden if the president determined that a breach of the peace posed a serious and direct threat to the security of the United States. Moreover, even if the act imposed insurmountable barriers to the use of certain instruments, the president could still rely upon the virtually unrestricted emergency powers granted by IEEPA. In fact, IEEPA served as the statutory authority for continuing export controls from the expiration of the act in 1983 until its reauthorization in 1985.[129]

None of this, however, implies that the domestic constraints on economic statecraft were insignificant. Even though Congress did not tie the president's hands, considerable political capital had to be expended to prevent the passage of legislation that would have circumscribed administrative authority. In addition, the impact of congressional influence on executive branch behavior often comes from a bargaining relationship rather than legislated mandates. A number of studies of trade policy found that Congress influenced the executive branch less by passing trade bills and more by using legislation to signal the executive branch that if it is not more deferential to its priorities, more restrictive legislation might be considered later.[130] In the legislative battle over the 1985 bill, the House actually passed legislation that would have weakened reexport controls to CoCom allies, a change that would have compromised even the more modest export control aims of the State Department pragmatists. Therefore, the battle over reauthorization of the Export Administration Act was designed to put the executive branch on notice that there were limits to congressional tolerance of unilateral actions that inflicted disproportionate costs on American business and the U.S. economy.

In sum, most scholars and policy analysts saw the pipeline case as a paradigm for the futility of extraterritorial sanctions, reinforcing the lessons drawn from the 1970s regarding the impact of transnational relations and hegemonic decline on unilateral economic statecraft. The case studies in part II will test the accuracy of these predictions against subsequent efforts by political actors to conscript corporate conduct abroad into their sanctions efforts.

NOTES

1. *Eagle Defiant: United States Foreign Policy in the 1980s* (Boston: Little, Brown, 1983), 31.

2. *Turmoil and Triumph: My Years as Secretary of State* (New York: Scribner's, 1993), 141.

3. Richard E. Feinberg, *The Intemperate Zone: The Third World Challenge to U.S. Foreign Policy* (New York: W. W. Norton, 1983), 38–40.

4. Feinberg, *The Intemperate Zone*, 96–97.

5. Mastanduno, *Economic Containment*, 96.

6. See U.S. Congress, House, Committee on International Relations, *Export Administration Act: Agenda for Reform*, Hearings, 95th Cong., 2d sess., 1978, 1–44.

7. Mastanduno, *Economic Containment*, 141.

8. William J. Long, *United States Export Control Policy: Executive Autonomy vs. Congressional Reform* (New York: Columbia University Press, 1989), 74.

9. Long, *United States Export Control Policy*, 80.

10. U.S. Congress, Senate Committee on Banking, Housing, and Urban Affairs, *International Emergency Economic Powers Legislation*, Report, 95th Cong., 1st sess., 1977, 2.

11. U.S. Senate, *International Emergency Economic Powers Legislation*, 2–3.

12. Carter, *International Economic Sanctions*, 189.

13. The major exception was that TWEA allowed the executive to vest or assume ownership over foreign assets. Under IEEPA, it could only freeze those assets. See Malloy, *Economic Sanctions and U.S. Trade*, 168.

14. U.S. Congress, Senate Committee on Banking, Housing, and Urban Affairs, *Export Administration Act of 1979*, Report, 96th Cong., 1st sess., 1979, 5.

15. Born, "A Reappraisal of the Extraterritorial Reach of U.S. Law," 66–67.

16. Gladwin and Walter, *Multinationals under Fire*, 244–246.

17. On the "no exceptions policy," see Martin, *Coercive Cooperation*, 196. On the grain embargo, see Robert L. Paarlberg, *Food Trade and Foreign Policy: India, the Soviet Union, and the United States* (Ithaca, N.Y.: Cornell University Press, 1985), 189–194.

18. Mastanduno, *Economic Containment*, 241–242.

19. This was superseded in 1984 by the Foreign Extraterritoriality Measures Act (FEMA) after the pipeline sanctions. See De Mestral and Gruchalla-Wesierski, *Extraterritorial Application of Export Legislation*, 113.

20. Gordon, "Extraterritorial Application of United States Economic Laws," 154.

21. Seyom Brown, *The Faces of Power: Constancy and Change in United States Foreign Policy from Truman to Reagan* (New York: Columbia University Press, 1983), 607; *New York Times*, 22 May 1982, 15.

22. Miles Kahler, "The United States and Western Europe: The Diplomatic Consequences of Mr. Reagan," in *Eagle Resurgent?*, eds. Oye, Rothchild, and Lieber, 311.

23. For more on this distinction, see Mastanduno, *Economic Containment*, 232.

24. Jentleson, *Pipeline Politics*, 173.

25. Mastanduno, *Economic Containment*, 241.

26. John Lewis Gaddis, *Russia, the Soviet Union, and the United States: An Interpretive History*, 2d ed. (New York: McGraw-Hill, 1990), 323–324.

27. Mastanduno, *Economic Containment*, 240.

28. Alexander M. Haig, *Caveat: Realism, Reagan, and Foreign Policy* (New York: Macmillan, 1984), 253.

29. Henry Nau, *The Myth of America's Decline: Leading the World Economy in the 1990s* (New York: Oxford University Press, 1990), 298.

30. Mastanduno, *Economic Containment*, 243.

31. *New York Times*, 19 July 1981, A10.

32. Nau, *Myth of America's Decline*, 299–301.

33. Jentleson, *Pipeline Politics*, 205.

34. David D. Driscoll, *Sovereign Debt: The Polish Example*, Congressional Research Service (CRS) Report No. 82–25E, 4 January 1982, 13–19.

35. Cohen, *In Whose Interest?*, 180.

36. Beverly Crawford, "How Regimes Matter: Western Control of East–West Trade Finance," *Millennium: Journal of International Studies* 16 (winter 1987): 441–442.

37. Driscoll, "Sovereign Debt," 5.

38. Cohen, *In Whose Interest?*, 189–190.

39. *New York Times*, 28 April 1981, D1.

40. Cited in Cohen, *In Whose Interest?*, 191.

41. *Wall Street Journal*, 7 January 1982, 34; *New York Times*, 6 February 1982, 38.

42. See Beverly Crawford, *Economic Vulnerability in International Relations: The Case of East–West Trade, Investment, and Finance* (New York: Columbia University Press, 1993), 191.

43. Testimony of Marc Leland, Assistant Secretary of the Treasury for International Affairs, U.S. Congress, Senate Committee on Appropriations, *Polish Debt Crisis*, Hearings, 97th Cong., 2d sess., 1982, 25–26.

44. Testimony of Undersecretary of State for Political Affairs Lawrence Eagleburger, U.S. Congress, Senate Committee on Banking, Housing, and Urban Affairs, *Polish Debt*, 97th Cong., 2d sess., 1982, 19.

45. Cohen, *In Whose Interest?*, 195–196.

46. Crawford, *Economic Vulnerability in International Relations*, 192.

47. The decision elicited the oft-quoted statement from George Will that the Reagan administration "evidently loves commerce more than it loathes communism." Cited in *New York Times*, 22 January 1982, 1.

48. *Wall Street Journal*, 26 February 1982, 34.

49. *New York Times*, 1 February 1982, 1.

50. Quoted in "Does Business Love Foreign Dictators?" *Business and Society Review* 41 (spring 1982): 4.

51. Cohen, *In Whose Interest?*, 193.

52. Crawford, "How Regimes Matter," 444.

53. Anthony Blinken, *Ally Versus Ally: America, Europe, and the Siberian Pipeline Crisis* (Westport, Conn.: Greenwood Press, 1987), 97.

54. Lowenfeld, *Trade Controls for Political Ends*, 275–276.

55. Haig, *Caveat*, 254.

56. See the text of President Reagan's 21 June news conference in *Cumulative Digest of United States Practice in International Law, 1981–1988: Vol. II* (Department of State Publication 10120, July 1994), 2502.

57. See Kahler, "The United States and Western Europe," 306.

58. Crawford, *Economic Vulnerability in International Relations*, 158–159.

59. David W. Hunter, *Western Trade Pressure on the Soviet Union: An Interdependence Perspective* (New York: St. Martin's, 1991), 76–77.

60. Mastanduno, *Economic Containment*, 248–249.

61. Martin, *Coercive Cooperation*, 234–239.

62. Lowenfeld, *Trade Controls for Political Ends*, 279.

63. *New York Times*, 24 January 1982, 1.

64. Mastanduno, *Economic Containment*, 244.

65. Cited in Peter Schweizer, *Victory: The Reagan Administration's Secret Strategy That Hastened the End of the Soviet Union* (New York: Atlantic Monthly Press, 1994), 102–103.

66. *New York Times*, 30 May 1982, A1.

67. Quoted in *BusinessWeek*, 22 February 1982, 62.

68. Mastanduno, *Economic Containment*, 252–254.

69. Blinken, *Ally Versus Ally*, 102.

70. See Lionel Olmer's statement in *Current Digest of U.S. Practice in International Law, 1981–1988*, 2503.

71. Nau, *The Myth of America's Decline*, 312.

72. Jan Malia Lundelius, "Reaction Sanctions and Foreign Incorporated Subsidiaries: Between a Rock and a Hard Place," *Temple International and Comparative Law Journal* 1 (fall 1985): 38.

73. Homer E. Moyer Jr. and Linda A. Mabry, *Export Controls as Instruments of Foreign Policy: The History, Legal Issues, and Policy Lessons of Three Recent Cases* (Washington, D.C.: International Law Institute, 1985), 109–113.

74. Moyer and Mabry, *Export Controls as Instruments of Foreign Policy*, 110.

75. *New York Times*, 11 January 1982, A13.

76. *New York Times*, 5 October 1982, A6.

77. Blinken, *Ally Versus Ally*, 105.

78. *International Legal Materials*, 1982, 893–895.

79. *International Legal Materials*, 894, 896–897.

80. Griffin and Calabrese, "Coping with Extraterritorial Disputes," 13.

81. *Washington Post*, 25 August 1982, A20.

82. Lowenfeld, *Trade Controls for Political Ends*, 297–298.

83. *New York Times*, 27 August 1982, 1.

84. Lowenfeld, *Trade Controls for Political Ends*, 296.

85. *Financial Times*, 7 September 1982, 5.

86. *International Legal Materials*, 1983, 66–74.

87. Shultz, "Light-Switch Diplomacy," *BusinessWeek*, 28 May 1979, 24.

88. Shultz, *Turmoil and Triumph*, 137–140.

89. Jentleson, *Pipeline Politics*, 197–203; for a more favorable view of the agreement from one of its participants, see Nau, *The Myth of America's Decline*, 315–318.

90. Jentleson notes that the administration did offer the Europeans two alternatives—American coal and Norwegian gas. The former was unlikely to satisfy European needs while the latter was not only more expensive, but beyond the authority of Washington to guarantee. See *Pipeline Politics*, 185–188.

91. Kobrin, "Enforcing Export Embargoes through Multinational Corporations," 37.

92. Martin J. Hillebrand, "East–West Economic Relations, Export Controls, and Strains in the Alliance," in *Controlling East–West Trade and Technology Transfer: Power, Politics, Policies*, ed. Gary K. Bertsch (Durham, N.C.: Duke University Press, 1988), 380.

93. William A. Root, "Trade Controls That Work," *Foreign Policy* 56 (fall 1984): 74.

94. *International Legal Materials*, 1982, 894, 896.

95. Shultz, "Trade Interdependence and Conflicts of Jurisdiction," 36.

96. Root, "Trade Controls That Work," 72.

97. Office of Technology Assessment (OTA), *Technology and Soviet Energy Development*, November 1981, 191.

98. Lindell, "Foreign Policy Export Controls and American Multinational Corporations," 38.

99. *New York Times*, 24 August 1982, D1.

100. Kobrin, "Enforcing Export Embargoes through Multinational Corporations," 37.

101. Abraham S. Becker, *Economic Leverage on the Soviet Union in the 1980s* (Santa Monica, Calif.: The Rand Corporation, July 1984), 48.

102. Spindler, *The Politics of International Credit*, 201 (emphasis in the original).

103. Neff, *Friends But No Allies*, 216.

104. Neff, *Friends But No Allies*, 214–215.

105. Shultz, *Turmoil and Triumph*, 138.

106. The classic exposition of the realist critique of legalism is in Hans J. Morgenthau, *Politics among Nations*, 5th ed. (New York: Alfred A. Knopf, 1973), 11–12; but also see his discussion of compliance with international law on pp. 311–313.

107. On the role of reputation and reciprocity as bases for compliance with international law, see Robert O. Keohane, "Reciprocity in International Relations," *International Organization* 40 (winter 1986): 1–27; and Harvey Starr, *Anarchy, Order, and Integration: How to Manage Interdependence* (Ann Arbor, Mich.: University of Michigan Press, 1977), 97–101.

108. Testimony of Erskine Chapman in U.S. Congress, Senate Committee on Foreign Relations, Subcommittee on International Economic Policy, *Soviet-European Gas Pipeline*, Hearings, 97th Cong., 2d sess., 1982, 8–10.

109. Jentleson, *Pipeline Politics*, 209.

110. Shultz, "Light-Switch Diplomacy," 24.

111. Shultz, *Turmoil and Triumph*, 138.

112. OTA, *Technology and East–West Trade: An Update*, May 1983, 57.

113. U.S. Congress, House Committee on Foreign Affairs, Subcommittee on Europe and the Middle East and on International Economic Policy, *Export Controls on Oil and Gas Equipment*, Hearings, 97th Cong., 2d sess., 1982, 125.

114. Moyer and Mabry, *Export Controls as Instruments of Foreign Policy*, 114.

115. See chapter 6.

116. Testimony of Douglas Rosenthal in U.S. Senate, *Soviet-European Gas Pipeline*, 41.

117. Sarah J. Cogswell, "In the Wake of the Pipeline Embargo: European-United States Dialogue," *Florida State University Law Review* 12 (spring 1984): 82–83.

118. Symposium, "Economic Sanctions as an Instrument of U.S. Strategic and Foreign Policy," *Journal of Comparative Business and Capital Market Law* 6 (March 1984): 73.

119. See Krasner, *Defending the National Interest*, 84–85.

120. Hufbauer, Schott, and Elliott, *Economic Sanctions Reconsidered*, 76.

121. U.S. Senate, *Soviet-European Gas Pipeline*, 7–17; also see U.S. Congress, Senate Committee on Foreign Relations, Subcommittee on International Economic Policy, *Economic Relations with the Soviet Union*, Hearings, 97th Cong., 2d sess., 1982, 196.

122. *Congressional Quarterly Weekly Report*, 14 August 1982, 1961.

123. *Congressional Quarterly Weekly Report*, 2 October 1982, 2467.

124. See U.S. Congress, House Committee on Foreign Affairs, Subcommittee on International Economic Policy and Trade, *Extension and Revision of the Export Administration Act of 1979*, Hearings, 98th Cong., 1st sess., 1983, 79.

125. Prepared statement from the Business Roundtable in U.S. House, *Extension and Revision of the Export Administration Act of 1979*, 45.

126. Long, *United States Export Controls*, 92–93.

127. *Congressional Quarterly Weekly Report*, 7 May 1983, 597.

128. Long, *United States Export Control Policy*, 93.

129. Carter, *International Economic Sanctions*, 74.

130. For a general argument on this type of congressional influence, see James M. Lindsay, *Congress and the Politics of U.S. Foreign Policy* (Baltimore: Johns Hopkins University Press, 1994). On specific applications to trade policy, see Robert A. Pastor, *Congress and the Politics of U.S. Foreign Economic Policy* (Berkeley: University of California Press, 1980); I. M. Destler, *Congressional Trade Politics*, 3d ed. (Washington, D.C.: Institute for International Economics, 1995).

Part Two

Contemporary Case Studies

Chapter Four

The Decline and Partial Return of Foreign Subsidiary Sanctions

> To many Americans there is nothing anomalous in Washington's commanding a U.S.-owned subsidiary in a foreign country not to sell technologically advanced products to the Soviet Union. It has not yet dawned on some people in this country how grossly offensive such a policy may be to other governments. The lesson may be borne home one day if Saudi Arabia directed a Saudi-owned subsidiary in the United States to terminate its exports to Israel.
>
> —Raymond Vernon[1]

In an article written in the late 1970s, Raymond Vernon called for the adoption of "radically new principles governing the status of foreign owned subsidiaries." Vernon acknowledged that the global spread of business and banking placed significant corporate activity beyond the reach of national laws and this could frustrate the achievement of certain public interests. Nonetheless, governments must understand "that foreign-owned affiliates lie wholly inside the jurisdiction of the countries in which the affiliates do business" and should resist the temptation "to issue commands to such enterprises as vehicles for political intervention." Instead, they should rely on diplomacy to negotiate multilateral rules governing corporate conduct abroad.[2]

While Vernon's argument covered a wide array of issues ranging from antitrust to corporate disclosure, it can also be applied to economic sanctions. As illustrated in part I, U.S. efforts to extend sanctions to the foreign operations of U.S. firms led to repeated conflicts with allies in the 1950s and 1960s. As those conflicts escalated in the mid-1970s, the United States scaled back the extraterritorial dimensions of its regulations. The Reagan administration's attempt to resurrect this practice during the Polish crisis was frustrated by allies, reinforcing the case against extraterritorial sanctions.

These experiences seem to have chastened successive administrations toward use of this weapon. The Reagan administration maintained the legal right to apply U.S. law to foreign subsidiaries. That right was not exercised in any of the five postpipeline sanctions it imposed under IEEPA (Nicaragua and South Africa in 1985, Libya in 1986, Panama and Iran in 1987).[3] The decision to limit the reach of U.S. regulations reflected recognition of the difficulty of extending U.S. law into other jurisdictions and the costs of such exertions on alliance relations. Efforts to strengthen multilateral sanctions after 1982 featured persuasion rather than coercion. The results, however, were modest. The fact that this did not trigger extraterritorial controls indicates a partial accommodation of U.S. sanctions policy to economic globalization.[4]

As the administration tried to rein in the scope of its controls, many in Congress tried to expand them. Legislators often expressed frustration and anger with trading partners, who were seen as taking a free ride on U.S. sanctions. They dismissed the prudential arguments against extraterritoriality as little more than obsequiousness toward allies who should be more deferential to U.S. leadership. In the 1980s, several sanctions and export control bills contained the very types of extraterritorial provisions about which the executive branch had become more skeptical.[5] In the 1990s, congressional activism induced a reluctant executive branch to reach foreign subsidiaries in two cases—the passage of the Cuban Democracy Act in 1992 and the 1995 executive orders preventing U.S. oil companies from buying Iranian crude oil for sale to third countries or investing in Iran's energy sector.

Examining these case studies provides an opportunity to test the lessons drawn from the pipeline case—namely, that the American political system has lost the ability to control or influence the operations of American MNCs in third counties for the purpose of economic sanctions. If the model is correct, overseas corporate behavior will be independent of U.S. foreign policy when Washington is deterred from employing extraterritorial sanctions. If jurisdiction is directly asserted, such efforts will be frustrated by the countervailing power of host countries and the self-interested behavior of private actors, as was the case with the Cuban sanctions in the mid-1970s or the pipeline sanctions in the early 1980s. Either way, American MNCs will be free to use their offshore operations to pursue their global interests regardless of the impact on public strategies of economic statecraft.

The evidence supports a partial confirmation of the model. Foreign subsidiaries were theoretically freer to trade with targets, either because they were exempted from the regulations or because host countries enacted laws blocking U.S. government or parent company interference. Yet they were often reluctant to exercise that freedom in ways that violated U.S. preferences because of the perceived risks in the American political system. When the executive branch was strongly committed to sanctions, most firms did not use loopholes in the law for fear of jeopardizing their relationship with the federal government. In cases in which the most intense pressures came from Congress, mobilized interest groups, or public sentiment, firms were often deterred by potential problems with customers, shareholders, and the risk that Congress might pass more restrictive legislation. Even in the absence of conscious public decisions to manipulate private behavior, these risks often persuaded MNCs to police their foreign subsidiaries beyond the requirements of the law.

NICARAGUA

In 1985, the Reagan administration imposed a trade embargo on the Sandinista government in Nicaragua—the first use of this economic weapon since the pipeline case. The sanctions were the culmination of a ratcheting up of economic pressure, beginning with an aid cutoff in 1981 and a suspension of 90 percent of its sugar quota in 1983.[6] The official rationale for the sanctions was to punish the Sandinistas for their intervention in the insurgency in neighboring El Salvador. The underlying strategy was to destabilize or weaken a regime viewed as an ideologically illegitimate client of the Soviet Union.[7]

This effort at economic warfare confronted many of the same factors that had frustrated sanctions in the past—namely, U.S. corporations did not share administration preferences and allies were opposed to sanctions. First, prior to the imposition of sanctions, the American business community adopted a nonideological approach to the Sandinistas. It worked out a number of compromises with the revolutionary government, the most significant of which was the restructuring of the $1.6 billion debt the Sandinistas inherited from the Somoza regime. A comparable modus vivendi was reached with foreign investors as the Sandinistas backed away from some of their more ideological positions regarding nationalization and labor relations.[8]

A number of surveys indicated that most U.S. investors were suspicious of the Sandinistas' ideology, but viewed confrontation as counterproductive. Most firms in Nicaragua opposed the aid cutoff and sugar quota suspensions, arguing that political progress (that is, a more nonaligned foreign policy and a mixed economy through supporting the private sector) was more likely if business was separated from politics.[9] A *Business Latin America* survey of twelve American managers in Nicaragua reported that only two agreed with U.S. aims and, of those, one opposed sanctions because it "pushes Nicaragua to be more dependent on the bad guys."[10] The 1985 sanctions elicited opposition from corporate trade associations, such as the National Association of

Manufacturers, which asserted that it would harm the reputation of "U.S. firms as reliable suppliers."[11]

Second, the United States could not persuade any other country, including its Central American clients, to join the embargo. This mitigated the economic impact of the sanctions because Nicaragua used the period of hostility preceding the sanctions to find new trading partners. From 1980 to 1984, it treated the United States as a "market of last resort." Its exports to the United States decreased from $218 million to $58 million while imports decreased from $247 million to $110 million.[12] When the embargo was finally enacted, Washington's closest allies uniformly opposed it. The EC not only refused to take parallel steps, but crafted a Central American aid package that included Nicaragua. Mexico announced a $26 million trade deal to exchange oil, raw materials, and agricultural chemicals for those exports Nicaragua could no longer sell in the U.S. market.[13] A 1987 study prepared by the Congressional Research Service concluded that the absence of international support combined with Managua's strategy of diversifying its trade partners severely limited the embargo's impact on the Nicaraguan economy.[14]

Moreover, the 1985 sanctions applied only to trade in goods and services between U.S. and Nicaraguan territory. They did not touch the affiliates of U.S. firms in third countries.[15] Since no one followed the U.S. lead in imposing sanctions, the offshore operations of U.S. firms were outside the scope of the controls. This potentially weakened the most significant cost imposed by unilateral sanctions—namely, denying access to components and replacement parts for U.S.-made equipment purchased during the Somoza era. For the sanctions to bite, noted the *Financial Times*, they "would have to embrace U.S. subsidiaries overseas and include pressures against other major trading partners, both of which will entail heavy political battles for the Reagan administration."[16]

These were battles the Reagan administration chose not to join because it wanted to avoid a repetition of the pipeline imbroglio. At the Bonn Summit of the G-7 leaders, U.S. allies pressed for assurances that U.S.-owned subsidiaries would not be affected.[17] The State Department consequently recommended that the Nicaraguan regulations should be "carefully designed" to avoid "potential conflict with the laws and policies of our friends and allies."[18] As a result, Canada allowed Nicaragua to move its trade office from Miami to Toronto. Ottawa did assure Washington that it would not allow its territory to serve as a conduit for the transshipment of U.S.-origin goods. If, however, Canadian subsidiaries of U.S. firms provide the same goods without U.S.-origin content, there would be no restrictions. These were Canadian, not U.S. firms, for whom U.S. law did not apply.[19]

Acceding to these jurisdictional limits was less corrosive of alliance relations. It also invited, as one former OFAC official observed, "easy evasion of the trade restrictions," which would "restructure rather than restrict U.S.-

Nicaraguan trade."[20] This is precisely what happened, as corporations did not police their subsidiaries beyond the letter of the law. Without extraterritorial controls, U.S. firms could legally sell spare parts from their affiliates overseas. As a result, Nicaraguan public and private producers were able to obtain Pratt and Whitney engines from Germany and parts for John Deere tractors from Brazil and Costa Rica.[21] In addition, most U.S. firms reportedly had few difficulties or compunctions about sourcing their import needs through their global networks. IBM procured spare parts from its Canadian affiliate, Xerox supplied copiers from Mexico, and Texaco bought lubricants from its operation in El Salvador—the country the United States was ostensibly protecting from Nicaraguan "aggression."[22]

In some ways, the inability to control overseas business activity allowed corporate self-interest to soften the impact of sanctions. While this may have helped some Nicaraguan industries, its overall impact was relatively small. The principal reason for this was Nicaragua's severe foreign exchange crisis, which eroded its ability to import from third country subsidiaries or anyone else. This problem was primarily a function of several factors beyond U.S. control—namely, the inheritance of a war-ravaged economy, economic mismanagement, declining terms of trade, and the regime's ambivalence toward the private sector. These factors were further exacerbated by the policies of the Reagan administration—that is, its influence in multilateral development banks (MDBs) to block all lending after 1982 and its support for the contra war, whose primary toll was economic.[23] These economic conditions limited the ability of foreign subsidiaries to obtain needed imports. *Business Latin America*, for example, reported that almost all firms would be willing to use the foreign subsidiary loophole as long as it was legal. That same survey indicated that their main problem was not finding sources for imports of capital goods and spare parts. It was having the foreign exchange to pay for them.[24]

In sum, the exclusion of foreign subsidiaries from the Nicaraguan embargo had a minor impact on the strategy of economic destabilization. It did allow U.S. companies operating abroad to trade items that were banned from U.S. territory. Their interest in pursuing this trade, however, was limited by the Sandinistas' foreign exchange crisis, something the administration attacked more effectively through other policies. As a result, the coercive impact of banning this trade was small relative to the risks of another extraterritorial conflict with allies so soon after the pipeline sanctions.

LIBYA

Through the 1980s, the Reagan administration gradually increased diplomatic and economic sanctions against the Libyan regime of Mu'ammar

Qaddafi because of its support for international terrorism. On 7 January 1986, it used IEEPA to impose comprehensive trade and financial controls following allegations of Libyan involvement in the bombings at the Rome and Vienna airports. The sanctions banned all U.S.-Libyan trade and ordered the departure of U.S. oil companies with investments in Libya. On 8 January, they were expanded to freeze Libya's assets in the domestic and foreign branches of U.S. banks.[25] The regulations did not cover U.S. firms licensed abroad. As in the Nicaraguan case, the aim was to "avoid the disruptive conflict that might come from broad extraterritorial application of new controls."[26]

Both allies and firms saw the sanctions as contrary to their interests. First, the United States tried to secure allied cooperation. In contrast to the pipeline case, this featured persuasion rather than coercion as Deputy Secretary of State John Whitehead was dispatched to European capitals. This effort produced an EC decision to embargo arms and a Canadian decision to tighten controls on the export of high technology. In addition, the administration worked out a "gentleman's agreement" with its allies not to exploit the sanctions by operating the concessions U.S. firms were forced to abandon. In contrast to the Nicaraguan case, a modest consensus on perceptions of threat made some level of cooperation feasible. Internalizing the lessons of the 1982 conflict, George Shultz called the U.S. approach a "long-term consciousness-raising effort."[27]

Given the Europeans' awareness of their energy vulnerability, persuasion ran up against severe limits. The United States wanted to sever or reduce allied energy links with Libya because, as one State Department official noted, Libya "is essentially a single-element economy, and . . . if you can get to [its] petroleum and petrochemical industry, you're really cutting past the jugular."[28] The Europeans opposed punitive energy sanctions. They regarded Qaddafi as a relatively minor nuisance who was being inflated to disproportionate importance by the Reagan administration. More importantly, they had more extensive commercial ties with Libya than did the United States. Several governments were dependent on imports of Libyan crude and had thousands of expatriates working in Libya. For economies trying to cope with unemployment and recession, these were concrete interests they did not want to sacrifice for an uncertain long-term confrontation.[29]

Second, private economic actors opposed the sanctions and wanted to maintain their trade and investment ties with Libya. At the time of the sanctions, five independent oil companies—Occidental Petroleum, Amerada Hess, Conoco, Marathon, and W. R. Grace—operated joint ventures with the Libyan National Oil Company (LNOC) to lift roughly 300,000 barrels per day (b/d). Libyan crude was more important to the independents than it was to the major oil companies because they had fewer alternative sources of supply and placed a higher premium on maintaining access. This appeared to foreshadow a repetition of what happened in the early 1970s when Qaddafi was then able to exploit this same vulnerability to force the independents to make concessions in pricing, taxation, and ownership that challenged and ultimately undermined traditional industry practices.[30]

The limits of multilateral agreement and absence of extraterritorial controls meant that much of this corporate activity was theoretically beyond the reach of U.S. sanctions. The regulations could not have prevented a foreign subsidiary of one of the departing oil companies from operating its old concession or buying crude from it as long as no U.S. person was involved in the transaction. Moreover, at least one of the companies, Occidental, operated its Libyan concession from its U.K. subsidiary—in other words, outside the formal reach of the regulations.[31] According to Treasury, as long as no U.S. citizens were directly involved in the transactions, such subsidiaries were exempt from the regulations because they "are not considered U.S. persons."[32] Allowing this kind of private behavior could have thwarted one of the more significant costs imposed by the sanctions—that is, the loss of guaranteed outlets for Libyan crude during an oil glut, something that would have forced LNOC to sell its crude at discounted prices on the spot market.

None of the independents took advantage of these potential loopholes. When the 1986 sanctions ordered the companies out of Libya, their response was that as American companies, they would obey U.S. law. Moreover, they were willing to go beyond the formal requirements of the law and prevent their non-U.S. affiliates from operating their concessions or buying Libyan crude.[33]

One reason why the administration was able to secure private cooperation was the use of informal pressure comparable to the moral suasion element of the CACRs. While the administration limited the reach of its regulations, it also arranged meetings between high-level State Department officials, including Secretary Shultz, and oil company CEOs. The aim of these meetings was, according to one of the participants, "to lay the burden of Americanism on them" and "talk U.S. companies into being good patriotic citizens."[34] Secretary Shultz hoped that by "jawbon[ing] American companies," they would be persuaded to "close down, restrict, or terminate activities in Libya."[35]

Beyond corporate patriotism, private cooperation can be understood in terms of the changing perceptions of interest and risk of the independents. The companies were less dependent on Libyan crude in the 1980s than they were in the 1970s given the emergence of an oil glut. Most of these companies had diversified in ways that made them less vulnerable to the loss of Libyan oil. For example, Occidental Petroleum acquired Cities Service, more than doubling its crude reserves, and expanded production in Peru and the

North Sea.[36] Other firms, such as Conoco and Marathon, had been bought by large diversified firms, such as DuPont and U.S. Steel, for whom the oil represented a small part of their overall operations.[37]

While the costs of losing access to Libya decreased, the risks of flouting American preferences rose. Given the extreme antipathy toward Libya in the United States, a continued association with Libyan oil might have been risky vis-à-vis Congress, shareholders, and customers. It may also have complicated relations with the U.S. government, as noted by a representative of DuPont, the owner of Conoco: "As a widely diversified firm, we need to maintain a good working relationship with Treasury and State. We're dependent upon them for so many services that it would be stupid to needlessly risk that relationship over maintaining a prerogative that isn't even all that profitable."[38] As a result, the risks of flouting a policy for which there was strong support in the executive branch, the Congress, and the public elicited voluntary home office cooperation in policing its affiliates' behavior.

An exception to this pattern of cooperation was the Coastal Corporation, a Houston-based oil exploration company. In 1979, Coastal worked out a deal with Libya in which it would invest in oil exploration in exchange for supplies of crude oil. The 1986 sanctions prevented the company from continuing to make good on its side of the bargain. Its Bermuda subsidiary then worked out an arrangement with LNOC in which it used the $45 million it owed Libya in order to purchase the Holborn group of refineries in Hamburg, Germany. LNOC agreed to provide the refinery with 75,000 b/d at a cost in exchange for accumulating a 50 percent interest over the next five years.

The deal did attract the attention of U.S. policymakers because it provided Libya with a guaranteed export outlet. According to the OFAC director, this augmented Libya's hard currency earnings and increased "its ability to promote and finance terrorist activity."[39] Treasury investigated the transaction, but was unable to make a legal case because it could not prove that the parent had directed the subsidiary or that the subsidiary had been created for the expressed purpose of establishing this joint venture with Libya.[40] OFAC did declare the Holborn refineries to be Special Designated Nationals (SDNs) of the Libyan government, authorizing the seizure of their assets in the United States and barring U.S. persons from dealing with them—penalties which had a negligible impact because they had no U.S. assets and all of their business was conducted in Europe. Without the ability to penalize Coastal's U.S. operations, Treasury was unable to break up the deal.[41]

The contrast between Coastal's risk-taking behavior and that of the independents can be understood in terms of differences in corporate structure and culture. Unlike the independents, Coastal was not part of a large multinational structure and was less concerned about the impact of flouting the spirit of the regulations on relations with the U.S. federal government for other parts of its operations. Moreover, its founder and CEO, Oscar Wyatt, had developed a reputation as a something of a buccaneer who was willing to make deals that offended public sentiment.[42]

Outside of the oil companies, another twenty-five to thirty U.S. firms did business with Libya before the embargo. Most either provided oilfield services or had construction and engineering contracts for several of the large projects Qaddafi initiated during the oil boom, such as the Great Man-Made River (GMMR), a project designed to tap water beneath the desert for use in coastal cities. Since the 1986 sanctions did not apply extraterritorially, these firms could legally do business with Libya through foreign subsidiaries as long as no U.S. persons were involved and the U.S. content of traded goods and technology was less than 20 percent U.S.-origin. Several firms utilized this exemption. For example, two U.S. firms (Halliburton and Price Brothers), which had been heavily involved in the GMMR, shifted their work to their U.K. subsidiaries and removed all U.S. citizens from the project. Schlumberger, a major supplier of oilfield equipment with executive offices in New York, continued to supply Libya through its Dutch subsidiary. Its spokesperson asserted that it had every right to do so because its subsidiary "is not a United States company . . . [and] the executive order didn't forbid foreign companies from working in Libya."[43]

Nonetheless, a General Accounting Office (GAO) study found that trade between overseas affiliates and Libya declined by 73.6 percent during the first year of the sanctions, even though these activities were legally unaffected.[44] In part, this was due to factors unrelated to the sanctions—such as a severe decline in Libya's creditworthiness because of its serious arrears to foreign firms—something that also induced a pronounced contraction in European business activity with Libya even though those firms' home governments opposed U.S. sanctions.[45] The main reason for this contraction was the dramatic decrease in the world price of oil and the growth of alternative low-sulfur sources in Angola and the North Sea. Libya's oil revenues, which accounted for almost all of its foreign exchange earnings, plummeted from $22 billion in 1980 to $5 billion in 1986, contributing to a drain on its reserves and an acute shortage of foreign exchange.[46]

Yet the extreme hostility of the U.S. government toward Libya compounded these economic factors. Many U.S. firms complied voluntarily with the spirit of the regulations for reasons similar to those of the oil companies— that is, a desire not to assume the onus of visibly flouting U.S. foreign policy. These factors had a more pronounced deterrent effect in the early 1990s after Libyan intelligence agents were identified as responsible for the 1988 downing of Pan Am flight 103 over Lockerbie, Scotland. As one State Department official noted, "They can pay a financial cost in other ways if they become branded as Libya-lovers. Most firms are risk-averters not buccaneers."[47]

Moreover, uncertainties regarding when a company was overstepping the line had a dissuasive impact on subsidiary deals with Libya. For a transaction to be legal, the home office must not be uninvolved in facilitating it (and *facilitation* is not precisely defined) and the U.S.-origin content must be less than 20 percent.[48] Given the intense bipartisan congressional and public support for the sanctions, administrative agencies were likely to act against any transgression that could have been construed as approaching a violation. For example, Halliburton was forced to plead guilty in federal court and pay $3.81 million in fines when it transferred oilfield equipment to its U.K. subsidiary, which, in turn, used it in its Libyan operations.[49] Given the difficulty of knowing the exact legal boundaries and the administrative difficulties of a firm segregating its Libyan activities from anything in the United States, it was difficult to know when a firm was transgressing the law. And OFAC's willingness to penalize major corporations in high-profile cases increased the credibility of sanctions if a firm crossed the line. All of these factors added to the inhibitions against Libyan business.

In sum, while the Reagan administration was unable to directly command affiliate behavior, official and public antipathy toward Libya redefined corporate calculations on interest. As a result, American oil companies voluntarily prevented affiliates from doing business with Libya, thereby making it more difficult for Libya to export its crude during a period of market surplus. These factors also discouraged foreign subsidiaries from participating in engineering and construction contracts, though not to the same degree. One reason for the difference between the oil companies and the other firms was that the administration made the former a priority since they enabled Qaddafi to earn additional foreign exchange, releasing resources for activities the United States opposed. Since construction contracts, such as the GMMR, were characterized as resource absorbing, public officials did not apply a parallel strategy of moral suasion to subsidiaries involved in these projects.[50]

THE CUBAN DEMOCRACY ACT

The Cuban Democracy Act (CDA), signed by President Bush on 23 October 1992 reimposed the Cuban embargo on foreign subsidiaries, the first use of this device since the pipeline sanctions. The bill overturned the 1975 Treasury exemption and rejected the logic that undergirded it—that is, extraterritorial sanctions would lead to acrimonious and futile confrontations with allies and place U.S. corporations in the untenable situation of having to choose between the laws of the host and home countries.[51] That logic held during the more zero-sum Cold War approach of the early 1980s. The Reagan administration did try to discourage allied trade with Cuba.[52] It never reimposed the pre-1975 restrictions on foreign subsidiaries because the diplomatic costs in relations with allies outweighed the amount of Cuban trade likely to be caught in an expanded sanctions net. As a result, from 1982 until 1987, OFAC approved 1,236 of the 1,279 licenses applications made for foreign subsidiaries, whose trade with Cuba averaged $259 million per year.[53]

That trade expanded almost threefold by the end of the decade to $705 million in 1990 and $718 million in 1991, primarily because the Soviet Union sharply cut back its Cuban subsidies in order to tend to its economic crises at home. Most of the increased trade involved imports of consumable goods no longer available through credit or barter deals with the Soviet bloc.[54] All of this trade took place in hard foreign currency; no one was willing to extend credit because of Cuba's debt crisis and its loss of a superpower guarantor of its obligations. Of the $4 billion in hard currency trade by Cuba in 1991, almost 20 percent was conducted by foreign subsidiaries, most notably the European and Canadian subsidiaries of U.S. grain companies, such as Cargill and Continental Grain.[55]

For the most part, these transactions took place without legal harassment. The director of OFAC testified that the overwhelming majority of license applications were approved as long as they fit into the formal criteria for the exemption.[56] A major grain exporter concurred, noting that "we are active with the Cubans and we know the licensing procedures; it is all very smooth and automatic by now."[57]

The expansion of this trade—and administration inaction in preventing it—generated strong interest group and congressional opposition. The Cuban-American National Foundation (CANF), the principal Cuban-American lobby, saw the disappearance of Cuba's Soviet subsidy as an opportunity to increase economic pressure in order to force Castro from power. From its perspective, U.S. firms operating abroad were filling the gap left by the Soviet Union and prolonging the life of the regime. As a result, they lobbied Congress to extend the embargo to foreign subsidiary trade.[58]

These efforts produced a strong congressional coalition in favor of extraterritorial sanctions, led by the Florida delegation, conservative Republicans, and some Democrats, most notably Representative Robert Torricelli (D-N.J.). The device advanced to achieve this end was an amendment first introduced by Senator Connie Mack (R-Fla.) in 1989, which sought to repeal the 1975 exemption for foreign subsidiary trade. Proponents referred to the regulation as a "loophole" in the law and a "ridiculous gesture of good will," rather than a means of avoiding chronic disputes with allies over economic sovereignty.[59]

Over the next three years, the Mack Amendment was appended to several pieces of unrelated foreign relations bills. Finally, in 1992, it became part of the Cuban Democracy Act, a bill sponsored by Representative Torricelli.

The Bush administration had tightened the embargo by issuing more restrictive rules governing the U.S.-content of foreign exports to Cuba, broadening the definition of strategic goods excluded from the regulations, and establishing a six-month denial of entry to ships that called on Cuban ports.[60] It nonetheless opposed extraterritorial sanctions and vetoed a 1990 bill that contained the Mack Amendment. In line with its predecessors, it believed that the economic costs imposed on Cuba by the bill were likely to be outweighed by the costs imposed on alliance relations and U.S. business. Administration officials testified that the 1975 exemption was not a loophole, but a conscious decision to avoid disputes with allies and place companies in untenable conflicts of jurisdiction. President Bush noted this explicitly in his memorandum of disapproval after vetoing the bill containing the Mack Amendment: "Extraterritorial application of U.S. law . . . could force foreign subsidiaries of U.S. firms to choose between violating U.S. or host country law."[61]

This logic was unpersuasive to congressional sanctions proponents. First, they denied that the measure was extraterritorial. Although it attached a legal consequence to behavior outside U.S. territory, enforcement could only take place against the home office in the United States, not in another jurisdiction.[62] Second, they dismissed administration arguments about the need to take allied sensitivities about sovereignty into consideration. Representative Torricelli spoke for most CDA supporters when he asserted that allies ought "to give some deference to us in the region" and that the administration should not allow a "$400 million annual exception to the embargo because people in Ottawa and London might get upset."[63] Ileanna Ros-Lehtinen (R-Fla.) predicted that allies would cooperate with the United States because they "would not want to risk their very substantial economic relationship [with the United States] over a small unreliable market like Cuba."[64]

While the administration remained concerned about the diplomatic repercussions, domestic factors would lead it to embrace the CDA. In the spring of 1992, many Democrats, including their presumptive presidential nominee, Bill Clinton, endorsed the CDA as a means of winning Cuban-American votes and political contributions.[65] As a result, the administration dropped its opposition and instructed the State Department to negotiate a compromise with Congress and the CANF. It did succeed in limiting the Mack Amendment to prospective contracts, averting the almost certain political fallout from mandating the abrogation of contracts legally entered into on foreign soil.[66] In one crucial way, however, the CDA was more severe than the pre-1975 regulations. The Mack Amendment removed administrative discretion over issuing licenses, eliminating what had in the past been an important "safety valve" in defusing bilateral conflicts.[67] While this seemed likely to exacerbate conflicts with allies, electoral considerations forced the administration's hand. As one former political appointee at State explained it, "[T]he worst that the Canadians and the British could do to President Bush in 1992 paled in comparison to what Florida voters could do."[68]

The international reaction to the passage of the CDA was uniformly negative. All of America's closest allies and trading partners condemned it as contrary to international law. Representative of these protests was a formal note from the European Commission that "it could not accept that the U.S. unilaterally determines and restricts European Union (EU) economic and commercial relations with any nation that has not been collectively determined by the UN Security Council as a threat to peace and order."[69] The extension of U.S. regulations to foreign activity also enabled Havana, for the first time, to persuade the UN General Assembly to formally condemn the U.S. embargo by a vote of 59 to 3 with 71 abstentions. Each succeeding year, the resolution passed with increasingly wider margins.[70]

Canada and Great Britain went beyond formal protest to invoke legislation banning compliance with foreign directives contrary to public policies that encouraged trade with Cuba. On 9 October, Canada's attorney general issued a blocking order under the FEMA, barring Canadian-based subsidiaries from complying with the CDA and requiring them to report all directives from the U.S. government or the home office.[71] Britain invoked the PTIA, which forbids British persons (including U.S.-owned subsidiaries) from complying with foreign laws, which could harm U.K. interests.[72] Trade Secretary Peter Lilley defended the order by stating that "it is for the British Government, not the U.S. Congress, to determine the UK's policy on trade with Cuba. We will not accept any attempt to superimpose U.S. laws on UK companies."[73]

In theory, the passage of the CDA and the issuance of the blocking orders set the stage for another major confrontation over extraterritorial sanctions. Despite predictions made in 1992, there have been no serious confrontations between the United States and its allies over specific cases. The principal reason for this is the adoption of conflict-avoidance strategies by both private and public actors. On the corporate side, the foreign subsidiaries of U.S. firms have discreetly terminated their Cuban relationships. An OFAC study reported that licensed trade had dropped to $1.6 million after passage of the CDA, all from preexisting contracts.[74] While the possibility remains that companies may continue to engage in unlicensed trade, most of the evidence indicates that this has also ceased. There have been no cases of subsidiaries appealing to London or Ottawa for diplomatic protection against U.S. sanctions regulations.[75]

Corporate acquiescence to extraterritorial controls stands in contrast to the 1970s when subsidiaries were more assertive in siding with host countries in protecting their Cuban trade. One reason for this change was that economic opportunities in the 1990s were bleaker than in the 1970s, when Cuba earned an export windfall because of a steep rise in the price of sugar and the Soviet Union was willing to guarantee Cuba's obligations. More important, however, was the change in the domestic political situation in the United States. Unlike the 1970s, the sanctions had powerful interest group and congressional backing. The removal of the exemption procedure meant that Ottawa and London could no longer persuade Washington to issue a license. Unlicensed trade would impose serious risks on the parent and lead to certain punishment if discovered. As one international lawyer noted, since the CDA had a strong constituency, "It would be politically hazardous for any administrative agency to disregard the embargo's prescriptions."[76]

Moreover, companies that sought host country support against the U.S. embargo faced the risk of adverse publicity in the United States. The CANF compiled a "Hall of Shame" to expose business dealings with Cuba, including U.S. parents whose subsidiaries trade with Cuba. To get out of this spotlight, a number of companies, such as PepsiCo and Tenneco, ordered their Canadian and U.K. subsidiaries to stop trading with Cuba prior to the CDA.[77] This was also one of the reasons why few corporations were willing to testify against a bill that most of the corporate community opposed.[78]

Host countries were also less aggressive in moving beyond principled opposition to the enforcement of their preferences. Both Canada and the United Kingdom investigated several companies that ceased their Cuban trade after passage of the CDA. The investigations were triggered by complaints from local companies that U.S.-owned firms had refused to bid on Cuban-related contracts.[79] As of this writing, there have been no prosecutions. British and Canadian officials explained this outcome in terms of the limits (and intentions) of the law. Under both the FEMA and PTIA orders, a mere correlation between passage of the CDA and termination of Cuban business is a necessary but insufficient condition for triggering the law. As one Canadian official responsible for enforcing FEMA noted, "If a company refused to bid on a contract, how is the government to know about that and, if so, whether it was because of the CDA or some other commercial reason?"[80] The "smoking gun" required for a prosecution is a directive either from the parent or from a U.S. government agency. Such evidence is likely to be forthcoming only if the subsidiary wants to trade with Cuba and is blocked by the parent or by OFAC.[81] As a British trade official noted, "The point of the PTIA is not to force companies to do business they don't want, but to protect companies that want the business from foreign legislation."[82] In other words, the legislation is less a means of vindicating economic sovereignty than of providing a service to subsidiaries that are interested in Cuban trade but have been prevented from pursuing it by the home office or the U.S. Treasury Department. Given the certainty of enforcement in the United States and the understandable reluctance of subsidiaries to put their home offices at risk, it has been a service without any takers.

Ottawa and London were less aggressive in challenging the embargo than they were in the 1970s and early 1980s because the CDA engaged matters of principle, not significant economic interests. Cuba's trade prospects diminished in the 1990s because of its economic crisis and its loss of a superpower guarantor of its economic obligations. Moreover, unlike the Ford-Canada case, where all Canadian automakers were U.S.-owned, there were numerous locally owned firms that could replace their U.S.-owned competitors. In neither the United Kingdom nor Canada was any significant trade lost to the country as a whole.[83] Finally, diplomats from both countries understood that Cuba was an emotional issue in the U.S. Congress and that the executive branch had only reluctantly accepted the CDA. They also recognized that there were more serious issues on the diplomatic agenda. For example, the primary Canadian concerns were the passage of NAFTA and the controversies over acid rain and softwood lumber. A low-profile approach of objecting in principle better served Canadian interests than enforcement actions that might lead to a public confrontation that could poison the bilateral relationship.

Washington shared this conflict-avoidance strategy. Even though the law was more restrictive than the CACRs, the executive branch used what limited discretion existed in the regulations to defuse potential conflicts. First, the one major concession that State obtained from Congress was an exemption for preexisting contracts. Its purpose was to avoid a repetition of the *Fruehauf* and Dresser cases in which the host government intervened against extraterritorial laws that forced the abrogation of contracts. Canadian and British officials asserted that such an outcome would more likely trigger enforcement actions through blocking legislation than the mere termination of Cuban trade.[84] The exemption was therefore interpreted generously to avoid overt violations of host country law.[85]

Second, Washington interpreted the regulations narrowly, issuing licenses in areas not expressly forbidden by the regulations. The exact language of the CDA bars foreign subsidiaries from trading goods and commodities. If a transaction did not narrowly fit the language of the law, Treasury licensed transactions to defuse crises. For example, a U.K. subsidiary of a U.S. firm sold pharmaceuticals to Mozambique under a letter of credit confirmed by the London office of a Cuban bank. When Britain's Department of Trade and Industry refused to issue a consent order to vacate the contract, Treasury reluctantly issued a waiver on the grounds that this was a financial transaction not covered by the law. Similarly, when a British sugar company used a U.S.-owned subsidiary to refine Cuban sugar, Treasury issued an exemption on the grounds that this was a secondary transaction rather than direct trade.[86] State and Treasury officials noted that these exemptions were of little economic significance, but were necessary to avoid confrontations.[87]

Finally, while Treasury acknowledged that the law required enforcement even in cases of foreign sovereign compulsion, it still has some discretion on the size of the penalty. That would hinge on the degree of influence the parent corporation has over the subsidiary and its willingness to use it. An illustration of this is the 1997 controversy surrounding the sale of Cuban pajamas by Wal-Mart's Winnipeg outlet after a customer complaint to a local television station. The Canadian subsidiary was instructed by the home office in Arkansas to remove the offending pajamas from all its stores after consultation with OFAC on the applicability of the CDA.[88] However, the decision—including the consultation with the home office—was reported in the Canadian press at a time of strong Canadian anger over the passage of the Helms–Burton law. As a result, Ottawa informed Wal-Mart Canada that its actions violated FEMA. The Canadian affiliate then defied the instructions of the home office and restocked its stores with the Cuban pajamas. Some legal analysts have speculated that the split between the subsidiary and the parent—each conforming to the law of the country in which it is located—was a means of averting legal liability in both countries.[89] Treasury officials, however, contend that the law makes the parent liable for the actions of its subsidiary even if it lacks effective control, though the size of the civil penalty will probably depend on a good faith effort to exercise whatever control is feasible.[90]

For the most part, the CDA has successfully enjoined U.S. corporate conduct abroad. That outcome did not impose significant new costs on the Cuban economy. Virtually all Cuban trade captured in the widened sanctions net took place in hard currency for readily available goods. If Cuba has hard currency, it can buy anywhere. If most of the sanctioned trade is in agricultural goods and light manufactures, there are several foreign suppliers that could replace U.S. subsidiaries. As a result, efforts to reach foreign subsidiaries only worked to the benefit of wholly foreign-owned competitors.[91]

Moreover, many exports banned by the CDA have found their way to Cuba through transshipment by third parties.[92] Several observers have noted the abundance of U.S. brand-name items at Cuban stores that accept dollars. They have been sold principally to the tourist industry, one of Cuba's largest hard-currency earners. At times, the United States has tried to stop this by identifying businesses created for the expressed purpose of selling U.S. goods to Cuba as Special Designated Nationals (SDNs)—that is, trading with them is equated with trading with Cuba. For the most part, this trade is part of the normal commercial intercourse between Cuba and third countries. Under current law, American exporters are not required to demand of their foreign customers certification against reexport to Cuba comparable to the Export Administration Act regulations on controlled technologies. According to OFAC, American exporters are not liable for the transshipment of their goods to Cuba unless they know or have reason to know that Cuba is the final destination.[93]

In sum, domestic political risk in the United States discouraged MNCs and host countries from challenging the CDA. Corporations were deterred by the strong domestic constituency behind the sanctions, which increased the credibility of penalties for proscribed behavior. Allies did not move beyond protest to the enforcement of the blocking orders as long as compliance with U.S. law was discreet and did not involve the abrogation of a binding contract. Expanding the sanctions, however, did not impose significant new costs on the Cuban economy because it primarily caught hard currency trade for widely available goods, for which there were many suppliers.

IRANIAN OIL SANCTIONS

The next attempt to bring foreign subsidiaries into a U.S. sanctions regime was the 1995 effort to sever the relationship between U.S. oil companies and Iran. The use of oil as an instrument to pressure Iran dates back to 29 October 1987 when the Reagan administration issued the Iranian Transactions Regulations, which banned all Iranian imports including oil. The decision was taken reluctantly. Officials from the Departments of State and Energy argued that an oil boycott would be difficult to monitor and futile without multilateral compliance. Congress, however, passed a comprehensive embargo, and the administration preempted congressional action through an executive order.[94] The regulations did not apply to offshore transactions in third countries, technically exempting foreign subsidiaries that purchased Iranian oil for reexport to third country markets. U.S. oil companies did not use this loophole. The costs of compliance were relatively low, given the surplus of oil in world markets. The domestic political risks were correspondingly high given Iran's unsavory reputation in the American political system.[95]

The regulations were partially relaxed by the Bush administration in November 1990 when U.S. oil companies were quietly authorized on a case-by-case basis to import Iranian oil in order to replenish the escrow account in the Hague for the settlement of U.S. claims dating back to the hostage crisis.[96]

The decision coincided with the exploration of a diplomatic opening with Iran. This effectively gave a green light to U.S. oil companies to resume their offshore ties with Iran.[97] While the U.S. market was still closed to Iranian exports, the companies were no longer inhibited from using foreign subsidiaries to purchase Iranian crude for refineries in Europe and Asia. Among the firms involved were major oil companies, such as Exxon, Mobil, and Caltex, and independents, such as Coastal and Philbro-Salomon. The Energy Department reported that this trade amounted to 734,000 b/d in 1994, or roughly 30 percent of Iran's exports.[98]

In March 1995, Conoco signed an agreement to develop Iran's Sirri offshore oil fields, the first investment by an American firm in Iran's energy sector since the Iranian revolution in 1979.[99] According to Conoco officials, the transaction was consistent with existing regulations since it was to be operated through its Dutch subsidiary and none of the oil would be exported to the United States.[100] While the company asserted that it did not need Washington's approval to go ahead, it did keep the State Department informed during three years of negotiations with National Iranian Oil Corporation (NIOC). The message it received was that while the deal was inconsistent with the policy of isolating Iran, it was also technically legal and would not face administrative roadblocks.[101]

These developments posed a problem for the Clinton administration in terms of both foreign policy strategy and domestic politics. In terms of the former, it adopted a zero-sum approach to Iran, branding it as an outlaw state because of its support for terrorism, efforts to acquire weapons of mass destruction, and opposition to the Arab-Israeli peace process. It therefore established a policy of "dual containment" seeking to isolate both Iran and Iraq simultaneously.[102] The economic component of this strategy was to place Iran in a sanctions net comparable to that around Iraq. This would exacerbate its foreign exchange shortage and "make it even tougher for the Iranian government to obtain hard currency and thereby constrict its ability to fund those policies that threaten our interests."[103]

Building multilateral support for this endeavor was difficult because, unlike the Iraqi embargo, there was no consensus within the UN Security Council for punishing Iran. Moreover, Western allies, particularly the EU, encouraged civilian commercial ties with Iran. The Europeans saw compelling economic interests to be preserved—that is, Iran was a significant market for exports and a major source of imported oil. The policy was also justified on diplomatic grounds. The EU was guided by Germany's policy of "critical dialogue," which viewed economic engagement as more likely to moderate Iranian behavior than was isolation.[104] Given these differences, the administration tried to strengthen multilateral policies in areas in which consensus was attainable. The strategy was partially successful on arms sales and dual-use nuclear technology. On the other hand, U.S. efforts had only a minor impact in persuading allies to end official credits and no success in limiting energy-related transactions, which the United States saw as strategic but the Europeans saw as vital to their own national economic security.[105]

U.S. oil company activity in Iran—plus the roughly $500 million in annual nonstrategic exports allowed by the 1987 sanctions—seemed to contradict the official policy of economic isolation and weaken the credibility of U.S. leadership. This precipitated a bureaucratic debate in early 1995 over whether regulations should be tightened to cover offshore energy deals with Iran. The Commerce Department, supported by Treasury and Energy, opposed such measures. Without multilateral support, they reasoned, Iran could still sell its oil and offer exploration contracts to non-U.S. competitors. Unilateral action would only handicap U.S. companies without imposing more than an inconvenience on Iran's economy.[106]

The State Department advocated a harder-line position. In part, State objected to any deal that alleviated Iran's hard-currency crisis. Of particular concern was the Conoco precedent, which provided Iran with new technology that could dynamically increase its export earnings.[107] More troublesome was its impact on U.S. efforts to negotiate stronger multilateral export controls or persuade countries to back off from controversial deals, such as a $1 billion Russian sale of a nuclear reactor and a $450 million Japanese loan for a hydroelectric dam.[108] Whenever the United States raised these concerns, its allies accused the United States of double standards, a retort pointedly made by German Chancellor Helmut Kohl at a joint news conference with President Clinton when he asserted that U.S., not German, companies were the largest purchasers of Iranian oil.[109] Ending this trade would, in the words of one State Department official, "eliminate that excuse, and place the U.S. in the strongest position to encourage other nations to adopt similar or parallel steps."[110]

The bureaucratic debate coincided with the introduction of extraterritorial sanctions legislation by the new Republican Congress. The chief policy entrepreneur on Iranian sanctions was the chair of the Senate Banking Committee, Alfonse D'Amato (R-N.Y.). In early 1995, Senator D'Amato sponsored two bills—S.277, which extended sanctions to foreign subsidiaries that traded with or invested in Iran, and S.630, which established a secondary boycott on foreign firms that traded with Iran.[111] In order to build support for these measures, Senator D'Amato's office sent a "Dear Colleague" letter to every member of Congress, which included a 1980 photograph of blindfolded hostages in the U.S. embassy in Teheran with the caption, "[S]hould we be subsidizing Iranian terrorism?"[112] His House cosponsor, Peter King

(R-N.Y.), was no less inflammatory, accusing U.S. companies of putting "profits before patriotism and blood money before national interest."[113] The bills also received strong support from pro-Israeli organizations, such as the American-Israel Political Action Committee (AIPAC) and the World Jewish Congress (WJC).[114]

The administration opposed both measures. One official testified that direct extension of U.S. law to foreign subsidiaries would "invite prolonged . . . diplomatic dispute . . . [and] the potential for litigation on an international basis involving the extraterritoriality of American law."[115] Extending sanctions to foreign firms with no U.S. connection would contradict the long-standing U.S. view that secondary boycotts, such as the Arab Boycott of Israel, violate international law.[116] Advocates of a tougher line shared these concerns since the aim of enjoining U.S. business with Iran was to establish greater credibility in building a stronger multilateral consensus. Attempts to bludgeon allies into submission through extraterritorial laws would increase "the risk of alienating countries whose cooperation we need to maximize the effectiveness of our policy toward Iran."[117]

In order to preempt congressional action, the Clinton administration used IEEPA to issue two executive orders. On 15 March, it targeted the Conoco deal by prohibiting any U.S. person from participating in the development of Iran's petroleum industry. On 6 May, the Iranian Transactions Regulations were extended to the purchase of Iranian crude for export to non-U.S. destinations.[118] Both orders limited their formal reach to firms incorporated in the United States in order to avoid diplomatic confrontations with allies. Since both the Conoco deal and the reexport of Iranian oil were transacted through foreign subsidiaries, they were theoretically exempt from the new regulations.[119]

Despite these potential loopholes, the administration was able to gain the compliance of private actors without the direct extension of U.S. law. Conoco withdrew from the Sirri deal the day before the issuance of the first executive order.[120] U.S. oil companies that had purchased Iranian crude pledged to seek alternative sources of supply. According to industry sources, they have policed their subsidiaries and no longer buy Iranian oil directly for their overseas refineries.[121]

The oil companies "voluntarily" complied for two reasons. First, they were deterred by political risk in the United States because none wanted to be seen as bailing out what most Americans saw as a rogue state—the same factor that inhibited legal opportunities foregone from 1987 until 1991. In the Conoco case, the company negotiated the deal because it interpreted the State Department's position as a mixed message—that is, we prefer you don't do it, but "you will risk your own money and assume your own investment risk." The deal was to be finalized only after consultations with public officials.[122]

The company had not anticipated Iran's unilateral announcement of the deal and the ensuing domestic firestorm. As a result, DuPont, which owned Conoco, informed Washington that, as a "good corporate citizen," it would follow whatever lead the government would set for it. To do otherwise would have incurred significant risk in terms of alienating both branches of the U.S. government on a highly charged political issue. It also would have created a conflict on DuPont's board of directors since 24.2 percent of DuPont's stock was owned by the Bronfman family, the owners of Seagrams, who were prominent members of the WJC and strong supporters of Clinton's policy toward Iran.[123] The oil companies stopped buying Iranian crude for much the same reason. As one international lawyer noted, "[A]fter the controversy surrounding the Conoco case, I wouldn't advise my clients to dabble in Iranian oil. There are a lot of other sources of supply out there."[124] In fact, some firms anticipated the legal changes and terminated their Iran supply relationships before the regulations were formally imposed.[125]

A second reason for corporate compliance was the ambiguity of the regulations. While the sanctions were carefully crafted to be territorial in scope, they did attach liability to the parent if it facilitated the subsidiary's transaction. This created a means through which control could be applied if voluntary cooperation was not forthcoming. For example, the performance of Conoco's Sirri deal was guaranteed by DuPont's Delaware headquarters, providing a potential legal nexus for asserting jurisdiction.[126] In addition, the home office was required to submit to OFAC reports on all subsidiary transactions, in effect furnishing it the information that might be used to assert a violation.[127] As a State Department official explained: "The fact that there is an embargo that might touch foreign subsidiaries has a chilling effect. They never quite know when they are overstepping the line."[128]

The executive orders constrained foreign oil company activity without a confrontation with allies comparable to the one that followed the passage of the CDA. They did not, however, impose more than marginal costs on the Iranian economy. First, while the sanctions did force short-term adjustments on the Iranian economy, they were mitigated by the willingness of non-U.S. firms to replace their American competitors. In July 1995, Iran was able to sidestep the sanctions on energy investments by turning to Total, Conoco's French competitor, to develop the Sirri fields, a transaction that was assisted by the French government.[129] Preventing U.S. oil companies from buying Iranian crude did force NIOC to discount prices to meet its OPEC quota. Iran was nonetheless able to sell the oil because of the willingness of European oil companies to serve as alternative customers.[130]

Second, the gesture of ending U.S. business with Iran had, at best, a marginal impact in erecting a higher multilateral wall around Iran's economy. The

United States did dissuade Japan from extending its loan and Russia from including a less proliferation-resistant gas centrifuge in its nuclear export package.[131] The policy had no perceptible impact on broadening European cooperation, in large measure because the Europeans already controlled everything deemed to be of strategic importance. While some of the sanctions literature indicates that credible leadership in building multilateral sanctions requires a willingness to incur costs, this presumes that allies share the leader's perception of the interests at stake.[132] In the Iranian case, the reason why the EU was unwilling to go along with restrictions on energy trade had less to do with the apparent inconsistencies of U.S. policy—though this was a good talking point—and more to do with commercial interests and definitions of national economic security. As a result, the EU continued to support trade and investment in Iranian energy even after the United States eliminated what appeared to be a double standard.

In sum, the outcome paralleled that of the CDA without the diplomatic friction generated by formal extraterritorial jurisdiction. The foreign operations of U.S. companies were susceptible to U.S. pressure and MNCs complied with the spirit as well as the letter of the regulations. Without multilateral cooperation, however, Washington was unable to translate that compliance into the imposition of significant costs on the Iranian economy.

CONCLUSION

The four cases examined in this chapter all conform to some of the lessons of the pipeline case. In all but one case, the United States limited the scope of its sanctions to avert a confrontation with allies. As a result, U.S. companies were able to pursue business opportunities through their foreign subsidiaries that would have been banned from U.S. territory—such as the sale of spare parts to Nicaragua, engineering and construction contracts with Libya, and the export of grain to and import of sugar from Castro's Cuba. When extraterritorial controls were imposed through the CDA, the result was universal condemnation and the enactment of blocking orders that theoretically barred subsidiaries from complying with U.S. sanctions.

In each case, however, corporate behavior diverged less sharply from U.S. economic statecraft than indicated by the pipeline experience. While political actors may have been less able to command MNCs to substitute public preferences for private interests, they were able to influence the latter by amplifying corporate calculations of risk so that prudent business decisions reinforced economic statecraft.

In some cases, considerations of external economic risk—often exacerbated by U.S. policy—deterred firms from using their subsidiaries for major new ventures, making regulatory control unnecessary. Nicaragua's for-eign exchange crisis dissuaded foreign subsidiaries from moving beyond arms-length trade to the injection of new investments or credits. Libya's loss of creditworthiness—due both to the oil glut and to the loss of guar-anteed export outlets from U.S. sanctions—led to a sharp decline in for-eign subsidiary trade. In the Panamanian sanctions (see chapter 5), third country subsidiaries were excluded from the ban on payments to the Pana-manian government in order to minimize conflict with allies. This exemp-tion was largely irrelevant since U.S. financial sanctions virtually dried up U.S.-Panamanian trade.[133]

Yet even without the direct infliction of costs, U.S. hostility created uncer-tainties that deterred investments that anticipated a long-term payoff, partic-ularly if the target's creditworthiness depended on U.S. support. This was most evident in Nicaragua and (as will be shown in chapter 7) South Africa. In the former case, U.S. hostility toward the Sandinistas augmented the risks facing investors and lenders before destabilization took its toll. Nicaragua's creditworthiness was dependent upon U.S. aid, MDB loans, and maintaining political stability, all of which were threatened by the Reagan administration's policies. In the latter case, congressional sanctions against loans and new in-vestments in South Africa did not reach the foreign subsidiaries of U.S. cor-porations and banks, theoretically freeing them to channel capital to South Africa from their operations in countries with looser sanctions. Neither in-vestors nor creditors took advantage of that option, in part because South Africa's liquidity crisis and political violence increased perceptions of risk. These perceptions were magnified by a congressional ban on International Monetary Fund (IMF) loans and the increased likelihood of sanctions. This meant that lenders and investors had to factor into their calculations the low likelihood that the international financial community would assist South Africa with its troubles relative to the threat of punitive sanctions.[134]

While arms-length trade was more immune to external risk, it was suscep-tible to the risks in the American political system. If there was a strong com-mitment in the executive branch—as in the Libyan and Iranian sanctions—oil companies usually enforced the sanctions beyond the letter of the law so as not to jeopardize their relationship with the U.S. federal government. If there was a strong public, interest group, or congressional constituency, corpora-tions were often deterred by the threat of adverse publicity and the complica-tions that might create with customers, shareholders, and workers. Moreover, if there was a strong congressional or interest group constituency behind the sanctions—as in the case of the CDA or the Iranian executive orders—com-panies recognized that violations of the sanctions were likely to be enforced so that the administration can maintain credibility with Congress to hold the line against more restrictive sanctions.

These calculations of risk were most salient to firms for whom the stake in question represented a small fraction of their overall operations.[135] In this sense, there is a significant difference between the pipeline sanctions and the preceding case studies. In the former, firms such as Dresser, Caterpillar, and General Electric were suffering record losses during a severe recession and were dependent on their business with the Soviet bloc and those European firms that did business with the Soviet Union. By contrast, the oil companies that departed Libya and Iran were part of large multinational structures that were less dependent on any single source of supply. This was true not only for such giants as Exxon, but for the independents, such as Occidental, whose vulnerability Qaddafi had exploited in the 1970s.[136] By the 1980s, the perceived risks of defying U.S. policy were greater than those of losing Libyan oil, particularly with diversification and the softening of energy markets. The fact that Coastal was not part of a larger multinational structure and was more dependent on Libyan crude explains, in part, why it was more willing to risk public antipathy and official scrutiny as the only U.S. firm that assisted Libyan oil exports.

Finally, foreign subsidiaries are more likely to comply with home state preferences if the risks in the American political system exceed those of flouting the sovereignty of the host country. This is likely only if compliance does not overtly violate local law or threaten what the host country defines as vital national interests. The pipeline sanctions did both—namely, forcing firms to abrogate legally binding contracts and challenging allied interests in maintaining employment during a severe recession, augmenting national economic security, and promoting détente. By contrast, European host countries did not oppose informal efforts to rein in the subsidiaries of U.S. oil companies from buying Libyan or Iranian crude. Such devices were less offensive to national sovereignty and less threatening to energy security given the oil glut. Moreover, they provided opportunities for their national corporations to replace the departing U.S. subsidiaries. While allies protested the CDA's formal sanctions more strenuously, they chose not to enforce their blocking orders against the mere correlation between the CDA and termination of Cuban trade as long as compliance was discreet (unlike the Wal-Mart case) and did not involve the breaking of a contractual obligation. Both the British and Canadian governments recognized the domestic political forces behind the Cuban sanctions and their reluctant acceptance by the executive branch. As a result, they tried to avoid a public confrontation to prevent domestic political fallout from complicating more important diplomatic issues.

As in the embargoes of the 1950s and 1960s, the primary source of foreign subsidiary compliance with home country preferences lies in domestic politics. The central difference is that interest group politics and public concerns about terrorism have replaced anticommunism as the principal sources of political risk. Yet as with these Cold War efforts, extending the reach of sanctions is not the same as imposing additional costs on targets. The departure of U.S. oil companies from Libya and Iran imposed some short-term dislocations, but eventually opened the doors to European competitors. The CDA enjoined U.S. subsidiaries from hard-currency trade for widely available goods, transactions easily replaced by others. Therefore, the key weakness of U.S. sanctions was not the globalization of American business, but the limits of multilateral compliance.

NOTES

1. Raymond Vernon, "Multinationals: No Strings Attached," *Foreign Policy* 33 (winter 1978–1979): 128.
2. Vernon, "Multinationals," 129.
3. See John Ellicott, "From Pipeline to Panama: The Evolution of Extraterritorial Trade and Financial Controls," in *Private Investors Abroad—Problems and Solutions in International Business in 1988*, ed. Cecil J. Olmstead (New York: Matthew Bender, 1989), 3.
4. An exception was the Reagan administration's approach to high-technology exports. Through Operation Exodus, it sometimes successfully used the dominant position of U.S. suppliers in items, such as supercomputers, to gain the compliance of foreign producers. See Shambaugh, *States, Firms, and Power*, ch. 4.
5. For examples, see Ellicott, "From Pipeline to Panama," 13–15.
6. For a chronology of sanctions against Nicaragua, see Hufbauer, Schott, and Elliott, *Economic Sanctions Reconsidered*, 175–180.
7. William Leogrande notes that between 1981 and 1985 there were bureaucratic divisions between those who supported the overthrow of the regime and those who advocated coercive diplomacy. After 1985, the former position won out. See "Making the Economy Scream: U.S. Economic Sanctions against Sandinista Nicaragua," *Third World Quarterly* 17 (June 1996): 330.
8. See chapter 5.
9. Purcell, "The Perceptions and Interests of United States Business," 121.
10. *Business Latin America*, 22 May 1985, 166.
11. U.S. Congress, House Committee on Foreign Affairs, *The Imposition of Economic Sanctions and a Trade Embargo against Nicaragua*, Hearings, 99th Cong., 1st sess., 1985, 41.
12. *New York Times*, 2 May 1985, 10.
13. See Hufbauer, Schott, and Elliott, *Economic Sanctions Reconsidered*, 185; and Leogrande, "Making the Economy Scream," 339.
14. Glennon J. Harrison, *The U.S. Trade Embargo against Nicaragua Two-and-a-Half Years Later*, CRS, Report to Congress 87-870E, 30 October 1987, 3–5.
15. Malloy, *Economic Sanctions and U.S. Trade*, 399.
16. *Financial Times*, 8 May 1985, 4.
17. *Globe and Mail*, 8 May 1985, 9.

18. U.S. Department of State, "Sanctions against Nicaragua," n.d. (DOS/FOIA), 2.

19. *Financial Times*, 11 July 1985, 4.

20. Malloy, *Economic Sanctions and U.S. Trade*, 413.

21. *Globe & Mail*, 28 May 1985, 1–2; *Wall Street Journal*, 4 August 1987, 30.

22. *Wall Street Journal*, 14 November 1986, 34; *Fortune*, 22 May 1985, 8.

23. See chapter 5.

24. *Business Latin America*, 22 May 1985, 166–167.

25. Hufbauer, Schott, and Elliott, *Economic Sanctions Reconsidered*, 140–143.

26. Memorandum, Shultz to Reagan, "Libyan Trade Sanctions," 3 January 1986 (DOS/FOIA). The asset freeze was applied to the foreign branches of U.S. banks. Both Treasury and State officials saw branches as different from subsidiaries because they are not incorporated in the host country. The Libyan government successfully challenged this in the British courts in the *Bankers' Trust* case. See Mahvash Alerassool, *Freezing Assets: The USA and the Most Effective Economic Sanction* (New York: St. Martin's, 1993), 55–58.

27. *New York Times*, 13 January 1986, 8.

28. Statement by Michael Armacost, Department of State, in Whitehead to American Embassies, "Departmental Press Briefing," 2 January 1986 (DOS/FOIA), 14.

29. *Financial Times*, 27 August 1986, 4.

30. See Turner, *Oil Companies in the International System*, 154–161.

31. *Platt's Oilgram News*, 9 January 1986, 1.

32. *Middle East Economic Digest*, 10 May 1986, 22.

33. *Platt's Oilgram News*, 31 January 1986, 3. Telephone interviews. Office of Foreign Assets Control on 16 June and 5 August 1988 and 31 May 1995.

34. Interview, Former Deputy Secretary of State John Whitehead, 14 August 1995.

35. Shultz to American Embassies, "Press Briefing—U.S. Economic Sanctions—Libya," 1 July 1986 (DOS/FOIA), 3.

36. *Petroleum Economist*, April 1984, 154.

37. *Wall Street Journal*, 21 June 1985, 32.

38. Interview, Robert Bonczak, General Counsel, Conoco, 6 July 1988; also see *Middle East Economic Digest*, 28 January 1986, 7.

39. *Platt's Oilgram News*, 7 August 1991, 4.

40. Telephone interview, Office of Foreign Assets Control, 31 May 1995; for Coastal's legal justification, see Michael Beaty, "Rebuttal," *Financial World*, 22 January 1991, 8.

41. *Platt's Oilgram News*, 2 August 1991, 1.

42. For a critical view of Wyatt, see Adrienne Linsenmeyer, "Saddam Hussein's Oil Man," *Financial World*, 8 January 1981, 30.

43. See *Middle East Economic Digest*, 10 May 1986, 22; *Business Week*, 27 January 1986, 55; *New York Times*, 9 December 1996, D9, and 2 December 1997, A1; *Christian Science Monitor*, 30 January 1986, 3.

44. U.S. General Accounting Office, "Libyan Trade Sanctions," Report NSIAD-87-132BR, May 1987, 19.

45. *Middle East Economic Digest*, 6 June 1987, 18.

46. *Middle East Economic Digest*, 11 October 1986, 25.

47. Interview, Department of State, Office of Economic Sanctions Policy, 6 April 1995.

48. OFAC, *Libya: What You Need to Know about the U.S. Embargo*, 20 May 1997, 2.

49. *Oil Daily*, 19 July 1995, 2.

50. Interview, Office of Economic Sanctions Policy, 20 April 1995.

51. Testimony of Wayne Smith in U.S. Congress, House Committee on Ways and Means, *Cuban Democracy Act of 1992; And Withdrawal of MFN Status from the Federal Republic of Yugoslavia*, Hearings, 102d Cong., 2d sess., 1992, 244.

52. See Morley, *Imperial State and Revolution*, 337, 346; and Gareth Jenkins, "Western Europe and Cuba's Development in the 1980s and 1990s," in *The Fractured Blockade*, eds. Alistair Hennessy and George Lambie, 310.

53. Donna Rich and Kirby Jones, "Opportunities for U.S.-Cuban Trade," Johns Hopkins University, Cuban Studies Program, June 1988, 6.

54. OFAC, "An Analysis of Licensed Trade with Cuba by Foreign Subsidiaries of U.S. Companies," July 1991, in U.S. House, *Cuban Democracy Act of 1992*, 91–106; also see Donna Rich Kaplowitz, *Anatomy of a Failed Embargo: United States Sanctions against Cuba* (Boulder, Colo.: Lynne Rienner, 1998), 145–147.

55. Kaplowitz, *Anatomy of a Failed Embargo*, 152–155.

56. Testimony of R. Richard Newcomb, Director of OFAC, in U.S. Congress, House Committee on Foreign Affairs, *Cuba and the United States: Thirty Years of Hostility and Beyond*, Hearings, 101st Cong., 1st sess., 1989, 126.

57. Rich and Jones, "Opportunities for U.S.-Cuban Trade," 7.

58. *New York Times*, 29 October 1992, A18.

59. U.S. Congress, Representative Ileanna Ros-Lehtinen (R-Fla.), *Congressional Record*, 102d Cong., 1st sess. (30 October 1991), 29210.

60. See Michael Krinsky and David Golove, *United States Economic Measures against Cuba: Proceedings in the United Nations and International Law Issues* (Northampton, Mass.: Aletheia Press, 1993), 102–104; and Kaplowitz, *Anatomy of a Failed Embargo*, 147–148.

61. *Public Papers of the Presidents of the United States: George Bush, 1990*, vol. 2 (Washington, D.C.: GPO, 1991), 1620.

62. See the statement of Rep. Torricelli in U.S. House, *Consideration of the Cuban Democracy Act*, 403.

63. *Consideration of the Cuban Democracy Act*, 402, 403.

64. *Congressional Record*, 102d Cong., 1st sess., 30 October 1991, 29210.

65. Walt Vanderbush and Patrick J. Haney, "Policy Toward Cuba in the Clinton Administration," *Political Science Quarterly* 114 (fall 1999): 392.

66. *Congressional Quarterly Weekly Report*, 9 May 1992, 1261, and 23 May 1992, 1462.

67. U.S. Congress, House, Committee on Foreign Affairs, *Cuban Democracy Act of 1992*, Report, 102d Cong., 2d sess., 3.

68. Confidential interview, 24 May 1995; also see Vanderbush and Haney, "Policy Toward Cuba in the Clinton Administration," 392–395.

69. Cited in the *Guardian* (U.K.), 9 October 1992, 15.

70. Kaplowitz, *Anatomy of a Failed Embargo*, 156–157.

71. Selma Lussenberg, "The Collision of Canadian and U.S. Sovereignty in the Area of Export Controls," *Canada–United States Law Journal* 20 (1994): 147–149.

72. *Financial Times*, 21 October 1992, 7.

73. Cited in Gareth Jenkins, "Trade Relations between Britain and Cuba," in *Cuba's Ties to a Changing World*, ed. Donna Rich Kaplowitz (Boulder, Colo.: Lynne Rienner, 1993), 118.

74. See Testimony of OFAC Director Newcomb in U.S. Congress, Joint Hearing before the Subcommittees on Economic Policy, Trade, and Environment; Western Hemisphere Affairs; and International Operations, *U.S. Policy and the Future of Cuba: The Cuban Democracy Act and U.S. Travel to Cuba*, Hearings, 103d Cong., 1s sess., 1993, 21–22.

75. See *Cuba Report*, April 1993, 4; *Ottawa Citizen*, 21 November 1993, D11; *Financial Post*, 23 January 1996, 1; Personal interviews, Gilles Lauzon, Justice Canada, and Douglas Forsythe, DFAIT, 25 and 28 August 1995.

76. John L. Ellicott, "Sovereignty and the Regulation of International Business in the Export-Control Area," *Canada–United States Law Journal* 20 (1994): 138.

77. Allan Gotlieb, "Canadian-Cuban Trade Relations," in *Investing in Cuba: Problems and Prospects*, eds. Jaime Suchlicki and Antonio Jorge (New Brunswick, N.J.: Transaction Publishers, 1993), 86–87.

78. Only three firms lobbied against the Cuban Democracy Act—Cargill, Continental Grain, and United Technologies. See Kaplowitz, *Anatomy of a Failed Embargo*, 155. A lawyer representing two United Technologies subsidiaries that did business with Cuba (Otis and Carrier) informed me that their experience in testifying against the CDA—both in terms of the lack of congressional receptiveness and the political flak—would probably deter them from doing so again in the future. Confidential telephone interview, 31 July 1995.

79. For reporting on these cases see *Observer* (London), 11 November 1993, D1; *Cuba Business*, November 1992, 1.

80. Lauzon interview (n. 75).

81. After the passage of Helms–Burton, the mandate of FEMA was broadened to cover the correlation between foreign directives and the termination of Cuban trade. See Peter Glossop, "Canada's Foreign Extraterritoriality Measures Act and U.S. Restrictions on Trade with Cuba," *International Lawyer* 32 (spring 1998): 93. Despite the tightening of the law, there were no prosecutions through 2000.

82. Interview, Nicholas Davidson, First Minister for Trade, British Embassy in the United States, April 1995.

83. Ernest H. Preeg, *Doing Good or Feeling Good with Sanctions: Unilateral Economic Sanctions and the U.S. National Interest* (Washington, D.C.: Center for Strategic and International Studies, 1999), 15.

84. Davidson and Lauzon interviews (nn. 82 and 75).

85. Ellicott, "Sovereignty and the Regulation of International Business," 138; not for attribution interview, Office of Economic Sanctions Policy, Department of State, 14 April 1995.

86. Ellicott, "Sovereignty and the Regulation of International Business," 143–144; Davidson interview (n. 82); confidential interview, Office of Foreign Assets Control, 29 May 1995.

87. Personal interview with Robert Gelbard at State and telephone interview with R. Richard Newcomb, Director of OFAC, who were the two principal officials from State and Treasury who worked on the CDA.

88. *Washington Post*, 14 March 1997, A29.

89. *New York Times*, 14 March 1997, D4.

90. Confidential telephone interview with former OFAC official, 4 June 1998.

91. *Business Latin America*, 22 August 1994, 2.

92. *San Diego Union Tribune*, 15 December 1996, A-39.

93. See Clara David, "Trading with Cuba: The Cuban Democracy Act and Export Rules," *Florida Journal of International Law* 8 (fall 1993), 385.

94. Kenneth Katzman and Lawrence Kumins, *Iran: U.S. Trade Regulations and Legislation*, CRS, 24 March 1995, 6.

95. See *Oil Daily*, 4 November 1987, 1; *Washington Post*, 8 November 1992, A1.

96. *Public Papers of the Presidents of the United States: George Bush, 1991*, vol. 1 (Washington, D.C.: GPO, 1992), 584–586.

97. *Middle East Economic Digest*, 31 May 1991, 19; *Oil Daily*, 30 April 1991, 1.

98. Cited in Katzman and Kumins, *Iran: U.S. Trade Regulations and Legislation*, 4.

99. *Financial Times*, 7 March 1995, 7.

100. *Oil and Gas Journal*, 13 March 1995, 32.

101. Testimony of J. Michael Stinson, Vice President of Conoco, in U.S. Congress, Senate Committee on Banking, Housing, and Urban Affairs, *The Comprehensive Iranian Sanctions Act of 1995—S.277*, Hearing, 104th Cong., 1st sess., 1995, 30–31.

102. See Anthony Lake, "Confronting Backlash States," *Foreign Affairs* 73 (March/April 1994): 48–53.

103. Testimony of Peter Tarnoff, Undersecretary of State for Political Affairs, in U.S. Congress, Senate Committee on Banking, Housing, and Urban Affairs, *The Iran Foreign Sanctions Act—S.1228*, Hearing, 104th Cong., 1st sess., 1995, 3.

104. Charles Lane, "Germany's New Ostpolitik," *Foreign Affairs* 74 (November/December 1995): 77–79.

105. Lane, "Germany's New Ostpolitik," 82–85.

106. *Financial Times*, 10 March 1995, A2, and 30 March 1995, A3.

107. *New York Times*, 1 April 1995, 5.

108. See *New York Times*, 17 March 1995, A1; and *Washington Post*, 18 February 1995, A6.

109. *Public Papers of the Presidents of the United States: William Jefferson Clinton, 1995*, vol. 1 (Washington, D.C.: GPO, 1996), 186.

110. Testimony of Robert H. Pelletreau, Assistant Secretary of State for Near East Affairs, in U.S. Congress, House Committee on International Relations, Subcommittee on International Economic Policy and Trade, *U.S. Sanctions on Iran: Next Steps*, Hearings, 104th Cong., 2d sess., 1995, 12.

111. *Oil Daily*, 11 April 1995, 1.

112. *Oil Daily*, 23 February 1995, 1.

113. *Oil Daily*, 3 May 1995, 1.

114. *Washington Post*, 2 April 1995, A26.

115. Tarnoff testimony (n. 103), 10.

116. Tarnoff testimony (n. 103), 11, 15.

117. Pelletreau testimony (n. 110), 12.

118. *Department of State Dispatch*, 8 May 1995, 387–389.

119. *Oil Daily*, 9 May 1995, 1.

120. *Oil and Gas Journal*, 20 March 1995, 38.

121. *Oil Daily,* 2 May 1995, 1; *Platt's Oilgram News*, 21 July 1995, 10, and 20 October 1995, 5.

122. Stinson testimony (n. 101), 31.

123. See *New York Times*, 14 March 1995, D5, and 15 March 1995, A1.

124. Confidential interview, 7 April 1995.

125. *Oil Daily*, 30 January 1995, 1.

126. Personal interview, Office of Economic Sanctions Policy, Department of State, 14 April 1995.

127. *Platt's Oilgram News*, 9 May 1995, 1.

128. Interview (n. 126).

129. *Financial Times*, 18 July 1995, 4.

130. Jahangir Amuzegar, "Adjusting to Sanctions," *Foreign Affairs* 76 (May/June 1997), 32.

131. *See Nikkei Weekly*, 22 May 1995, 4.

132. Lisa Martin suggests that the Carter administration's willingness to accept self-imposed costs through the grain embargo increased U.S. credibility in establishing the "no exceptions" policy on CoCom exemptions. By contrast, the Reagan administration decision to remove the embargo undermined U.S. attempts to get the Europeans to back off deals that were more important to it, such as the natural gas pipeline. See *Coercive Cooperation*, 193–198, 234–239. Another difference between the two cases is that the former (strategic denial) was an area of alliance consensus, whereas the latter (linking energy trade to Soviet behavior) was not. No matter how willing the Reagan administration was to accept self-imposed costs, the Europeans were unlikely to back off the pipeline deal given their vision of détente, their commercial interests, and their perceptions of national economic security. See chapter 3.

133. Joseph C. Lombard, "The Survival of Noriega: Lessons from the U.S. Sanctions against Panama," *Stanford Journal of International Law* 26 (fall 1989): 306–308.

134. See chapter 7.

135. See Krasner, *Defending the National Interest*, 75–82.

136. Kenneth A. Rodman, *Sanctity versus Sovereignty: The United States and the Nationalization of Raw Material Investments* (New York: Columbia University Press, 1988), ch. 8.

Chapter Five

Direct Investors: Instruments of Coercion or Hostages of the Target State?

In specific instances, possibly in *Nicaragua if the internal political situation should stabilize in the future*, there may be an increasing willingness on the part of U.S. banks and companies to deal with socialist countries in Latin America even in the face of a contrary U.S. policy.

—John Purcell[1]

On the whole, the [oil] companies are now keeping their heads down and concentrating on optimizing their relations with whatever governments they have to deal with. The evidence from Angola, and more tentatively from Libya, is that when such companies are in the middle of ideological disputes they now tend to side with the status quo.

—Louis Turner[2]

The previous chapter posed the question of whether Washington could enlist the cooperation of U.S. investors in third countries. This chapter investigates whether this cooperation can extend to direct investments in the target country itself. Can security planners use these investments as instruments of economic statecraft? Or does their location within the target state make them hostages to that country and potential frustrators of coercive strategies?

During the early Cold War era, MNCs were often willing and able to play the former role, acting as conduits for U.S. pressure against radical regimes. In part, this was due to an ethnocentric orientation that equated their private interests with the promotion of Cold War aims. Such strategies also coincided with their perceptions of investment security since leftist regimes opposed by Washington often threatened their property rights with nationalization. This support was often reciprocated by the state, which used diplomatic and economic pressure against regimes that challenged U.S. investments.[3]

Given this mind-set, MNCs often cooperated with U.S. foreign policy aims. In 1960, for example, Texaco and Standard Oil were initially willing to accept under protest Castro's demand that they refine crude oil imported from the Soviet Union in 1960 in order to avoid expropriation. They reversed that decision after a meeting with U.S. Treasury Secretary Robert Anderson, who wanted to use the expropriation to precipitate a crisis that would trigger the enactment of punitive sanctions.[4] In Guatemala and Chile, United Fruit and ITT funneled money into local organizations that opposed the leftist Arbenz and Allende governments.[5] Given the perceived coincidence of private and public interests, MNCs were willing to allow their direct investments to be used as conduits or "fifth columns" through which the United States could project its power into host countries.

A number of studies written in the 1970s and 1980s indicate that this was a relationship on which security planners could no longer depend. One of the key reasons for this was the change in corporate thinking about investment security in the Third World. The rise of economic nationalism in the early 1970s convinced most MNCs that their long-term interests were no longer served by interventionist strategies. Calling on the home state for overt pressure or involving oneself in local political struggles may have worked in an earlier era. By the 1970s, it would more likely undermine rather than enhance their investment security by delegitimizing their position in the local political system.[6]

A much better strategy was to adapt to local conditions, even if momentarily difficult, and rely on market forces to make host countries reasonable. This logic applied not only to economic nationalists, but to radical and communist regimes as well. As a result, MNCs developed business relationships that would have been unthinkable in the more zero-sum approach of the early Cold War era. Oil companies in Angola and Libya formed amicable ties to regimes that the Reagan administration sought to destabilize.[7] Mining companies that supported the white minority regime in Rhodesia prospered under Zimbabwe's first black (and Marxist) leader, Robert Mugabe.[8] In China, a state-owned facility near Canton that had been used to "re-educate" intellectuals during the Cultural Revolution was purchased by the Coleeco company to manufacture such revolutionary items as Cabbage Patch Dolls.[9] In other words, the 1970s taught companies that global markets created powerful incentives that, as one radical critic noted, forced "even self-proclaimed communists to behave like 'good capitalists' out of necessity if not conviction."[10]

In order to justify these relationships, multinationals adopted a cosmopolitan worldview that sought to insulate commerce and investment from political manipulation. MNCs opposed economic sanctions whether the call came from Cold War conservatives against radical regimes (Angola, Nicaragua), from human-rights-oriented liberals against white minority regimes or rightist authoritarians (South Africa, the Argentine or Chilean juntas), or from across the political spectrum in opposition to rogue states (Iran, Libya). To the extent to which companies involved themselves in foreign policy, they did so as conduits for the host country's desire for better relations, not as agents of the home country's strategy of coercion. John Purcell's survey found that direct investors in Central America justified nondemocratic practices in both left-wing Nicaragua and right-wing Guatemala.[11] Louis Turner's study of the international oil industry found that U.S. investors in Angola and Libya lobbied their governments for better relations when Washington's preferences were precisely the opposite.[12]

If this analysis is correct, we would expect that Washington could no longer use direct investors within the target country as instruments of economic pressure. Attempts to extend U.S. laws into those states can be effectively blocked through host country sovereignty. And, given changes in corporate perceptions of interest, firms are more likely to defend their rights to engage in "business as usual" with radical or rogue regimes than act as tools of American foreign policy.

The following case studies (including one—Rhodesia—that preceded the pipeline case) support many features of this model. In each case, corporate preferences coincided with the target state's desire to normalize relations and this led MNCs to lobby on behalf of this interest. Yet it was not this change in corporate outlook that impaired economic statecraft. In each case, MNCs initially followed Washington's lead despite their skeptical view of the sanctions. In some cases, they withdrew without explicit government directives because they anticipated the risks associated with increasing U.S. hostility.

There were two circumstances in which direct investors continued operations in ways that alleviated U.S. economic pressure on the target. First, in some cases, most notably in Angola and Nicaragua, public officials concluded that interfering with direct investors would either be counterproductive or impose costs on U.S. business disproportionate to their contribution to destabilization strategies. As a result, U.S. corporate activity in both countries reflected official ambivalence regarding their presence rather than corporate defiance of U.S. foreign policy. Second, when Washington tried to reach direct investors, corporate compliance was often blocked by the sovereign power of the territorial state. In each case, the United States was forced to fudge the enforcement of sanctions to remove U.S. firms from untenable conflicts of jurisdiction.

ANGOLA

Angola is often cited as a classic clash between corporate diplomacy and economic statecraft. From 1975 through the 1980s, the United States opposed the

Angolan government as a Soviet proxy because of the presence of Cuban troops. In the mid-1980s, the CIA provided covert assistance to insurgents who tried to overthrow the regime. At the same time, Gulf Oil (which was bought by Chevron in 1985) was the largest investor in Angola and provided the government more revenues from royalties and taxes than the CIA provided to the rebels. In fact, corporate taxes enabled Luanda to pay for the Cuban troops in hard currency, two-thirds of which were used to protect its most important strategic asset—oil production—from the "freedom fighters" the United States was funding.

Gulf's Angolan operations were initially controversial for a very different reason—that is, Angola was a Portuguese colony and one of the last outposts of white minority rule in Africa. In 1966, Gulf discovered oil in Cabinda, a coastal enclave, and began producing in 1968. By 1971, production reached 150,000 b/d and oil exports became the colony's principal source of foreign exchange.[13] This attracted the attention of citizen groups in the United States who tried to mobilize boycotts of Gulf products, alleging that the company's tax and royalty payments subsidized colonial rule. Gulf responded that its investment did not constitute an endorsement of colonialism: "[W]e do not engage in public debate about their political system . . . an international company must remain neutral."[14]

This same logic informed Gulf's approach to postcolonial Angola. After a coup in 1974, Portugal agreed to grant Angola independence. In January 1975, it brokered the Alvor Accords, which established a transitional coalition of the three main factions to govern Angola prior to scheduled elections in November. The accords quickly broke down and fighting resumed between the MPLA (Popular Movement for the Liberation of Angola), backed by the Soviet Union and Cuba, and UNITA (Union for the Total Independence of Angola) and the FNLA (Front for the National Liberation of Angola), supported by the United States through the CIA. By July, the MPLA, with aid from Cuban troops, controlled the capital city of Luanda as well as the Cabinda oil enclave. Despite these changes, Gulf continued to pay a $10 per barrel royalty to the Banco Angola, now under MPLA control. In September and October, it paid the MPLA $116 million, dwarfing the amount the CIA spent to sustain the opposition.[15] As in the case of payments to the Portuguese colonial authorities, Gulf claimed its role was politically neutral, honoring its contractual obligation to whomever was in charge without making political judgments.

This time it was the Ford administration that took issue with Gulf's apolitical stance. Secretary of State Kissinger saw Angola as an important Cold War battleground because Soviet support of the MPLA, particularly the deployment of Cuban troops, represented a challenge to détente. It had sent

$300,000 in CIA support to UNITA and the FNLA in January 1975 with plans to provide an additional $50 million. These plans were aborted by congressional passage of the Clark Amendment in December 1975, banning CIA involvement in the Angolan civil war.[16] Gulf's operations may have been neutral in intention, but their effect was to help consolidate the power of what was seen as a Soviet proxy while U.S.-supported factions were denied any assistance.

As a result, high-level State Department officials appealed to Gulf to suspend payments to Luanda, particularly since another $125 million was due by 15 January 1976. The company was initially reluctant to comply because it feared the seizure of its assets. Despite the political risk, it shut down its operations, withdrew its personnel, and deposited its tax and royalty payments in an interest-bearing escrow account, which would be held for the recognized political authority after the civil war ended.[17]

By mid-February 1976, it was clear that the MPLA had won the civil war and it was recognized by the Organization of African Unity (OAU) and the EC as the legitimate government of Angola. Around the same time, Luanda expressed an interest in reestablishing ties with Gulf. It preferred Western MNCs to the Eastern bloc because the latter lacked technology and expertise in offshore exploration and the former could better earn hard foreign currencies from exports to Western markets. At the same time, it accused the United States of economic warfare and threatened to transfer Gulf's assets elsewhere if the company was not allowed to return.[18] Recognizing the situation, the State Department gave Gulf a green light to release the escrow funds to Luanda and negotiate its return. On 9 March, Gulf resumed operations in a production-sharing accord with the state-owned oil company, Sonagol. By July, production returned to pre-independence levels.[19]

During the remainder of the 1970s, Gulf increased production from its Cabinda operations. Other U.S. companies joined Gulf in extensive offshore exploration in joint ventures with Sonagol. Angola was an attractive site for these investments because of its rich oil deposits, high-quality oil, and the fact that it stayed outside of OPEC, meaning that companies could export whatever they produced.[20] Corporate executives also found Angola to be a reliable business partner, Marxist ideology notwithstanding. They described their relationship as "businesslike" and "nonideological" and placed the political orientation of the MPLA outside the legitimate purview of corporate decision making.[21] As Louis Turner observed, "Angola is the most interesting example of the way today's oil companies can come to terms with governments of virtually any hue."[22]

This modus vivendi was not entirely inconsistent with U.S. foreign policy. Both the Ford and Carter administrations withheld diplomatic recognition of the MPLA because of the presence of Cuban troops. Contrary to corporate preferences, they also favored repeal of the Clark Amendment to retain the covert option. Oil company activity, however, was never linked to the regime's political orientation, in part because of the high premium placed on the development of new energy sources after the OPEC price increases. In addition, forcing the U.S. firms out would only have benefited foreign competitors. Therefore, public officials not only accepted U.S. business in Angola as a fait accompli, they also facilitated it through Eximbank financing of exports to support oil exploration and development.[23]

The Reagan administration came into office committed to a more confrontational Cold War approach. In the Third World, it pursued what later became known as the Reagan Doctrine. As explained by Chester Crocker, undersecretary of state for African Affairs, it endorsed support for "anti-communist insurgents [to] . . . raise the price of the Soviets' Third World empire."[24] In Angola, however, this strategy was not pursued as aggressively as it was in Nicaragua or Afghanistan. In part, this was because the Clark Amendment banned covert intervention. In addition, Crocker did not define the situation as a pure zero-sum game. Instead, he supported a strategy of linkage in which U.S. support for the end of South African colonialism in Namibia would be tied to the removal of Cuban troops in Angola and a negotiated settlement with the main insurgent group, UNITA. Persuading Congress to repeal the Clark Amendment would assist this strategy by maintaining "the option of backing our diplomacy with physical power."[25]

Oil company activity in Angola worked at cross-purposes with this strategy. From 1981 through 1985, Gulf invested $1.4 billion in exploration and was joined by seventeen other Western companies.[26] Angola also raised considerable sums from the international financial community given its oil prospects and its reputation as a reliable business partner. As a result, Angola emerged as Africa's second largest exporter of oil behind Nigeria, tripling its output from 1981 through 1985. In 1985, oil exports represented 90 percent of the regime's export earnings, 75 percent of which were provided by Gulf's Cabinda operations.[27]

Given the economic interests at stake, the oil companies opposed administration preferences. They dismissed its Cold War frame of reference by describing their business activities as apolitical. One executive went further, suggesting that separating business from politics was more likely to wean Angola from the Soviet Union than was confrontation because "they're not getting what they want from the Eastern bloc." For the companies, the highest priority was to maintain stability. Ironically, this was enforced by the Cuban troops who were protecting the companies' oil operations, which were Angola's most valuable strategic assets. These shared interests persuaded the companies to act as conduits for Angola's interest in better relations and in opposing repeal of the Clark Amendment.[28]

The Reagan administration did not interfere with this business even though oil exports provided the MPLA the foreign exchange it needed to pay for Soviet arms and Cuban troops. While it linked diplomatic ties and large-scale assistance to U.S. conditions, oil company activity was never part of the equation. As a result, it did not initially reverse its predecessors' policy that encouraged U.S. business in Angola. Nor did it rescind Eximbank policies that judged export-financing decisions on economic merits rather than political strategy.[29] In fact, in 1981, Eximbank approved an $85 million loan to finance exports related to offshore exploration by the Gulf-Sonagol joint venture.[30]

The decision to exclude oil from the Reagan Doctrine came under strain as the civil war intensified in the mid-1980s. In January 1985, UNITA declared Cabinda-Gulf a military target and increased attacks on its facilities.[31] The administration also persuaded Congress to repeal the Clark Amendment in August 1985 and resumed aid to UNITA. In early 1986, UNITA's leader, Jonas Savimbi, made a high-profile trip to Washington, which included a White House visit, to build support for a more interventionist policy.[32]

As a result, oil company operations became more controversial in the American political system. Conservative activists charged Chevron (which purchased Gulf in 1985) with subsidizing Soviet imperialism and organized protests, boycotts, and shareholder resolutions against the company's Angolan activities. Congress introduced a number of restrictive bills, which ranged from denying federal contracts to firms that did business with Angola to a comprehensive trade embargo that would have mandated disinvestment.[33]

The administration also appeared to reverse its initial approach. At a news conference on 28 January 1986, Crocker changed the tone of American policy by stating that U.S. oil companies "should be thinking about U.S. national interests as well as their own corporate interests in making their decisions."[34] Shortly thereafter, National Security Decision Directive (NSDD) 212 instructed officials to warn senior management of the risk "that commercial dealings with Angola may someday be banned or restricted." In step with these changes, the administration blocked the sale of Lockheed civilian aircraft and ended the extension of Eximbank credits to Angola because of its contribution to "acquiring the military and economic resources necessary to sustain its war effort."[35]

These changes influenced private calculations of risk, but did not lead to any significant departures. Chevron sold 20 percent of its Cabinda stake to its Italian competitor, AGIP, a hedge against worst-case scenarios. Nonetheless, its Angolan stake was too valuable to consider disinvestment because of its high success rate in offshore exploration and low production costs. The only other firms to cut back were Texaco, which spun off 40 percent of its operations, and Mobil, which sold its exploration rights to Mitsubishi. Other firms, such as Conoco, dismissed the likelihood of mandatory disinvestment and increased their investments.[36] To many observers, the oil companies were defying Washington by elevating their commercial interests above the national interest.

Yet the companies' ability to stay in Angola was neither an example of an unaccountable corporate diplomacy nor a bureaucratic oversight. Despite its change in tone, the administration never altered its initial decision to exclude oil from its linkage strategy. To Crocker, military aid to UNITA was the most effective prod on the MPLA. If economic instruments were to be used, the most practical levers were blocking Angola's entry into the IMF or linking reconstruction aid to acceptance of the U.S. formula.[37]

Adding oil to the strategy would have been counterproductive. Crocker acknowledged that petroleum exports eased the pressures on the MPLA. Yet he testified that extending the logic of linkage to the oil companies would not have cut off Angola's oil income because "there is a very long line of eager bidders from other countries who will fill the shoes of the Americans were they to leave under one circumstance or another."[38] Even those restrictions adopted in 1986 were designed primarily to dissuade Congress from imposing imprudent sanctions. As Crocker noted in his memoirs, they imposed costs on U.S. business rather than Angola since U.K. and French export credit agencies replaced Eximbank and Airbus captured the sale that Lockheed was forced to forego.[39]

The oil companies understood these preferences. Chevron officials stated that they were not informed of any policy change and U.S. officials denied any new pressures on the companies to curtail their operations.[40] Corporate decision makers consequently concluded that the risks of being forced out of Angola were low relative to the benefits of staying. As a result, the outcome was less an example of MNCs freeing themselves from state control than the fact that economic globalization persuaded public officials that unilateral sanctions were a futile and costly option.

RHODESIA

In 1967, a Rhodesian minister dismissed sanctions imposed against his country, noting that "whatever any particular government says . . . is quite different [from] what their [*sic!*] businessmen do."[41] Indeed, the subsidiaries of Western oil companies in Rhodesia and South Africa enabled the rebel regime to circumvent a potentially crippling oil embargo. The question is whether differences between governments and MNCs reflected the former's loss of control over the latter or their lack of commitment to the sanctions.

The sanctions against Rhodesia (now Zimbabwe) were initiated by Great Britain on 11 November 1965, after Ian Smith, the leader of its Southern Rhodesian colony, issued the Unilateral Declaration of Independence (UDI) to preserve white minority rule. Sanctions were designed to reverse the UDI and force the rebel regime to proceed with decolonization based on universal franchise. Multilateral support followed when the UN Security Council imposed selective sanctions in 1966 and comprehensive sanctions in 1968.[42]

U.S. sanctions were issued under the United Nations Participation Act. They were based on Security Council resolutions and paralleled British practice. The regulations covered both U.S. persons and subsidiaries within Rhodesia, although the latter would be exempted if their activities did not involve international trade and took place under duress. Since TWEA was not invoked, third country subsidiaries were exempt. As a result, U.S. firms in South Africa, a country that opposed the embargo, could legally trade with Rhodesia as long as no U.S. citizens or U.S.-origin components were involved.[43]

The omission of Rhodesian and South African subsidiaries from the regulations potentially weakened what U.S. and U.K. officials saw as their most potent economic weapon—namely, the oil embargo. Oil was a key area of vulnerability for Rhodesia's economy since it had no indigenous production and imported almost all of its transportation fuel.[44] Moreover, Rhodesia was a landlocked country dependent on the transportation of oil by rail links from the port of Beira in the Portuguese colony of Mozambique. To cut off this source of supply, the Security Council authorized Britain to erect a naval blockade around Beira to interdict vessels shipping oil to Rhodesia.[45]

The weak link in this strategy was the risk that South Africa and Portugal would circumvent the sanctions because of their shared interest in preserving white minority rule. In order to prevent this outcome, the U.S. and British governments obtained commitments from their oil companies to cooperate with the sanctions beyond the letter of the law. The companies agreed to instruct their South African subsidiaries to prevent the sale of oil to Rhodesia, directly or through intermediaries. To reduce the risk of transshipment, the companies also agreed that their South African subsidiaries would not import oil more than 10 percent in excess of their 1964 import requirements. That way, if South African distributors sold oil to Rhodesia, they would be unable to satisfy domestic demand. Both public and private actors assumed that South Africa's dependence on imported oil would dissuade Pretoria from forcing the companies to violate these commitments.[46]

South Africa, however, was determined to assist Rhodesia. From the onset of the sanctions, Pretoria informed the companies that they could not make sales conditional on guarantees against reexport to Rhodesia. The companies were initially reluctant to comply, citing the risk that their home governments may cut off supplies. Pretoria believed it could "call the bluff of the Western nations."[47] As a result, five Western oil companies (Mobil, Caltex, British Petroleum, Shell, and Total) were required to sell oil to independent South African dealers who served as conduits for the Rhodesian state purchasing agency, GENTA. The oil was then shipped through Mozambique by rail to the companies' refineries in Rhodesia, now operated by Rhodesian nationals.[48] In effect, South African sovereignty negated commitments made by the oil companies to their home governments.

Corporate involvement in sanctions-busting came to light in the mid-1970s when an antiapartheid organization obtained photocopied documents from Mobil South Africa revealing the "paper chase." The documents were forwarded to the Center for Social Action of the United Church of Christ, which publicized them in the United States.[49] This prompted congressional hearings in 1976 and an OFAC investigation in 1977.

In defending itself, Mobil cited both the territorial limits of U.S. regulations and foreign sovereign compulsion. First, its general counsel testified that the sanctions applied only to U.S. persons, not foreign subsidiaries. Mobil's New York headquarters established a clear policy of preventing Rhodesian sales. Its Durban refinery, however, was incorporated under the laws of South Africa, which did not observe the Rhodesian embargo. As long as no U.S. citizens were involved in any Rhodesian transaction, its subsidiary's business was outside the scope of U.S. regulations. Therefore, Mobil's instructions to discourage Rhodesian exports exceeded the requirements of the law and it could not be held responsible if the subsidiary acted on its own.[50]

Second, Mobil claimed that host country law prevented it from policing its subsidiary's behavior and complying with the Treasury investigation. Its Rhodesian affiliate was subject to government mandates to distribute oil and faced criminal liability if it disobeyed.[51] Its South African subsidiary was barred by South African law from making destination commitments on the final point of sale. As a result, it could not turn away any creditworthy South African customer, even if the final destination was Rhodesia.[52] Finally, both countries invoked their Official Secrets Act, under which the release of information involving national security—which included oil supplies—was a criminal offense. Mobil was consequently unable to determine whether its South African refinery colluded with its Rhodesian affiliates in any transshipment scheme.[53]

One senator referred to Mobil's defense as an "incredible assumption" since it implied that "if any given companies in South Africa . . . violate the sanction, nobody could find out whether they had or not."[54] Nonetheless, that is what the Treasury Department concluded in May 1977. OFAC acknowledged the limits of its jurisdiction—that is, the duress argument in Rhodesia and the exclusion of foreign subsidiaries in South Africa. Nonetheless, the companies were still liable—in the former case if they participated in the procurement of oil from abroad; in the latter case, if U.S. citizens or U.S.-origin goods were involved. Yet OFAC was blocked by the Official Secrets Act from questioning managers or inspecting company records in either country. Given the inaccessibility of the primary evidence, it was unable to determine whether Mobil had violated the law.[55]

At the same time, comparable charges were made against Shell and BP in Great Britain, in what became known as the "oilgate" scandal. This led to the creation of the Bingham Commission, a government inquiry that found that both companies had helped Rhodesia obtain oil through intermediaries and they had done so with the knowledge and approval of senior management. In addition, high-level government officials were informed of these transactions and did nothing to stop them.[56]

As with Gulf and Chevron in Angola, this case has often been cited as an illustration of the independence of MNCs from home state control. One scholar, for example, challenged a state-centered approach to the study of sanctions, arguing that questions of international compliance must focus not only on a multilateral consensus, but on whether "massive interlocking international economic elites apply and enforce the sanctions."[57] Senator Dick Clark (D-Iowa), who chaired the hearings on the allegations against Mobil, suggested that the oil companies were pursuing their own foreign policy "totally to the disinterest [*sic*!] of the United States."[58]

Yet, despite the dramatic contrast between official policy and corporate behavior, the outcome is better understood in terms of state policies—the strength of host country commitment to sanctions-busting and the ambivalence of home countries toward enforcement. In terms of the former, oil company defenses were somewhat self-serving. Mozambique, for example, did not have an Official Secrets Act and there was nothing to prevent the companies from investigating subsidiaries there.[59] In addition, the Bingham Commission found that Shell and BP policies evolved from reluctant compliance to active complicity because they wanted to maintain their favorable business position in South Africa and discourage that country from turning to other sources of supply.[60]

Nonetheless, as long as these firms were located in South Africa, there were limits as to how far they could comply with home country directives. Pretoria was determined to wreck the sanctions. Direct investors became hostages to that policy since South African sovereignty could block home country regulations and compel subsidiaries to act as instruments of sanctions busting. The only way to have prevented the companies from assuming this role would have been to make a credible threat of cutting off oil supplies to South Africa and Portugal. In fact, this is precisely what executives from

Royal Dutch Shell told the British government in 1965. Since making good on that threat would almost certainly result in the expropriation of its assets, Shell stated that it would not do this on its own without an explicit directive from the government.[61]

The reason why neither London nor Washington issued such instructions leads to the second reason why multinationals collaborated with sanctions busting—the ambivalence of home country preferences. The United Kingdom ruled out extending sanctions to Portugal, a NATO ally, and South Africa, a major economic partner.[62] Since it became clear that sanctions would not work within these constraints, what eventually mattered was maintaining their form rather than their substance. In 1968, the Foreign Office learned of the possibility of direct British sales to Rhodesia. It was satisfied when Shell and BP worked out a "swap" arrangement with the French company Total, which sold its oil directly to Rhodesia while the British companies sold an equivalent amount of oil to Total's customers in South Africa.[63] This pretense ended in 1971 when Shell and BP resumed direct exports to Rhodesia. British officials were unaware of this change, in large measure because they stopped meeting with the oil companies over Rhodesia from 1969 through 1976—an indication of the low priority given to enforcement.[64]

While there is no comparable hard evidence of official knowledge on the U.S. side, oil company actions were not inconsistent with public priorities. During the 1960s, Washington was as ambivalent about strict enforcement as was London and joined it in the UN Security Council by opposing the extension of sanctions to South Africa and Portugal. The Nixon administration further relaxed enforcement of the sanctions. In what became known as the "Tar Baby Option," it concluded that "the whites are here to stay" and that revolutionary violence only increased opportunities for the Soviet Union.[65] Part of that strategy was to scale back economic restrictions against white minority regimes. In Rhodesia, this meant support for congressional passage of the Byrd Amendment, which exempted Rhodesian chrome from the comprehensive sanctions the United States had agreed to five years earlier.[66] Mobil could reasonably have inferred from this that it had little to fear in terms of official scrutiny.

The oil embargo may have been vitiated by the differences between what "governments say . . . and businessmen do," but this was largely because neither the U.S. nor the U.K. governments were committed enough to their words that they were willing to punish South Africa and Portugal. Without any kind of credible threat of retaliation, the companies were hostages to host country strategies of sanctions-busting, something about which those countries were not ambivalent. Corporate behavior may have evolved from reluctant acquiescence to willing complicity, but that was the logical outgrowth of choices made in London and Washington.

NICARAGUA

A 1982 study by John Purcell suggested that changes in corporate perceptions of interest made it less likely that U.S. investors would join an "interventionist coalition" against radical regimes.[67] This prediction was put to the test by the Reagan administration's effort to wage economic warfare against the Sandinista government in Nicaragua in order to undercut the regime's base of support. These destabilization efforts took place against the backdrop of pragmatic adjustments between Nicaragua and the foreign (mostly U.S.) business community outlined in the Purcell study. These compromises were put into effect after early challenges by the Sandinistas to the foreign business community. The most important of these was the restructuring of the $1.6 billion debt inherited from the Somoza regime. Managua retreated from suggestions that it would repudiate the debt because of its need to maintain creditworthiness with private and public lenders for reconstruction assistance. As a result, it agreed to honor its obligations in exchange for a liberal rescheduling plan from its private creditors.[68]

The Sandinistas also accepted ideological compromises in the areas of state control and labor relations. First, while the government was more interventionist than its predecessor, it retreated from some of its more ambitious schemes. In 1980, for example, Nicaragua tried to impose greater state control over agricultural exports. Castle & Cooke, which had managed and marketed Nicaragua's banana production since 1961, responded by halting its purchases of Nicaraguan bananas. Given low barriers to entry in primary production and corporate control over the major distribution networks, exports fell sharply. As a result, the Sandinistas backed down and offered the American firm a five-year contract on prerevolutionary terms.[69] For similar reasons, there was no general socialization of the economy as there was in Cuba. Expropriations were generally limited to Somocista properties and foreign-owned mines. The latter were compensated and did not elicit appeals to the State Department for diplomatic protection.[70]

Second, the Sandinistas retreated from their early support for strikes, factory occupations, and requirements that management must share decision making with workers. To increase productivity and exports, they placed a higher premium on labor discipline by banning factory takeovers by workers and intervening against strikes organized by the Nicaraguan Communist Party.[71] Surveys of corporate managers consequently gave the government high marks in mediating the resolution of labor disputes.[72]

For their part, foreign investors were cautious and ambivalent in their approach to the new regime. A *Business International* survey found that most were wary of the Sandinistas' ideology and their long-term commitment to a mixed economy. The most frequent complaints surrounded lack of clarity on the "rules of the game," severe limits on their ability to remit profits, and a decapitalization law in which workers can accuse employers of illegally transferring capital abroad.[73] At the same time, the settlement with the banks was seen as a positive sign that Managua was a potentially pragmatic business partner. In a 1981 survey, few managers referred to the Sandinistas as communists. The Council of the Americas sponsored business trips to Nicaragua and invited Sandinista officials to the United States.[74]

Most of these adjustments took place during the Carter administration, which believed that economic engagement would moderate the Sandinistas' domestic and foreign policies. In fact, Ambassador Lawrence Pezzulo had arranged meetings between the Council of the Americas and Sandinista officials in the U.S. embassy and persuaded Castle & Cooke that an arrangement that facilitated its relationship with Nicaragua would serve U.S. national interests.[75] President Carter did suspend aid in January 1981 following intelligence reports of Nicaraguan involvement in the Salvadoran insurgency. This, however, was part of a "carrot and stick" strategy to influence Sandinista behavior, not the first step toward destabilization.[76]

The Reagan administration dramatically changed the tone and substance of U.S. policy, canceling the remainder of the Carter aid package and incrementally increasing sanctions—suspending 90 percent of Nicaragua's sugar quota in 1983 and imposing a comprehensive trade embargo in 1985. Direct investors did not share the administration's perspective. Most endorsed containment objectives in the region, but opposed sanctions. This continued as the conflict between Managua and Washington intensified. Surveys of corporate mangers found that firms opposed the aid cutoff and sugar quota suspensions, arguing that political dividends would accrue from separating business from politics—that is, a more nonaligned foreign policy and a mixed economy through supporting the private sector.[77] Many cited the fear that an overt confrontation could arouse anti-U.S. nationalism throughout Latin America and that they might suffer "collateral damage."[78] MNCs also tried to maintain an apolitical stance within Nicaragua. While they joined private sector associations to register economic concerns to the government (e.g., exchange restrictions or the decapitalization law), they maintained their distance from the political agenda of the local private sector.[79] Standing on the political sidelines was seen as a better way of protecting their investments than intervening on behalf of the U.S. political interests.

Nor were the 1985 sanctions able to enlist the cooperation of direct investors. The forty-three U.S. firms with direct investments in Nicaragua, which accounted for approximately 15 to 25 percent of its industrial production, were unaffected. Some of these investors did sell their stakes because the sanctions prevented them from sourcing parts in the United States. Most stayed because they were able to make modest profits due to high tariff walls and a scarcity environment that enabled them to sell almost everything they produced. Their position was that as long as they could cover their costs, they did not want to abandon an asset so they could maintain market access when the political situation improved.[80] As a result, Exxon refined crude oil imported from the Soviet Union and Monsanto manufactured fertilizer using raw materials imported from the People's Republic of China.[81]

In some ways, the Reagan administration's unwillingness to extend sanctions to direct investors cushioned their impact on the Nicaraguan economy. The willingness of a major U.S. corporation, such as Exxon, to refine Soviet oil helped keep the Nicaraguan economy and military afloat. Given the strategic importance of the refinery, it received Sandinista military protection from the U.S.-backed contras. While such behavior conformed to the cosmopolitan outlook illustrated by Purcell, it also attracted the attention of anti-communist activist groups and some members of Congress in demanding that Exxon should either pull out or be forced to do so by the administration.[82]

Yet, in other ways, corporate self-interest reinforced U.S. policy. During the 1980s, no foreign corporation injected more than negligible capital into new or existing operations. As one oil company executive noted after defending his company's right to stay: "[W]ho, in today's conditions, would want to risk new money there?"[83] The primary reason for this was Nicaragua's chronically severe and deteriorating balance of payments deficits and foreign exchange shortage. This outcome was primarily a function of several factors beyond U.S. government control—namely, declining terms of trade, the inheritance of a war-ravaged economy, economic mismanagement, and Managua's ambivalent attitude toward the private sector. Nonetheless, the influence of these factors on corporate calculations of risk was magnified by the policies of the Reagan administration.

First, the Reagan administration succeeded in informally preventing multilateral loans from coming up for consideration despite the absence of an international consensus with U.S. aims and the loss of its formal veto power over regular loans from these institutions. Initially, it was less successful because it possessed a veto only over soft loans rather than regular loans from the World Bank and Inter-American Development Bank (IDB) and because European and Latin American members either did not share its perspective on Central America or objected to the politicization of these institutions.[84] As a result, in 1981 and 1982, each institution approved two significant ($109.4 million from the IDB and $49.7 million from the World Bank) projects in Nicaragua over U.S. government objections.[85] After September 1982 however, the Sandinistas were completely cut off from both institutions. The main reason for this was the threat of U.S. financial withdrawal—a threat made explicit in a 1986 letter from Secretary of State Shultz that stated that IDB approval of a \$59.8 million agricultural loan would jeopardize continued U.S. participation. Given the IDB's dependence on its largest contributor, it referred the loan back for technical review. This was done even though staff reports had deemed the loan to be technically feasible, Nicaragua had paid its arrears to those institutions, and representatives from Latin America, Canada, and Europe publicly protested American efforts at politicization.[86]

The second factor was U.S. support for the contra war. The contras were less successful in controlling territory and posing a military threat than they were in attacking economic targets—a fact acknowledged by one military official who praised the contras for hitting "soft targets . . . that are putting strains on the Sandinistas."[87] They harmed export production by timing their offensives with the coffee and cotton harvests, blocking critical supplies through the mining of the harbors, and destroying infrastructure. They also compelled Managua to reallocate capital and personnel away from productive enterprises and toward the military, further magnifying Nicaragua's debt and labor shortage.[88]

Even prior to these events, the Reagan administration's extreme hostility toward Managua had a chilling effect on prospective investors by creating an environment of severe uncertainty regarding the country's social and economic stability. With the change from the Carter approach, investors had to factor into their calculations the risk that the United States would, at best, no longer assist economic recovery, at worst, harm the economy through economic sanctions or support for local insurgencies. *Business Latin America*, for example, praised the Sandinistas' surprisingly liberal 1982 foreign investment code and noted positive signs, such as internal stability, minimal labor problems, and a good record on debt servicing. It nonetheless concluded that "little investment is likely . . . until the level of rhetoric between the United States and Nicaragua subsides."[89] In other words, investors were inclined to limit their exposure until bilateral conflicts were resolved.

The anticipation of political risk also prompted some foreign investors to disengage. Castle & Cooke's decision in September 1982 to terminate its banana-marketing contract with Nicaragua provides such an example. Corporate spokespeople cited commercial rather than political reasons for the pullout—such as, the depressed market for bananas and the fact that they were losing money.[90] Yet political circumstances influence commercial decisions. If a global firm plans to curtail its overseas operations, prudence dictates that the first cutbacks should be in countries where the risk of politicization is highest. The decision also imposed costs on Nicaragua by forcing it to heavily discount exports to sell them outside the established corporate distribution network.[91]

Compared to the disappearance of new investment, the continued operation of direct investors was viewed by the administration as a minor consolation to the Nicaraguan economy. In fact, State Department officials expressed sympathy with the position of these investors, whose primary interest was to protect their pre-1979 property rights. Public officials concluded that the private costs of forcing investors to abandon their property exceeded the impact of disinvestment on the Nicaraguan economy. As a result, they made no effort to force out direct investors.[92] This was acknowledged by an Exxon official, who stated that the administration knew of the company's position and did not challenge it.[93]

In sum, MNCs did not act as agents of the Reagan Doctrine in Nicaragua. The administration neither persuaded them that destabilization served their interests, nor exercised legal control over their direct investments. As a result, MNCs acted more like private firms interested in protecting their assets than as instruments of economic warfare. Nonetheless, Washington was able to induce corporate disengagement by imposing costs on the Nicaraguan economy and by creating an environment of severe uncertainty. As a result, it reinforced conditions that discouraged the kind of new investment necessary to sustain economic recovery, particularly during the early years of the revolution. Although MNCs were not persuaded to join an "interventionist coalition" to destabilize Nicaragua, U.S. policies heightened corporate perceptions of risk so that prudent investment strategies achieved the same ends.

LIBYA

The Reagan administration's 1986 sanctions against Libya were the culmination of a ratcheting up of pressure on the Qaddafi regime that began in 1981. Even before the imposition of formal sanctions, the administration saw economic pressure as a way to destabilize the regime or limit the resources available to it. Of particular concern were the thirty-five U.S. firms doing business in Libya, especially the seven oil companies which lifted Libyan crude oil in minority (49 percent) joint ventures with the Libyan National Oil Company (LNOC). In July 1981, the State Department advised the companies to remove their American personnel. In December 1981, it ordered them to leave when it revoked the passports of all U.S. citizens in Libya. Initially, the administration relied on persuasion, but its ultimate aim was the withdrawal of the companies to deprive Qaddafi of the financial freedom he derived from oil. As one State Department official noted, "We're playing confrontation politics and we want them out."[94]

As in the Nicaraguan case, private economic actors initially opposed public preferences and did not want to politicize their business ties with Libya.

The oil companies defended their right to stay in Libya to maintain their long-term access to its crude reserves. Some analogized their situation to the trouble they had in Sukarno's Indonesia in the 1960s; by staying, they were able to maintain the rights to their concessions after Sukarno was overthrown.[95] The companies consequently resisted U.S. advice to withdraw their American staff until they were legally required to do so, and then replaced them with foreign technicians.[96] Oil company officials also approached the State Department on behalf of Qaddafi after the expulsion of the Libyan embassy from Washington in May 1981.[97] Initially, the U.S. oil companies acted less as instruments of coercion and more as conduits for host state influence—helping Libya earn revenues that augmented its capabilities and making representations on its behalf in the American political system.

In November 1981, Exxon broke ranks and announced plans to withdraw. Despite the timing of the announcement with escalating Libyan-American tensions, company spokespeople and industry analysts attributed it to commercial rather than political motives—namely, Libya's high tax rate and its attempt to maintain a high posted price at a time of market surplus.[98] Yet, Exxon's departure was unprecedented. Oil companies usually responded to such policies by redirecting purchasing and production to cheaper sources until the host country provided more reasonable terms. Withdrawal, by contrast, entailed a cost in terms of long-term access to reserves—a cost no other company had accepted in comparable circumstances. This fact led one radical critic to suggest that Exxon's departure was motivated by political, rather than narrow commercial, considerations.[99]

Political considerations, however, cannot easily be separated from commercial calculations of risk. For Exxon, a large diversified firm with a strong global position, the loss of Libyan reserves was not crucial. Conversely, the risks of politicization from future U.S. sanctions or from public antipathy from appearing to bankroll a terrorist regime were potentially high. The decision also showed considerable foresight since Exxon was able to salvage $95 million in compensation (out of a book value of $123 million) for its assets.[100] Those companies that stayed until the 1986 sanctions were forced to suspend operations and virtually abandon their assets to the Libyan government.

The only other company to depart was Mobil, another large, diversified firm. In Libya, however, independent oil companies, such as Occidental, Marathon, Amerada Hess, Conoco, and W. R. Grace, lifted most of the oil. These firms, with fewer alternative sources of crude, had a much greater stake in Libya than did the majors. They placed a higher premium on maintaining access to their equity crude (i.e., oil they owned outright from their minority share of the concession) relative to the risks in the U.S. political system. As a result, they resumed lifting, albeit at lower levels. Libya also cut prices and offered discounts to prevent further departures and stimulate increased production.[101]

The 1986 sanctions ordered the remaining oil companies to end this relationship and withdraw from Libya. As noted in chapter 4, the companies agreed to comply with the letter and spirit of the sanctions even though the sanctions' lack of extraterritorial reach meant that the companies had the theoretical right to operate their concessions through foreign subsidiaries.

Despite a private willingness to follow the government's lead, this effort to reach investments inside Libya was problematical from the start. How were the companies supposed to dispose of their assets? Corporate officials convinced the administration that if they just walked away, Libya could confiscate their facilities citing breach of contract. This would provide a $1 billion annual windfall to Qaddafi because the equity crude lifted from the companies' minority share would be marketed by LNOC with all the profits going to the Libyan government. Such an outcome would threaten not only the oil companies' private interest in maintaining access to the oil, it would also undermine the foreign policy goal of maximizing economic pressure on Libya.[102]

The administration tried to elide this dilemma by having Treasury provide temporary licenses to the companies, allowing them to continue to operate their concessions—including the payment of taxes and royalties to the Libyan government—while they tried to dispose of their assets.[103] The terms of the exemption, however, prevented the companies from transferring control to their foreign subsidiaries or selling their equity stakes to European competitors. The former option was rejected because it would have been seen as subterfuge in the American political system and the limits of such arrangements would have been difficult to enforce without extraterritorial controls. It would also have undercut efforts to build a stronger multilateral consensus with allies because, as Treasury Secretary James Baker noted, "[A]t some point, I think the United States has to be able to make the case to its allies, if we're asking them to take action, that there are no longer United States companies operating in Libya with the consent of the United States Government."[104] The latter option was rejected for comparable credibility reasons. It would also have enabled Libya to find established outlets for its crude exports that would otherwise have to be sold at a discount on the spot market. The only potential buyer was therefore the Libyan state oil company. This was not an attractive option for the companies. Since they were effectively placed in the position of forced sellers to a single customer, LNOC had no incentive to pay anything resembling market price.[105]

Given the terms of the exemptions and the incentives of the parties, no progress was made in negotiations over the status of the concessions. After Qaddafi's escalation of terrorism and the U.S. air strikes against Libya, administration officials concluded that it was "increasingly difficult to justify politically . . . the continued presence in Libya of U.S. oil companies, especially the payment of taxes and royalties."[106] Treasury consequently set a 30 June deadline for the termination of operations and authorized the companies to negotiate the Standstill Agreement with Libya. The accord effectively placed the concessions in suspended animation for three years—that is, the companies retained title to the oil while LNOC assumed operational control. During this period, both sides agreed to forego legal actions: Libya would not confiscate the assets for nonperformance and the companies would not challenge Libya's right to lift and market its equity oil.[107]

The arrangement served the interests of both parties. The companies retained title to the oil so they did not have to abandon their investments and could return if political conditions changed. The Libyan government was able to export the oil without the legal challenges it might have faced had it seized the oil fields. The arrangement also left the door open for access to U.S. technology and expertise if relations improved in the future. Finally, the deal enabled Libya to use the self-interest of the oil companies—that is, the desire to regain access to crude reserves and the fear of confiscation after the expiration of the Standstill Agreement on 30 June 1989—to lobby Washington to ease the restrictions.[108]

The oil companies were partially successful in persuading the administration to relax some of the regulations. On 19 January 1989, the day before President Bush was to take office, President Reagan issued an executive order designed to facilitate the return of the oil companies to Libya. The directive modified the regulations to allow the companies to operate their Libyan concessions through their foreign subsidiaries. The official rationale reflected corporate arguments made in 1986—namely, to "protect U.S. interests from forfeiture or expropriation and to avoid the financial windfall that Libya has been receiving for the sale of U.S.-owned oil."[109] This exemption, however, had to be utilized within the context of the 1986 sanctions. This meant that the companies could not export oil into the U.S. market, employ U.S. citizens, or use U.S.-origin technology.

The change in the regulations did not lead to a change in the status of the concessions. One reason for this was the opposition of the Libyan government. Qaddafi wanted to use the companies' concerns about their assets—and their desire to bid for a new round of exploration and production-sharing contracts—to pressure Washington to terminate the sanctions so it could regain access to U.S. technology, spare parts, and personnel.[110] The companies had actively lobbied for exemptions for themselves and made clear to the U.S. government their opposition to the embargo. They nonetheless recognized that the conditions demanded by Tripoli were nonstarters in Washington and kept the State Department informed of all communications from the Libyan government.[111]

A more salient deterrent to any agreement was political risk in the United States. This was a significant factor when the exemption was issued in 1989. The decision was subjected to congressional criticism and bureaucratic debate because it coincided with a conflict with Libya over an alleged chemical weapons plant at Rabta.[112] These risks became prohibitive after the indictments of two Libyan intelligence officers for the downing of Pan Am flight 103 over Lockerbie, Scotland, and Tripoli's refusal to extradite them.

The Bush and Clinton administrations were able to use these events to mobilize stronger multilateral sanctions through the United Nations—that is, an arms and air transport embargo in 1992 and an asset freeze and embargo on oilfield equipment in 1993.[113] Neither of these sanctions touched oil exports because the Europeans did not want to lose access to their second largest supplier of oil.[114] As a result, the sanctions did not preempt the 1989 exemption and bar the companies from operating their concessions through their European subsidiaries.

When Libya removed all previous conditions for the companies' return, the Clinton administration considered extending its Libyan sanctions to foreign subsidiaries. It eventually concluded that this was unnecessary.[115] The central reason was the domestic political risk of business with Libya—a factor that has even deterred some foreign firms from Libyan involvements. As one industry analyst explained it: "They [the oil companies] do not mind sanctioning an entrance into some of the world's most disreputable countries . . . but as soon as the word Libya is mentioned, thoughts turn to Lockerbie, the IRA, Rabta, and scandal, and that's often it."[116]

The impact of this effort to reach oil company investments in Libya was mixed. At one level, it was unsuccessful in that there was no politically acceptable formula by which the companies could dispose of their assets consistent with the intent of the sanctions. Under the Standstill Agreement, which remains in effect, LNOC marketed the equity crude and reaped all the export earnings for itself—an outcome counterproductive to the sanctions. At the same time, the suspension of oil company activities forced Libya to operate the concessions less efficiently without access to the expertise and technology of the firms who had run the operations prior to 1986. In addition, Libya lost links with an integrated multinational network, which provides exporters with a measure of security during an oil glut. Absent those links, Libya was forced to sell roughly 300,000 b/d outside that network and had to offer steep discounts to sell its oil on the spot market.[117]

PANAMA

From 1987 to 1989, the principal goal of the Reagan and Bush administrations in Panama was the removal of its military strongman, General Manuel

Antonio Noriega. They came to this conclusion after several years of cooperation with Noriega in the prosecution of the contra war. The catalyst for the change in relations was the attack on the U.S. embassy by a mob of pro-Noriega supporters on 30 June 1987, following opposition demonstrations, and a U.S. Senate resolution demanding an investigation of the regime's human rights abuses and involvement in the narcotics trade. As a result, the United States imposed its first economic sanctions against Panama—the suspension of economic and military assistance and opposition to MDB loans. Resumption of aid was made conditional on reestablishing civilian political rule and eliminating the influence of the Panamanian Defense Forces (PDF) on the government.[118]

The crisis came to a head in early February 1988 after two federal grand juries indicted Noriega on charges of drug trafficking. The United States called for his removal and tried to use the indictments as a bargaining chip linked to his agreement to step down and go into exile. After negotiations failed, the State Department persuaded his hand-picked president, Eric Arturo Delvalle, to dismiss Noriega on 25 February. The next day, the Noriega-controlled National Assembly ousted Delvalle and replaced him with Manual Solis-Palma. Delvalle was forced to go into hiding, largely in areas under U.S. protection.[119]

In order to dislodge Noriega, Washington imposed economic sanctions. The strategy was to use what is currently referred to as "smart sanctions" that focus on a target state's base of power while minimizing costs on the population as a whole.[120] Policymakers reasoned that the regime's public finances represented its Achilles heel. Denying the government as much cash as possible would precipitate a budgetary crisis in which it would be unable to pay government workers or the PDF. This would either trigger a coup against Noriega or force his resignation. At the same time, the United States did not extend sanctions to trade or direct investors in Panama because such measures would be disproportionately costly to Panamanian civilians and U.S. business relative to the additional costs imposed on Noriega. As explained by the director of OFAC, the logic was to "maintain basic business activities while at the same time continue to deprive the Noriega regime of financial liquidity to the greatest extent possible."[121]

This strategy was set in motion by actions by Delvalle's "government-in-hiding" and was concocted by his ambassador to the United States, Juan Sosa, and the Washington law firm of Arnold and Porter. On 2 March, Ambassador Sosa initiated litigation to gain title to roughly $50 million in Panamanian government assets in the United States. He began by seeking a temporary restraining order against the transfer to Noriega of Panamanian funds deposited in Republic National Bank of New York. The State Department supported this action certifying Ambassador Sosa as the sole legitimate representative of Panama. This allowed for the application of section 25(b) of the Federal Reserve Act, which had been used during the Second World War to assert temporary custody over the assets of governments that had fallen to the Axis powers. As a result, the banks did not honor requests for withdrawal by the "illegal" Noriega-Solis regime and transferred the funds to a special account in the Federal Reserve Bank of New York for the officially recognized Delvalle government.[122]

This attempt to foment a "revolution by litigation" was augmented by formal sanctions imposed on 11 March.[123] Their aim was to deny additional resources to the Panamanian Treasury. Provisions included the suspension of trade preferences through the Caribbean Basin Initiative and the Generalized System of Preferences and the withholding of payments due to Panama for the operation of the Panama Canal and their deposit in Delvalle's escrow account in the Federal Reserve Bank of New York.[124]

These actions triggered an acute financial crisis, particularly since the U.S. dollar was Panama's sole national currency. Cutting off access to assets and other revenue sources in the United States meant that Panama's Treasury lacked sufficient funds to meet its monthly bills. This also created a cash shortage for commercial banks that could no longer obtain sufficient dollars from the Panamanian National Bank. It also led to a run on accounts by nervous depositors that was stemmed only when Noriega ordered the closure of the banks on 4 March.[125] Popular discontent within Panama intensified because government workers and pensioners were unable to cash their checks in order to purchase basic necessities. The economic crisis precipitated a failed coup attempt on 16 March and the declaration of a state of emergency on 18 March. The main opposition group, National Civic Crusade, called for a general strike on 21 March to force a change in leadership by bringing the economy to a halt.[126] With salaries due to the PDF and government workers by the end of the month, this appeared to be the regime's period of greatest vulnerability.

While the sanctions devastated Panama's economy, they did not bring down Noriega. Despite the economic distress, the regime managed to pay the salaries of the PDF and the 150,000 government workers, who represented its main base of support. It was able to do so, in part, because it suspended payments on its foreign debt and slashed public expenditures by 79 percent.[127] It was also able to raise roughly $3 to $5 million in tax payments from U.S. investors, such as Texaco and United Brands, who were outside the scope of the regulations.[128] As a result, U.S. firms helped Noriega ride out the economic storm by providing him the resources to co-opt those groups most crucial to the regime while using force to intimidate the opposition.

The administration tried to close this loophole. Utilizing IEEPA, it issued an executive order on 8 April that both formalized the court-ordered asset freeze and, more importantly, barred U.S. persons from making direct or indirect payments to any public sector entity in Panama. The latter provision was designed to staunch the flow of U.S. funds into the Panamanian Treasury from both the 450 U.S. firms doing business with Panama as well as the 100 U.S. firms with direct investments in Panama. It was initially construed broadly to encompass virtually any payment, including income and social security taxes, port fees, import duties, and utility payments.[129] The withheld funds were to be deposited in Delvalle's escrow account at the Federal Reserve Bank of New York. As the GAO noted, "The practical effect of these additional sanctions was to add U.S. firms to the total sanctions package."[130]

Yet, the ability of Washington to use direct investors as instruments of economic warfare was constrained by conflicts of jurisdiction. The new sanctions were extraterritorial, though not toward third country subsidiaries.[131] They did apply to U.S. firms incorporated in Panama. In order to obey the sanctions, U.S. investors had to violate Panamanian law.[132] Most initially complied with the executive order, conceding that in a conflict of jurisdictions, U.S. law prevails.[133] By doing so, however, they placed their Panamanian operations at risk. Refusal to pay utility bills led to a cutoff of electricity and other services. Barring the payment of import fees and port duties prevented U.S. firms from importing spare parts and supplies needed to maintain their operations. Nonpayment of corporate taxes placed them at risk of confiscation.[134] This led to a major lobbying campaign by corporate trade associations, such as the Council of the Americas and the American Chamber of Commerce for Panama. The latter sent a letter to the administration pinpointing the dilemma: "U.S. business cannot ignore the fact that there is a Government Authority in Panama with all the legal authority and mechanisms to enforce the law in tax matters."[135]

The administration was not unsympathetic to corporate entreaties. During the first two months of the sanctions, OFAC issued forty-six waivers, mostly for the payment of utilities.[136] When the Panamanian Transaction Regulations (PTRs) were issued in June, they provided a blanket exemption for utility and travel-related expenses. The regulations were subsequently amended to exempt social security taxes, port fees, and import duties. As explained by OFAC Director R. Richard Newcomb, the regulations were designed to "deny as much cash as possible to the Noriega regime [without] . . . forcing U.S. companies to cease business activity altogether."[137]

Even with these exemptions, the PTRs still covered corporate activities that ran afoul of Panamanian law. In such cases, investors were forced to find creative ways to elide jurisdictional conflicts. To get around the ban on in-

come taxes, the Panamanian government required U.S. firms to pay employees their gross wages and collected income taxes directly from Panamanian
workers.[138] In some cases, the PDF was sent to the company to collect the
taxes from the consumer. For example, Texaco signed a 1982 agreement with
the Panamanian government, which granted it a monopoly on wholesale distribution of gasoline and fuel oils in exchange for a profit-sharing agreement
with the government. A strict interpretation of the executive order would have
required Texaco to abrogate the agreement. Instead, PDF officials were sent
to the company to collect taxes directly at the pump, vitiating the intent of the
regulations.[139]

Some critics alleged that the administration's reluctance to punish these
practices compromised the sanctions and contributed to their failure. Representative Sam Gedjenson (D-Conn.) asserted: "When the going got tough, we
sacrificed our central goal of removing Noriega and provided 46 exemptions
that knocked the wind out of our sails."[140] Indeed, the GAO estimated that
Treasury exemptions covered roughly half the funds that could have been denied to the Panamanian government.[141] Therefore, the aim of protecting
American business from harm relieved some of the budgetary pressures facing the regime.

A case can be made that corporate tax payments may have tipped the balance in favor of Noriega's survival during his period of greatest vulnerability
in March 1988.[142] Once that knockout blow failed, strict enforcement of the
sanctions faced some serious practical obstacles. While Washington could
fine those firms that violated the PTRs, Panama could threaten them with
reprisals, confiscation, and the arrest of managers and employees. As a result,
direct investors were effectively controlled industries of the target state,
whose payment of taxes could not be blocked. The unwillingness to punish
these activities reflected less a half-hearted commitment to the sanctions than
a recognition that enforcement served no purpose other than to maintain the
pretense of sanctions that one observer called "the remains of a failed quick
fix."[143]

HAITI

As in the Panamanian case, economic sanctions against Haiti were designed
to press a military regime to relinquish power to an elected civilian leader.
That leader was Jean-Bertrand Aristide, a left-wing priest who, on 16 December 1990, was elected to the presidency with 67.5 percent of the vote, representing Haiti's urban and rural poor. His redistributive policies, and occa-
sional support for mob violence to back them up, threatened the country's

economic elites. As a result, he was overthrown on 30 September 1991 in a coup engineered by General Raoul Cedras.

Unlike the Panamanian sanctions, those imposed against Haiti had significant multilateral support. For the OAS, the coup presented the first test of the Santiago Commitment, a June 1991 resolution to respond collectively to threats to democratic rule in the Americas.[144] As a result, it condemned the coup and called for Aristide's reinstatement. This was backed up on 8 October with a trade embargo and a freeze on government bank accounts to force the junta to negotiate the return of constitutional processes.[145] On 28 October, the Bush administration complied with the OAS resolution, imposing a trade embargo and ordering U.S. firms to withhold payments to the Haitian regime. This complemented the freeze on government assets and suspension of non-humanitarian aid enacted immediately after the coup.[146]

The sanctions were globalized on 16 June 1993, when the UN Security Council passed Resolution 841 imposing a mandatory oil and arms embargo as well as a freeze on the regime's assets. UN and U.S. sanctions were suspended following the signature of the Governor's Island Agreement, in which the Cedras regime agreed to a timetable for the return of the Aristide government by 30 October. They were reimposed on 13 October after an armed gang, supported by the Haitian security forces, deterred thirteen hundred U.S. and Canadian peacekeepers from disembarking to assist in the democratic transition. The Security Council also authorized member states to take whatever action was necessary to insure implementation of the embargo. The United States assumed that role, deploying six destroyers to interdict ships transporting oil and arms to Haiti.[147] Despite the progressive tightening of sanctions over the next year, military intervention proved necessary to enforce the Security Council mandate.

The question of why the Haitian sanctions were unable to dislodge the regime is the subject of controversy. Some analysts point to the nature of Haiti's political and economic structure. Sanctions did impose enormous costs on the Haitian economy. That could not be translated into coercive power because of Haiti's "predatory state apparatus."[148] As a result, the costs were borne not by the junta and the economic elites that supported it, but by the population as a whole. Others argue that the problem was lax enforcement by the major powers, particularly the United States, against those states that were flouting the embargo.[149]

For the purposes of this chapter, the principal controversy surrounding enforcement involved the operation of Western oil companies in Haiti and the allegation that they weakened the impact of the international oil embargo. When OAS sanctions were first imposed, oil was viewed as Haiti's greatest area of economic vulnerability. It had no refinery capacity and its domestic stockpiles were estimated to last no more than four weeks. Three international oil companies—Texaco, Esso, and Shell—which imported gasoline and fuels from the United States, met all its energy needs.[150]

The OAS sanctions did not fully place the companies within their ambit. First, prior to Security Council action, sanctions applied only to OAS members. Of the three oil companies in Haiti, only Texaco was a U.S.-incorporated subsidiary technically subject to Treasury regulations. Since the Esso and Shell affiliates were incorporated in Europe, they were not legally barred from distributing fuel within Haiti, though they could no longer import anything from the United States.[151]

Texaco was also able to escape regulatory control. On 4 June 1992, it established a blind trust based in Bermuda to assume operational control of its Haitian distribution network. Its purpose was to avoid a conflict of jurisdictions, which might place its investment and employees at risk. Under the agreement, the subsidiary was allowed to distribute oil within Haiti, but only under duress. To support the embargo, the company pledged not to import any oil into Haiti. In addition, all profits derived from operations would be donated to humanitarian relief in Haiti and the trust would automatically dissolve once the sanctions were removed.[152]

The disclosure of this practice shortly after the military intervention triggered a public controversy and legal proceedings. Documents obtained by the Associated Press revealed that Texaco had distributed oil from at least twenty-six tankers and had paid millions of dollars in taxes to the Haitian government. In addition, OFAC never cleared the blind trust and advised the company that it was probably illegal. When Texaco noted the potential threat to its employees, it was advised to protect them while still complying with the regulations. As a result, Texaco was liable for $1.6 million in penalties. An intense bureaucratic controversy ensued over why OFAC had waited eleven months to inform Texaco of its liability and why no enforcement actions were taken.[153]

Texaco's defense of the blind trust may have been self-serving. A State Department investigation did not support its claims of duress and some industry analysts speculated that the company might have been motivated more by concern for not losing out to competitors not subject to U.S. regulations.[154] Nonetheless, the central weakness in the sanctions was less the lack of accountability over MNCs in distributing the oil than it was the inactivity of governments in preventing its import. Until 16 June 1993, the OAS sanctions applied only in the Americas, and many Europeans continued normal commercial relations with Haiti. Nor were sanctions binding on the member states and there was no enforcement mechanism against those who flouted them. Information gathered by the GAO found that Haiti received fuel supplies from

France, Colombia, Portugal, Senegal, and the Netherlands Antilles.[155] According to the Economist Intelligence Unit, oil imports increased by 30 percent during the first year of the embargo, albeit at higher prices.[156]

The dilemmas facing direct investors became more acute after the United Nations globalized the sanctions in 1993. When the United Nations reimposed sanctions to reverse the abrogation of the Governor's Island Accord, the oil embargo was seen as its most potent coercive instrument. Initially, the companies agreed to cooperate with the UN sanctions by halting the distribution of stockpiled fuels.[157] In other words, direct investors were initially willing to cooperate with international efforts to use Haiti's oil shortage to force the regime from power.

Haitian sovereignty prevented the companies from playing this role. In response to the companies' refusal to sell, fuel wholesalers quickly obtained court orders to force the release of the stockpiles and the Haitian military and police backed up the rulings.[158] As a result, the companies were compelled to release the gasoline even though this frustrated the sanctions of their home governments.[159] One UN official tried to make a virtue out of necessity by asserting that the companies' initial pledge may have exceeded the UN mandate, which applied only to the export of oil, not its distribution within Haiti.[160]

Again, the issue was not the role of direct investors circumventing the embargo, but the inability to staunch the flow of oil into Haiti. The UN sanctions were more tightly enforced than those by the OAS. Nonetheless, significant transfers of fuel did take place, principally by transshipment through the Dominican Republic. This further augmented domestic stockpiles and enabled the Cedras regime to weather the sanctions for another year.[161] While the oil companies' distribution system facilitated this strategy, it was a role they were compelled to play by threat of confiscation or violence. The real vulnerability in the sanctions lay in the limits of interstate enforcement, not the independence of MNCs from home state control.

CONCLUSION

This chapter began with the hypothesis that as MNCs move away from an ethnocentric frame of reference, direct investors in target states could no longer be used as instruments of home state economic pressure. These changes in corporate outlook are evident in each of the case studies. MNCs equated the protection of their assets not with U.S. strategies of destabilization but with normalizing ties with the countries in which they were doing business. This was even true of relations with Marxist-oriented regimes, such as Angola and Nicaragua. Direct investors were therefore reluctant to play the fifth-column role adopted by U.S. oil companies in Cuba in 1960. They were more likely to act as conduits for better relations (as in Angola and Libya) or the amelioration of economic sanctions (as in Nicaragua and Panama).

Yet opposition to sanctions did not automatically translate into a willingness to frustrate U.S. policy. In each case in which sanctions were applied, MNCs instructed local affiliates to follow U.S. regulations until circumstances on the ground made that impossible. In the Rhodesian and Libyan cases, their initial commitments went beyond the letter of the law. Those businesses that continued to operate despite U.S. destabilization efforts—namely, oil companies in Angola; direct investors in Nicaragua—were not really defying U.S. policy because they were never asked to leave. In the former case, oil was excluded from U.S. strategy because a forced withdrawal would only benefit European competitors. In the latter case, policymakers concluded that the hardship disinvestment imposed on U.S. firms outweighed the additional costs imposed by forcing their withdrawal from Nicaragua.

As in the case of third country subsidiaries, U.S. hostility heightened corporate calculations of risk, thereby dissuading companies from taking actions that would undercut the sanctions. This was most clearly evident in Nicaragua as no investor funneled new capital into the country, in large measure because of the implications of the Reagan administration's policies for the country's creditworthiness. Other investors anticipated worst-case scenarios (e.g., political violence, a financial crisis, the forced sale of assets) by withdrawing— for example, Castle & Cooke in Nicaragua; Exxon and Mobil in Libya. These considerations were less evident in Angola because its oil reserves made its creditworthiness less vulnerable to U.S. pressure, although Chevron, Mobil, and Texaco hedged their bets by spinning off parts of their operations.

Despite corporate willingness to follow Washington's lead, each case demonstrates the difficulties of conscripting direct investors into strategies of economic statecraft. First, forcing the departure of U.S. business often involves the abandonment of assets to the target state. This was precisely the dilemma facing the Reagan administration in Libya in its search for a formula with which the departure of the U.S. oil companies would not provide Qaddafi the opportunity to market and earn all the revenues from the companies' minority shares. This is also why mandatory disinvestment from South Africa would likely have been counterproductive had it been legislated. White South African business would have earned a windfall from U.S. firms, who would have been placed in the position of forced sellers unable to recoup anything resembling market price.[162]

Second, if the assets on the ground are of particular value, forced withdrawal could work to the advantage of non-U.S. competitors. This is what happened in Libya, as European firms replaced their American counterparts in exploration and production. It is also the central reason why the Reagan administration never ordered Gulf or Chevron out of Angola despite the foreign exchange their operations provided to the MPLA.

Finally, and most importantly, extending sanctions to U.S. firms in the target state creates a confrontation between U.S. authority over its citizens and a sovereign's control of its territory. It is a battle the United States is unlikely to win. While it can financially penalize its firms for the behavior of its direct investors, the host country can deny essential services, confiscate assets, and subject local managers to criminal penalties.[163]

This is not to argue that it is impossible for the United States to extend its regulations into a target state. In 1978, for example, Congress passed the Evans Amendment, which linked eligibility for Eximbank loans to the labor practices of South African-incorporated subsidiaries. The 1985 South African sanctions banned direct investors from selling anything to the South African military and police. Pretoria protested both laws as derogations of its sovereignty. It also had the ability to block compliance through either the Protection of Businesses Act, which prevented South African firms from obeying foreign directives, or the National Supplies Procurement Act, which empowered it to commandeer goods and services necessary for national security and order that the transaction be kept secret. In neither case did it interfere with U.S. extraterritorial controls, in large measure because they were seen as a relatively small price to pay to fend off the more serious threat of punitive sanctions.[164]

In Rhodesia, Panama, and Haiti, by contrast, extraterritorial controls were directed at resources that were critical to the survival of each regime. Target states consequently used the full range of their sovereign powers to make it impossible for U.S. firms on the ground to comply. As a result, policymakers were forced to fudge the enforcement of the regulations so as not to penalize firms for noncompliance compelled by local law.

NOTES

1. Purcell, "The Perceptions and Interests of U.S. Business," 123 (emphasis added).
2. Turner, *Oil Companies in the International System,* 230.
3. See Rodman, *Sanctity versus Sovereignty*, ch. 6.
4. Krasner, *Defending the National Interest*, 291.
5. Krasner found that in both cases, the motivation behind covert intervention was Cold War ideology, not corporate preferences. See Krasner, *Defending the National Interest*, 279–286 and 298–313. Nonetheless, the firms in question equated their private interests with public strategies of destabilization.

6. See Raymond Vernon, "Multinational Enterprises and National Governments: Exploration of an Uneasy Relationship," *Columbia Journal of World Business* 11 (summer 1976): 14; Theodore H. Moran, "Multinational Corporations and Dependency: A Dialogue for Dependentistas and Non-Dependentistas," *International Organization* 32 (winter 1978): 96–97; Rodman, *Sanctity versus Sovereignty*, ch. 9.

7. Turner, *Oil Companies in the International System*, 229–230.

8. See Gladwin and Walter, *Multinationals under Fire*, 176–178; and *Business Week*, 9 May 1983, 9.

9. *Economist*, 8 September 1984, 50.

10. Richard R. Fagen, ed., *Capitalism and the State in U.S.–Latin American Relations* (Stanford, Calif.: Stanford University Press, 1979), 6.

11. Purcell, "The Perceptions and Interests of U.S. Business," 121.

12. Turner, *Oil Companies in the International System*, 230.

13. Gladwin and Walter, *Multinationals under Fire*, 193.

14. David Vogel, *Lobbying the Corporation: Citizen Challenges to Business Authority* (New York: BasicBooks, 1978), 188.

15. Gladwin and Walter, *Multinationals under Fire*, 195.

16. Robert M. Price, "U.S. Policy toward Southern Africa: Interests, Choices, and Constraints," in *International Politics in Southern Africa*, eds. Gwendolen M. Carter and Patrick O'Meara (Bloomington: University of Indiana Press, 1982), 47–50.

17. *New York Times*, 21 December 1975, 2, and 23 December 1975, 7.

18. *New York Times*, 2 February 1976, 3.

19. Turner, *Oil Companies in the International System*, 79.

20. Price, "U.S. Policy toward Southern Africa," 66.

21. See testimony of Melvin Hill, President of Gulf Oil, in U.S. Congress, House Committee on Foreign Affairs, *Foreign Assistance Legislation for FY 82*, Hearings, 97th Cong., 1st sess., 1981, 289.

22. Turner, *Oil Companies in the International System*, 229.

23. Raymond W. Copson and Robert B. Shepard, "Angola: Issues for the U.S.," CRS, 5 December 1986, 5.

24. Chester A. Crocker, *High Noon in Southern Africa: Making Peace in a Rough Neighborhood* (New York: W. W. Norton, 1992), 290.

25. Crocker, *High Noon in Southern Africa*, 137.

26. *New York Times*, 31 January 1986, 3D.

27. Copson and Shepard, "Angola," 9.

28. *New York Times*, 27 June 1981, 37; and *Wall Street Journal*, 27 March 1981, 19.

29. See Crocker, *High Noon in Southern Africa*, 162, 203.

30. *Economist*, 1 August 1981, 34.

31. *New York Times*, 5 January 1985, 29.

32. Copson and Shepard, "Angola," 3.

33. See Investor Responsibility Research Center (IRRC), "Withdrawal of U.S. Companies from Angola—Chevron Corp.," Social Issues Series, Proxy Investment Reports, Analysis U, 6 April 1989, 10–12; and *Los Angeles Times*, 17 July 1986, 12.

34. *New York Times*, 29 January 1986, 15.

35. Kenneth Mokoena, ed., *South Africa and the United States: The Declassified History* (New York: New Press, 1993), 297–299.

36. *Petroleum Economist*, December 1987, 434–436; *Financial Times*, 14 September 1987, 20; *Washington Post*, 31 July 1986, 1A.

37. Crocker, *High Noon in Southern Africa*, 341.

38. U.S. Congress, Senate Committee on Foreign Relations, *Angola—Options for American Foreign Policy*, Hearings, 99th Cong., 2d sess., 1986, 18–19.

39. Crocker, *High Noon in Southern Africa*, 344.

40. *Offshore*, March 1986, 54; Telephone interview, George Keller, former CEO of Chevron, 28 July 1995.

41. Douglas G. Anglin, "United Nations Economic Sanctions against South Africa and Rhodesia," in *The Utility of International Economic Sanctions*, ed. Leyton–Brown, 44.

42. Anglin, "United Nations Economic Sanctions," 31–33.

43. See statement of Michael J. Matheson, Assistant Legal Advisor for Africa, Department of State, in U.S. Congress, House Committee on International Relations, Subcommittee on Africa, *United States Policy Toward Rhodesia*, 95th Cong., 1st sess., 1977, 7–8.

44. Harry R. Strack, *Sanctions: The Case of Rhodesia* (Syracuse, N.Y.: Syracuse University Press, 1978), 132–133.

45. Robin Renwick, *Economic Sanctions*, Harvard Studies in International Affairs, no. 45, 1981, 30.

46. Strack, *Sanctions*, 132–133.

47. David M. Rowe, "Economic Sanctions Do Work: Economic Statecraft and the Oil Embargo of Rhodesia," *Security Studies* 9 (August 1999): 273.

48. Strack, *Sanctions*, 135.

49. Gladwin and Walter, *Multinationals under Fire*, 178.

50. Testimony of George Birrell in U.S. Congress, Senate Committee on Foreign Relations, Subcommittee on African Affairs, *South Africa—U.S. Policy and the Role of U.S. Corporations*, Hearings, 94th Cong., 2d sess., 1976, 358–363.

51. Birrell testimony (n. 50), 359–360.

52. Birrell testimony (n. 50), 376–377.

53. Birrell testimony (n. 50), 378–379.

54. Statement of Senator James Pearson (R-Kans.) in U.S. Senate, *South Africa*, 381.

55. "Treasury Investigation of Charges Made against the Mobil Corporation," 23 May 1977, in U.S. House, *United States Policy Toward Rhodesia*, 26–27, 34–35, 55.

56. T. H. Bingham and S. M. Gray, *Report on the Supply of Petroleum and Petroleum Products to Rhodesia* (London: Her Majesty's Stationary Office, 1978, hereafter, Bingham Commission).

57. Harry R. Strack, "The Influence of Transnational Actors on the Enforcement of Sanctions against Rhodesia," *Naval War College Review* 28 (spring 1976): 54.

58. U.S. Senate, *South Africa*, 399.

59. Martin Bailey, *Oilgate: The Sanctions Scandal* (Seven Oaks, U.K.: Coronet, 1979), 32–33.

60. Bingham Commission, 118–119.

61. Renwick, *Sanctions*, 29.

62. Rowe, "Economic Sanctions Do Work," 282.

63. Bingham Commission, 105.

64. Brian White, "Britain and the Implementation of Oil Sanctions against Rhodesia," in *Foreign Policy Implementation*, eds. Steve Smith and Michael Clarke (London: George Allen & Unwin, 1985), 46–47.

65. Price, "U.S. Policy toward Southern Africa," 46–47.

66. Mohammed El–Khawas and Barry Cohen, *The Kissinger Study of Southern Africa: NSSM 39* (Westport, Conn.: L. Hill, 1976), 41–45.

67. Purcell, "The Interests and Perceptions of United States Business," 123.

68. Richard S. Weinert, "Nicaragua's Debt Renegotiations," *Cambridge Journal of Economics* 5 (June 1981): 187–194.

69. *Wall Street Journal*, 13 January 1981, 16.

70. See *Business Latin America*, 14 August 1981, 249; EIU, *Quarterly Economic Review of Nicaragua*, 1995 (1): 15; and *Business Week*, 10 January 1983, 43.

71. For reporting of specific examples, see *This Week in Central America*, 5 September 1980; *Central America Report*, 17 March 1980, 86.

72. James E. Austin and John C. Ickis, "Management, Managers, and Revolution," *World Development* 14 (July 1986), 783; *Business Latin America*, 12 August 1981, 249.

73. *Business International*, 12 August 1981, 264.

74. Purcell, "The Perceptions and Interests of United States Business," 107, 119.

75. Pezzullo to Muskie, "Conversation w/Junta Member Sergio Ramirez," 9 January 1981; and "Reaction to New Banana Agreement," 19 January 1981 (DOS/FOIA).

76. See Leogrande, "Making the Economy Scream," 339.

77. Purcell, "The Perceptions and Interests of United States Business," 121.

78. *Business International*, 12 August 1981, 264.

79. Austin and Ickis, "Management, Managers, and Revolution," 784–785; and "Managing after the Revolutionaries Have Won," *Harvard Business Review* 64 (May–June 1986): 108.

80. Austin and Ickis, "Managing after the Revolutionaries Have Won," 105.

81. Overseas Development Council, "The U.S. Embargo against Nicaragua: One Year Later," May 1986, 7.

82. See *Oil Daily*, 11 August 1987, 5; and statements by Representative Toby Roth (R-Wisc.), in U.S. Congress, House Committee on Foreign Affairs, *Review of the U.S. Economic Embargo against Nicaragua and Humanitarian Exports*, Hearings, 100th Cong., 1st sess., 1987, 4.

83. *Platt's Oilgram News*, 13 February 1987, 3.

84. *New York Times*, 17 September 1982, D15.

85. World Bank, *World Debt Tables: External Debt of Developing Countries, 1987–88*, vol. II (Washington D.C.: World Bank, 1988), 266.

86. *Financial Times*, 9 March 1985, 2; *New York Times*, 13 April 1986, 8.

87. *National Journal*, 9 January 1988, 86.

88. See Michael Conroy, "The Political Economy of the 1990 Nicaraguan Election," *International Journal of Political Economy* 20 (fall 1990): 47–69.

89. *Business Latin America*, 13 January 1982, 10; Business International, *Investing, Licensing, and Trading Abroad: The Central American Common Market*, May 1982, 5.

90. *Wall Street Journal*, 19 October 1982, 19.

91. *Financial Times*, 9 May 1985, 40.

92. Interviews, Department of State, 28 July 1988 and 12 January 1989.

93. *Oil Daily*, 11 August 1987, 5.

94. *Wall Street Journal*, 14 July 1981, 16; on the evolution of the Libyan sanctions, see Gideon Rose, "Libya," in *Economic Sanctions and American Diplomacy*, ed. Haass, 141–142.

95. *New York Times*, 20 December 1981, sec. III, 4.

96. *Oil and Gas Journal*, 21 December 1981, 35.

97. *New York Times*, 27 June 1981, 37.

98. *New York Times*, 13 November 1981, D5.

99. Terisa Turner, "U.S. Oil Giants Have Become Part of Reagan's Plan to Destabilize Libya," *Multinational Monitor* 2 (December, 1981): 12–14.

100. *Petroleum Economist*, February 1982, 69.

101. *Petroleum Economist*, December 1981, 531; *Oil and Gas Journal*, 23 November 1983, 3.

102. *Wall Street Journal*, 3 February 1986, 25.

103. *Platt's Oilgram News*, 3 February 1986, 1.

104. Shultz to American Embassies, "Libyan Sanctions: Implementation of Executive Orders," 6 February 1986 (DOS/FOIA).

105. See interviews with Shultz and Baker in *New York Times*, 6 May 1986, 14.

106. Platt (State) to Poindexter (NSC), "Libyan Economic Sanctions," 25 April 1986 (DOS/FOIA).

107. *Middle East Economic Survey*, 5 January 1987, 8(A).

108. See *Business Week*, 5 December 1988, 45; and *Wall Street Journal*, 13 January 1989, 4.

109. *Department of State Bulletin*, March 1989, 71.

110. EIU, *Libya*, Country Report, 1989, no. 3, 12, and no. 4, 11.

111. *Platt's Oilgram News*, 4 May 1989, 1, and 29 June 1989, 1; *Financial Times*, 30 June 1989, 6.

112. See *New York Times*, 16 January 1989, A1; and *Platt's Oilgram News*, 17 January 1989, 4.

113. Rose, "Libya," 135–137.

114. EIU, *Libya*, Country Report, 1992, no. 3, 15.

115. *Reuters*, 1 May 1995.

116. *Middle East Economic Digest*, 30 August 1991, 4.

117. *Middle East Economic Survey*, 10 March 1987, 3(A).

118. Mark Sullivan, "U.S. Sanctions and the State of the Panamanian Economy," CRS, 22 August 1988, 13–14.

119. John Dinges, *Our Man in Panama: How General Noriega Used the United States to Make Millions in Drugs and Arms* (New York: Random House, 1990), 296.

120. George A. Lopez and David Cortright, "Making Targets 'Smart' From Sanctions," paper presented at the annual meeting of the International Studies Association, Minneapolis, Minn., 18–22 March 1998.

121. See testimony of OFAC Director R. Richard Newcomb in U.S. Congress, House Committee on Foreign Affairs, *Policy Toward Panama in the Aftermath of the May 1, 1989 Elections*, Hearings, 101st Cong., 1st sess., 1989, 246–249.

122. Frederick Kempe, *Divorcing the Dictator: America's Bungled Affair with Noriega* (New York: G. P. Putnam, 1990), 265–268.

123. Term coined by William D. Rogers of Arnold and Porter, in *Washington Post*, 22 March 1988, D1.

124. Sullivan, "U.S. Sanctions and the State of the Panamanian Economy," 18.

125. Glennon Harrison, "Panama: Trade, Finance, and Proposed Economic Sanctions," CRS, 7 March 1988, 8.

126. Kempe, *Divorcing the Dictator*, 269.

127. "GAO Review of Economic Sanctions Imposed against Panama," Report no. GAO/T-NSIAD 89–44, 26 July 1989, 18.

128. EIU, *Nicaragua, Costa Rica, Panama*, Country Report, 1988, no. 3, 18.

129. Joseph C. Lombard, "The Survival of Noriega," 286.

130. "GAO Review of Economic Sanctions Imposed against Panama," 6.

131. Newcomb Testimony (n. 121), 247.

132. Ellicott, "From Pipeline to Panama," 13.

133. *New York Times*, 12 April 1986, A6.

134. *Business Latin America*, 27 June 1988, 201.

135. "Prepared Remarks of the American Chamber of Commerce and Industry in Panama," in U.S. House, *United States Policy Toward Panama*, 204.

136. *International Trade Reporter*, 27 April 1988, 633.

137. Newcomb testimony (n. 121), 250–253.

138. See "GAO Review of Economic Sanctions Imposed against Panama," 18; and Stephen J. Govoni, "Romancing Noriega: How United Brands Prospers Despite U.S. Sanctions," *Corporate Finance* 4 (September 1989): 38–43.

139. *Journal of Commerce*, 18 April 1988, 1(A), 19 April 1988, 7(B), and 4 December 1989, 7(B).

140. Cited in Lombard, "The Survival of Noriega," 270.

141. "GAO Review of Economic Sanctions Imposed against Panama," 13.

142. See Kempe, *Divorcing the Dictator*, 270.

143. Lombard, "The Survival of Noriega," 272.

144. Gideon Rose, "Haiti," in *Economic Sanctions and American Diplomacy*, ed. Haass, 59.

145. *New York Times*, 9 October 1991, A3.

146. *International Trade Reporter*, 30 October 1991, 1583–1584.

147. *UN Chronicle*, December 1993, 20.

148. See Rose, "Haiti," 61–64.

149. See Claudette Antoine Werleigh, "The Use of Sanctions in Haiti: Assessing the Economic Realities," in *Economic Sanctions: Panacea or Peacebuilding in a Post-Cold War World*, eds. David Cortright and George Lopez (Boulder, Colo.: Westview, 1995), 164–166.

150. *Oil Daily*, 11 November 1991, 4.

151. *Platt's Oilgram News*, 20 September 1994, 1.

152. *Associated Press*, 19 September 1994.

153. The details of those controversies are spelled in *Associated Press* reports on 29 September 1994 and 1 October 1994.

154. *Platt's Oilgram News*, 20 September 1994, 1.

155. Domingo E. Acevedo, "The Haitian Crisis and the OAS Response: A Test of Effectiveness in Promoting Democracy," in *Enforcing Restraint: Collective Intervention in Internal Conflicts*, ed. Lori Fisler Damrosch (New York: Council on Foreign Relations, 1993), 137n.

156. EIU, *Haiti*, Country Profile, 1993, 45.

157. *Latin American Weekly Report*, 4 November 1993, 506.

158. *Oil Daily*, 15 November 1993, 5.

159. *New York Times*, 17 November 1993, A9.

160. *Platt's Oilgram News*, 20 November 1993, 2.

161. EIU, *Haiti*, Country Report, 1994, no. 2, 35.

162. Charles M. Becker, "Economic Sanctions against South Africa," *World Politics* 39 (January 1987): 164.

163. Lombard, "The Survival of Noriega," 323.

164. See Brian F. X. Clark, "United States Labor Practices in South Africa: Will a Mandatory Fair Employment Code Succeed Where the Sullivan Principles Have Failed?" *Fordham International Law Journal* 7 (winter 1984): 381; and *A Fresh Look at South Africa* (New York: Business International Corp., 1982), 66.

Chapter Six

Targeting Foreign Corporations: Helms–Burton and the Iran–Libya Sanctions Act

I think the United States has the right to expect Canada to be deferential. Cuba is disproportionately so much more important to the United States than it is to Canada.

—Representative Robert Torricelli (D-N.J.)
on Canadian objections to the Helms–Burton Law[1]

This is bullying. But in America, you call it global leadership.

—Canadian Foreign Minister Lloyd Axworthy[2]

The 1990s have seen an expansion in the use of economic sanctions as an instrument of American statecraft. With the end of the Cold War, sanctions have been imposed against an increasing number of countries for a wider array of purposes with fewer limitations on their territorial scope. The most ambitious and controversial of these measures are the Cuban Liberty and Democratic Solidarity (Libertad) Act, better known as Helms–Burton, and the Iran–Libya Sanctions Act (ILSA). Both seek to isolate target states by penalizing foreign firms that invest in those countries. Unlike the foreign subsidiary sanctions discussed in the last two chapters, they apply to firms with no connection to U.S. persons, technology, or territory. As such, they have been denounced by trading partners as secondary boycotts contrary to international law.

That the United States would embark on such a course in the 1990s is at variance with the prediction that globalization and hegemonic decline would lead the United States to rein in, not expand, the territorial scope of its regulations. Some observers have seen in these acts evidence of a second era of American hegemony whereby the United States seeks to enforce its vision of world order more aggressively in a unipolar world. Like its predecessors, however, the Clinton administration was wary of secondary sanctions because of their corrosive impact on alliance relations and the world trading system. The impetus for these new sanctions lies in domestic politics—that is, interest groups, such as the Cuban-American National Foundation (CANF) and the American Israel Political Affairs Committee (AIPAC), public concerns about terrorism, and Congress, many of whose members expressed frustration with allies who were seen as taking a free ride on U.S. sanctions. The administration's eventual endorsement of both bills reflected domestic political imperatives more than it did a strategy of coercively bolstering unilateral sanctions regimes.

Critics of secondary sanctions have also cited the pipeline case in predicting that these measures are likely to fail since they are premised on a U.S. position in the world economy that no longer exists. Indeed, Helms–Burton and ILSA were universally condemned by allies who enacted blocking laws comparable to those that frustrated the pipeline sanctions in the early 1980s. The Clinton administration recognized this opposition and fudged the implementation of the laws to avert an escalation of conflicts with its chief allies and trading partners.[3] Nonetheless, both measures had something of a chilling effect on new investments, to a greater extent in Cuba than in Iran. The reason lies in the strong congressional and interest group coalitions behind both measures. This made credible the costs and risks of challenging sanctions, particularly if some unforeseen event creates a stronger momentum for reprisals. Their deterrent impact, however, diminished in the late 1990s. This was less the result of administration fudging or allied resistance than of changes in the domestic politics of sanctions, which reduced the likelihood that Cuban or Iranian investments would trigger the implementation of penalties.

SECONDARY BOYCOTTS AND U.S. FOREIGN POLICY

The secondary boycott is the most extreme and controversial form of extraterritorial sanctions. Unlike a primary boycott, which is limited to the sender state's territory, the secondary boycott tries to "dragoon the world at large into the boycott campaign by exposing anyone who deals with the enemy to like treatment."[4] The classic example is the Arab League's boycott of Israel. It not only bans trade between its member states and Israel, it also blacklists firms that trade with or invest in Israel and requires certification from prospective investors that they conduct no business with Israel. At times, this has been expanded to a tertiary boycott requiring the severance of business ties not only with Israel, but with all blacklisted firms that do business with Israel. As one legal scholar observed, the aim was to gain "foreign [private] compliance with the boycott without attempting to obtain the cooperation of foreign (i.e., non-Arab) governments."[5]

The United States officially protested these practices. It disagreed with the primary boycott on policy grounds, but recognized the sovereign right of Arab states to decide with whom they should or should not trade. The secondary and tertiary boycotts, by contrast, were opposed as encroachments on U.S. sovereignty since they "influence decisions and activities of American firms" in furthering the aims of foreign governments.[6] As a result, when Congress passed the antiboycott provisions of the 1977 Export Administration Act, the State Department persuaded it to exclude the primary boycott, whose removal was linked to a broader settlement of the Arab-Israeli conflict, and to focus only on the secondary and tertiary blacklists. As the Senate report concluded, the United States should not "acquiesce in attempts by foreign governments . . . to embroil American citizens in their battles against others."[7]

Nonetheless, the United States has used its economic power to go over the heads of its allies and secure the compliance of their firms with unilateral embargoes. While few U.S. programs replicate the Arab Boycott, Washington has occasionally used comparable devices. Under TWEA, for example, any vessel that shipped goods to Cuba or North Vietnam was barred from U.S. ports unless it certified that it would never do so again.[8]

A more indirect means toward the same end was to require that foreign firms certify that no content from a target state—for example, sugar and nickel from Cuba, crude oil from Libya—was incorporated into their exports into the United States. This increased the costs of doing business with those countries by forcing firms to segregate Cuban and Libyan raw material from those obtained elsewhere. When the Reagan administration enforced those measures more strictly in the early 1980s, it induced some foreign firms, most notably France's Creusot-Loire, to stop importing nickel from Cuba.[9]

The most significant means by which Washington tried to influence foreign companies was through their connection with U.S.-origin technology. Under the Export Control Act and its successors, foreign purchasers of U.S. technology had to submit to U.S. export control laws and not sell any goods incorporating that technology to third parties without authorization from the U.S. Department of Commerce. Companies that violated the terms of these agreements would be subjected to denial orders, effectively blacklisting them from the United States market.

Yet the United States was reluctant to move beyond reexport controls and impose direct secondary boycotts on foreign governments and firms, even when the United States enjoyed a preponderant position in the world economy. As shown in chapter 2, the Truman and Eisenhower administrations routinely waived Battle Act sanctions against allies that traded strategic goods to the Soviet bloc because of the costs to postwar economic recovery, which was the cornerstone of European containment. Eisenhower rejected the advice of his military advisers to penalize foreign firms that traded with China after the abolition of the China Differential because of the risks to the alliance and to CoCom. The Johnson administration gave more serious consideration to secondary sanctions against foreign firms that traded with Cuba after the British Leyland bus deal. It ultimately backed off from that strategy, in part because of the costs to U.S. leadership in promoting trade liberalization and opposing comparable practices by others, such as the Arab League's secondary boycott of Israel.

By the 1970s and 1980s, these considerations increasingly dissuaded policymakers from targeting foreign companies, a lesson reinforced by the pipeline experience. A partial exception was Operation Exodus, the Reagan administration's effort to staunch the outflow of critical technologies to the Soviet bloc. The United States was able to enlist foreign corporate compliance with this effort by denying or delaying licenses for technology imports by foreign firms until they agreed to submit to stricter reexport controls and audits and inspections by U.S. officials. These practices were sharply condemned by allies. The British attorney general characterized them as "unwarranted encroachments on U.K. jurisdiction and sovereignty," and the European Parliament went so far as to question the legitimacy of CoCom. Despite the protests, no European state blocked its nationals from complying with U.S. regulations because of their dependence on U.S. technologies.[10]

Yet Operation Exodus differed from both the pipeline sanctions (and the secondary sanctions of the 1990s) in some fundamental ways. First, the United States asserted jurisdiction over U.S. technology, not over foreign companies, more aggressively enforcing a practice that began with the Export Control Act in 1949. Second, U.S. efforts were successful only with respect to those technologies for which U.S. firms were the sole or dominant suppliers—such as, computers and telecommunications—for which there were no comparable alternative sources of supply. Finally, U.S. efforts to strengthen CoCom were within the boundaries of the allied consensus for strategic denial. They did not extend to areas of divergent interests—that is, denying energy-related technology in pursuit of economic warfare.[11]

Congressional moves to expand the territorial reach of sanctions emerged in the late 1980s. The first example was an amendment to the Dellums–Wolpe South African sanctions bill, which passed the House in 1988. It sought to strengthen South African sanctions vis-à-vis an administration that was seen as dragging its feet and allies that opposed stronger measures. The most controversial portion of the bill tried to cut the flow of oil to South Africa by conditioning eligibility for federal oil, gas, and coal leases on the severance of business ties with South Africa. The principal targets were both U.S. oil companies and foreign competitors, particularly Shell and BP, which had extensive U.S. interests. As one sanctions proponent explained it: "Who is going to risk the major market they have, which is the United States, for less than one percent of their total business."[12] The British government denounced the bill and threatened retaliation against U.S. firms bidding for contracts to develop North Sea oil.[13] Although the Senate never acted on the bill, one international lawyer described it as the "most extraterritorial measure ever to receive serious consideration by Congress."[14]

The second case was an amendment sponsored by Senator Jake Garn (R-Utah) to a 1988 trade bill, which punished foreign companies that violated CoCom regulations even if there was no connection to U.S. technology, ownership, or territory.[15] The law was a response to the revelation that a subsidiary of Japan's Toshiba Corporation and its Norwegian partner had illegally sold precision milling machines to the Soviet Union, improving its submarines' ability to evade detection. The Senate quickly voted for punitive sanctions, barring both the subsidiaries and their parents from the U.S. market for two to five years. The final sanctions bill was softened considerably as the result of an aggressive lobbying campaign by U.S. businesses that would have been adversely affected by losing access to Toshiba technology. The Reagan administration also opposed the original bill. It nonetheless used the threat of congressional sanctions as leverage to persuade Tokyo to strengthen its export controls and cooperate with the United States in the development of the Strategic Defense Initiative and Japan's next generation of fighter aircraft.[16]

The Garn Amendment was designed to deter future Toshibas. It mandated the blacklisting for any foreign firm, including parents, subsidiaries, and successors, that exported items on the CoCom list to the Eastern bloc. Unilateral sanctions would thereby compensate for the absence of a multilateral enforcement mechanism within CoCom.[17] In 1990, Senator Garn cosponsored a parallel bill with Senator Robert Dole (R-Kans.) that targeted firms that sold technology associated with chemical or biological weapons after the revelation that a German firm, Imhausen, had assisted in the construction of an alleged chemical weapons plant in Rabta, Libya.[18] The Reagan and Bush administrations initially opposed both bills because of mandatory provisions that would have antagonized allies and complicated efforts to negotiate more effective multilateral controls. They eventually signed on when Congress inserted a waiver provision that facilitated diplomatic solutions.[19]

While neither bill forced the hand of the executive branch, they were harbingers of congressional activism on sanctions in the 1990s. Part of this was spurred by the end of the Cold War, which expanded the sanctions agenda of Congress to a new range of issues, such as nuclear testing, environmental protection, and religious persecution. It also removed many of the inhibitions regarding the costs of alliance confrontations on national security. The sanctions efforts were given an added boost by the Republican congressional sweep in 1994. This placed Jesse Helms (R-N.C.) and Alfonse D'Amato (R-N.Y.) as chairs of the Senate Foreign Relations and Banking Committees, each of whom acted as policy entrepreneurs on Cuban and Iranian sanctions, respectively. In addition, much of the new class of Republican freshmen and their leaders were more aligned with the social and ideological agendas behind sanctions efforts than they were with the views of the business community and foreign policy establishment.[20] All of this set the stage for the most serious effort to reverse the lessons of the pipeline sanctions and to use U.S. economic power to bring to heel foreign corporations that ignored U.S. sanctions.

THE HELMS–BURTON LAW

The Cuban Liberty and Democratic Solidarity (Libertad) Act, better known as Helms–Burton, expanded the Cuban embargo to foreign corporations with no connection to U.S. ownership or technology. Its central target was the growing number of joint ventures between non-U.S. MNCs and Cuban state-owned enterprises. As with foreign subsidiary trade, these emerged in response to the economic crisis created by the loss of the Soviet subsidy. In order to earn desperately needed hard currency, Havana initiated a number of market-oriented reforms, including the liberalization of foreign investment laws. In 1991, it changed its investment regulations to allow profit repatriation, the right to hire and fire workers, tax exemptions, and majority foreign ownership in some sectors of the economy. In 1992, it revised Article 14 of the Cuban Constitution, which held that the state was the sole owner of the means of production. In 1995, it opened up the entire economy to foreign capital except for defense, public health, and education.[21] This represented a dramatic change for a revolution whose birthright was the expulsion of foreign business. As one Cuban official explained it, "We have no choice but to feed the Trojan Horse."[22]

In the early 1990s, Cuban state-owned enterprises negotiated a number of joint ventures in oil exploration, mining, biotechnology, pharmaceuticals, and tourism.[23] The most significant and controversial of these was with Canada's Sherritt-Gordon. In 1991, Sherritt obtained the right to mine, refine, and market nickel and cobalt from Moa Bay, a property owned by the U.S. firm, Freeport McMoran, prior to the Cuban revolution. It expanded operations in 1994 when it agreed to invest $12 billion over five years and sold Cuba a stake in its Alberta refinery in exchange for access to Cuban ores.[24]

These investments weakened the embargo by expanding Havana's ability to earn and conserve foreign exchange through tourism, exports, and increased energy self-sufficiency. Washington discreetly tried to discourage this development. At times, this involved using U.S. regulations, such as linking withdrawal from Cuba to certain privileges in the U.S. market, or strictly denying licenses for the export of foreign goods to Cuba that contain any U.S. content.[25] In addition, when foreign MNCs were negotiating for Cuban properties previously owned by U.S. citizens, they were sent "buyer beware" notices from the State Department warning that they might face legal challenges over their property rights from their former owners.[26] While these techniques dissuaded some potential investors, the number of joint ventures increased steadily to 230 by May 1995.[27]

This alarmed the CANF and its congressional supporters, who accused the administration of soft-pedaling the issue with allies. As a result, they sought to legislate a more punitive approach to arrest what they viewed as a private bailout of the Castro regime. Their opportunity came after the Republican congressional sweep in the 1994 midterm elections. Their device was the Cuban Liberty and Democratic Solidarity (Libertad) Act, sponsored by Senator Jesse Helms (R-N.C.) and Representative Dan Burton (R-Ind.).

For the purpose of deterring joint ventures, the most significant provisions of Helms–Burton are Titles III and IV. The former creates a private right of action that empowers U.S. citizens, including naturalized Cuban Americans, to sue foreign corporations for triple damages for "trafficking" in properties confiscated after the Cuban revolution. The term *trafficking* was consciously borrowed from the narcotics field to stigmatize what foreign businesses saw as normal investment opportunities.[28] The latter mandated visa denials to any person who continues to traffic in confiscated property ninety days after the enactment of the bill. It applied to corporate officers, shareholders with controlling interests, spouses, and minor children.[29]

The ostensible purpose of Title III was to remedy the injury imposed on U.S. property owners by Castro's confiscations.[30] Its underlying aim—explicitly acknowledged by its authors—was to multilateralize economic warfare by pressuring foreign firms to abide by U.S. law.[31] The text of the legislation, which defined trafficking as almost any commercial or financial activity, not just ownership, was designed to serve the latter rather than the former purpose. Such language was likely to encourage a large number of claims, many of dubious merit, and allow the courts to decide the scope of the law.[32] This may be a liability from the vantage point of creating predictable expectations for claimants and investors. To sanctions proponents, it was an asset that created greater uncertainty for prospective investors. As Senator Helms's chief foreign policy aide noted: "[H]ow will investors know what to expect? They will face a legal minefield. If they misstep, they could blow up."[33]

opponents

The administration initially opposed Helms–Burton. First, it warned that Title III could be interpreted as a secondary boycott, a practice the U.S. opposed when employed by the Arab League against Israel. Second, customary international law holds that a state is liable only for confiscating the property of foreign nationals, not its own citizens. Extending the right to sue to naturalized Cuban Americans who were Cuban citizens at the time created an international remedy for a domestic matter. It also set a precedent for reciprocal actions by others since similar devices could be used to make claims against U.S. firms that invest in former communist countries, such as Vietnam or the former German Democratic Republic.[34] Finally, Helms–Burton could be challenged as contrary to international trade agreements, such as the NAFTA and the WTO, undercutting the U.S. leadership in the world economy. As one former Commerce Department official noted: "A fundamental goal of United States policy is to expand the scope of national economic practices that are subject to the WTO and regional trade agreements. . . . Helms–Burton undermines America's ability to negotiate rules for trade that assure its exports and MNCs freer and fairer treatment abroad because it calls into question United States resolve to live by rules it prescribes for others."[35]

Proponents

Sanctions proponents dismissed these concerns. First, they denied that the sanctions were extraterritorial. Even if the result was to force foreign firms to make a choice between Cuba and the United States, enforcement would take place entirely within the United States to remedy a specific wrong perpetrated against U.S. citizens.[36] Second, they defended the extension of the right to sue to naturalized Cuban Americans on both legal (equal protection of the laws to naturalized and native-born citizens) and practical (increasing the number of potential litigants fourfold) grounds.[37] Finally, they criticized administration arguments as overly indulgent of allied sensitivities. Senator Helms discounted the costs of the bill by pointing to a 1992 EC warning that passage of the CDA would have a "grave and dangerous effect to bilateral EC/US trade relations": "Once other nations understood that we are serious . . . they respected our decision. The CDA did not hurt our trade relations with Europe."[38] Moreover, sanctions proponents believed that the administration got its priorities reversed in its concern about allied sensitivities. Representative Torricelli expressed this sentiment when he responded to a formal protest from Ottawa by declaring that "the United States has a right to expect Canada to be somewhat deferential."[39]

Through February 1996, the administration opposed Helms–Burton and promised to veto it if it included Titles III and IV. On 12 March 1996, the Clinton administration withdrew its objections and signed the bill. The catalyst for its reversal was the downing by a Cuban MiG-29 of two unarmed Cessna aircraft, leafleting the island for the Cuban exile group, Brothers to the Rescue.[40] In negotiations with Congress, the administration was able to remove the most legally indefensible sanctions, such as the secondary boycott on Cuban sugar. It also obtained the discretion to waive the right to sue under Title III every six months for reasons either of national interest or of expediting democracy in Cuba.[41] Yet, the final bill imposed some significant limits on presidential discretion. First, the Cuban embargo was from then on based on statutory law, not an executive order that the president could flexibly adapt to changed circumstances. Second, the administration could only suspend the right to sue under Title III; liability would still accumulate if an investor did not liquidate its stake within three months of the effective date of the law. Finally, there was no waiver provision for the visa denials under Title IV.[42]

The international response to Helms–Burton was near-universal condemnation. In both the United Nations and the OAS, the focus of recriminations shifted from Cuba to the United States. Both organizations passed resolutions challenging the legality not only of Helms–Burton, but of the embargo as a whole.[43] Allied trading partners also took steps to protect their companies' business activities with Cuba from U.S. law. Ottawa issued a blocking order under FEMA which denied legal validity to Helms–Burton by refusing to recognize any verdict, empowering the Canadian courts to deny access to records associated with any lawsuit, and requiring Canadian firms to report any directives associated with extraterritorial laws to the attorney general of Canada. It also contained a "clawback" provision permitting Canadian firms to recover any losses incurred by U.S. litigation.[44] The EU issued regulations that contained largely the same nonrecognition and clawback provisions. It also added a "watchlist" of U.S. citizens and companies that filed claims.[45] The aim was to discourage plaintiffs by diminishing the prospects for reaching a settlement and raising the prospect of retaliation, thereby bolstering the confidence of national firms to pursue Cuban investments without fear of litigation.

The EU also challenged Helms–Burton as a discriminatory trade practice and initiated a grievance proceeding before the WTO. The United States replied that the WTO was an inappropriate venue for resolving this issue because it was a foreign policy rather than a trade dispute. It consequently planned to use the WTO's national security exception (Article XXI) to deny the institution's competence and threatened to boycott the proceedings. EU officials were undeterred and, on 20 November 1996, the WTO established a dispute resolution mechanism to review the complaint.[46]

Given the conflicting domestic and international pressures over an issue not central to its priorities, the administration tried to defuse the issue. On 16 July, President Clinton announced that he would allow Title III to go into effect (meaning the liability would begin to accrue), but suspended the right to sue for six months citing a provision that allows a waiver to expedite the promotion of democracy in Cuba. Undersecretary of Commerce Stuart Eizenstat was dispatched as a special envoy to allied capitals to use the six-month deadline as leverage to build tougher multilateral policies toward Cuba.[47] There was, however, no waiver provision for Title IV. As a result, the State Department issued visa denials to nine executives of Sherritt, as well as officers from three other MNCs.[48]

The Eizenstat mission initially received a chilly reception. One EU diplomat noted in frustration that "the U.S. is always citing Congress as a reason for not doing things, but when did Washington ever pay attention to what our parliaments think."[49] Despite these sentiments, a tentative compromise was reached in January 1997, a few weeks before the deadline for the issuance of a second waiver, when the EU agreed to link improved political and economic relations to human rights. President Clinton cited this as progress in collective efforts to promote democracy in Cuba and once again waived the right to sue.[50]

Both sides took further steps to defuse the conflict through a Memorandum of Understanding between Eizenstat (now undersecretary of state for economic affairs) and EU Trade Commissioner Leon Brittan on 11 April 1997— three days before the WTO dispute resolution panel was scheduled to begin. That understanding was formalized at the meeting between President Clinton and EU leaders in London on 18 May 1998. Under its terms (which also covered ILSA), the EU allowed its WTO grievance to lapse in exchange for a promise by President Clinton to suspend the right to sue for the duration of his term in office. In addition, the EU agreed to establish binding legal "disciplines" to discourage investment in expropriated property in Cuba and elsewhere by drawing up a registry of claims and pledging to deny government support to firms that invest in contested properties. Activating the process, however, was conditional on the administration persuading Congress to revise Title IV to make it discretionary.[51]

Eizenstat lauded the disciplines as a historic breakthrough and a model of how Congress and the executive branch can successfully work together on sanctions issues—that is, having a flexible waiver provision enabled the administration to use extraterritorial sanctions as a bargaining chip to strengthen multilateral policies.[52] The disciplines, however, may never materialize. Congress is unlikely to amend Title IV because EU concessions fall short of the aims of sanctions proponents. The scope of the disciplines is narrower than Helms–Burton, focusing only on firms that purchase or acquire a controlling interest. They also apply only to expropriations in violation of international law, thereby excluding the assets of naturalized Cuban Americans. Finally, they do not ban investment in confiscated properties; rather, such firms are denied government credits, subsidies, risk insurance, and diplomatic assistance. As a result, the chairs of both committees overseeing the sanctions opposed the agreement and tried to make the law more restrictive.[53] Following the announcement of the framework in April 1997, the House voted to require the State Department to send formal reports to Congress to list all companies considered for visa denial—a procedural requirement designed to increase the pressure to name more foreign executives. Shortly thereafter, Representative Bill McCollum (R-Fla.) introduced legislation to strip Title III of its presidential waiver.[54]

In reality, the accord was designed less to break new ground than it was to defuse a crisis that would delegitimize the fledgling WTO, which both the United States and EU saw as vital to their economic interests. Had the WTO accepted the U.S. argument that national security exempted it from scrutiny, this would have opened the door to parallel claims by others. Were the WTO to rule against the United States, the administration announced it would have disregarded the decision, acceding to necessity because any other choice would have required legislative concurrence. That would not only set a damaging precedent, but also risk an anti-WTO backlash in Congress. Moreover, a successful complaint would only authorize the EU to take retaliatory action, something it had already done through its blocking orders and clawback provisions.[55] As a result, the EU was "forced to accept an apparent violation of WTO rules because of the impossibility of winning compliance of the U.S. Congress."[56]

Even though the blocking orders and the suspension of the right to sue have delayed litigation, Helms–Burton had some of the dissuasive impact on foreign investment that its authors had anticipated. The law magnifies the risks of Cuban ventures by raising the prospect of expensive entanglement in the litigious U.S. legal system. These risks are only partially assuaged by the promised waivers since they can only be made through the duration of the administration or the next serious Cuban-American crisis. As a result, Helms–Burton has induced a degree of corporate retrenchment since its introduction in 1995 and passage in 1996—to a minimal degree for existing investors and to a more significant degree for prospective investors.

Helms–Burton did persuade a few firms to liquidate their Cuban operations. Even though the right to sue was suspended, Title III went into effect. That provided a three-month grace period for companies to divest themselves of contested properties if they wanted to escape liability. The State Department announced that four firms availed themselves of this option—two Spanish hotel chains, a Mexican cement company, and Redpath Sugar, a Canadian subsidiary of the British firm Tate & Lyle, which terminated its annual purchase of one hundred thousand tons of Cuban sugar.[57] In the Redpath case, the Canadian Justice Department investigated the firm for a possible violation of FEMA, but no action was taken.[58] This demonstrates the limitations of blocking orders when risk-averse companies choose to forego Cuban trade because of their vulnerability in the United States.

Most firms calculated that the risks of litigation were less than the costs of abandoning capital already sunk into Cuban projects. For some firms, Helms–Burton posed little risk because they had few attachable assets in the United States. This was the case for most of the small Canadian energy and mining companies that had been actively involved in developing Cuban resources.[59] Others were not vulnerable to litigation because of the absence of expropriation claims. For example, British-American Tobacco (BAT) acquired a cigarette factory originally expropriated from American Tobacco, a company it now owns, making it the holder of a claim against itself.[60]

Even when there was a credible threat of litigation, the profitability of many Cuban ventures made staying a risk worth taking.[61] This was most clearly evident for Sherritt-Gordon despite being singled out by sanctions proponents. Sherritt tried to evade liability through a corporate restructuring that created two separate publicly traded companies — Sherritt International, which would be responsible for Cuban operations, and Viridian, which would take over the company's traditional non-Cuban activities.[62] The move did not dissuade the State Department from excluding nine company officers from entry into the United States under Title IV. Nonetheless, given the crucial role Cuban ores have played in revitalizing Sherritt's Canadian refineries, it calculated that the risks were heavily outweighed by the benefits. As a result, it expanded its investment in Cuba, contributing to a doubling of nickel output from 1994 to 1996. And to defy the U.S. embargo, it held its 1996 annual board meeting in Havana.[63]

Helms–Burton has been more successful in deterring prospective investments. This began with the introduction of the bill following the Republican congressional sweep in 1994. As a result, the number of new joint ventures dropped from seventy-four in 1994 to thirty-one in 1995 as risk-averse firms sought to protect themselves from worst-case scenarios. Even though that number rebounded to forty-two in 1996, there was a marked disappearance of many of the larger firms whose stakes in the United States made them vulnerable to lawsuits.[64] Neither the presidential waiver nor the clawback provisions reduced these risks significantly. Even if the latter enabled recovery of everything lost to claimants in the United States, this would represent a diversion of resources away from more lucrative opportunities to time-consuming litigation. As the president of the European-American Chamber of Commerce noted, claimants "have every incentive to name as many traffickers as possibly, thus sparking a witch hunt that would unfairly impose legal costs on many firms that have no commercial ties to former U.S. properties."[65]

The salience of these risks has been compounded by the impact of Helms–Burton on the ability of new investors to obtain finance or political risk insurance. After passage of Helms–Burton, OFAC issued notices to all banks with offices in the United States to exercise extreme caution in lending to firms that invest in expropriated Cuban properties.[66] Canada's *Financial Post* subsequently reported that many Canadian banks terminated loans to Cuban operations. In addition, a number of Canadian and European banks that were actively involved in financing Cuban sugar and nickel operations abruptly cut off those relationships.[67] All had substantial U.S. assets which, given the malleable definition of trafficking in Title III, made them vulnerable to lawsuits. In other words, foreign banks adhered to the rules of the U.S. embargo despite the opposition of their home governments. As one Dutch executive put it, "We have to operate within the legal framework however much we disapprove of it."[68]

Political risk insurers have also been influenced by Helms–Burton. They provide coverage for Cuban ventures only if the investor certifies that it has no connection with property claims in the United States — a guarantee that is difficult to prove. The risk associated with Helms–Burton, consequently, falls entirely on the investor.[69] As in the case of the banking community, Helms–Burton altered the incentives facing private actors. As one insurer observed, the market "tended to think that these laws were illegal outside the U.S. and that they will not matter. But in practice, they mattered a lot."[70]

In sum, Helms–Burton has deterred many non-U.S. firms from establishing joint ventures with Cuba despite the purported decline of American hegemony and near-universal opposition to the policy. Most of those firms were active in the United States and, hence, vulnerable to entrapment in the U.S. legal system. What made this vulnerability a credible risk to MNCs is U.S. domestic politics — namely, the strength of the Cuban-American lobby and its allies in Congress. As a result, investors, creditors, and insurers had to factor it into their calculations however much they and their governments objected.

THE IRAN–LIBYA SANCTIONS ACT

A second attempt to target foreign MNCs was the Iran–Libya Sanctions Act (ILSA), which followed the 1995 executive orders banning U.S. companies from developing Iran's energy resources or buying its oil for sale to third countries. While the aim of those directives was to make U.S. leadership more credible in forging stronger multilateral controls, little allied cooperation was forthcoming. The Europeans were unwilling to move beyond the strategic controls already in place because they argued that nonstrategic trade, particularly in energy, served their commercial interests, national economic security, and strategy of engagement with Iran. As a result, European firms replaced their U.S. counterparts in selling Iranian oil and the French energy company, Total, replaced Conoco in developing the Sirri offshore natural gas fields.

The expansion of European-Iranian energy ties widened executive-legislative differences over Iranian sanctions. The administration remained committed to using diplomacy and working within whatever allied consensus could be negotiated. Congress was less resigned to multilateralism. Sanctions proponents were angry at EU governments and companies, particularly Total, for what they saw as the exploitation of U.S. sanctions. They concluded that if the administration could not level the playing field multilaterally through diplomacy, then Congress would level it unilaterally through coercion.

Their first legislative initiative, sponsored by Senator D'Amato, was a secondary boycott that would have banned U.S. persons from dealing with any company that traded with Iran.[71] Later revisions were targeted at specific transactions that were seen as choke points for the Iranian economy, such as exports of energy-related equipment or investment in oil and gas exploration.[72] The logic of the legislation was to use the power of the U.S. economy to force foreign firms to comply with sanctions their governments had rejected. As explained by Senator D'Amato, "It will tell foreign companies that you will either trade with them [Iran] or with the United States. But you can't have it both ways."[73]

The administration initially opposed the D'Amato bill. Undersecretary of State Peter Tarnoff testified that it would create serious diplomatic fallout since it tried to attach liability to foreign activity with no legal connection to U.S. persons or technology. This would compromise U.S. leadership in world trade, particularly since the United States challenged the legality of the Arab League's secondary boycott of Israel. It would also alienate allies and "put at risk the cooperation on Iranian policy that we share with others."[74]

In December 1995, the administration tried to craft a compromise with Congress. This meant negotiations to modify those provisions most difficult to defend in terms of international trade law and to obtain discretion over implementation to defuse potential conflicts with allies.[75] Over the next six months, it made progress on both counts. First, it narrowed the scope of the sanctions to investments in the energy sector. Second, it removed mandatory import sanctions from the final bill because of the blatant violation of WTO rules.[76] Third, it limited the sanctions to investments negotiated after enactment of the bill, thereby exempting preexisting contracts. While that immunized Total's Sirri deal, it also minimized conflicts with European governments whose firms would have been forced to abrogate existing contracts to escape liability.[77] Finally, when Libyan sanctions were added to the legislation, the administration persuaded Congress to limit penalties to transactions already banned by the UN Security Council, thereby narrowing unilateral enforcement to those rules accepted multilaterally.[78]

The catalyst for passage of the bill was the crash of TWA flight 800 on 17 July 1996—a disaster that elicited fears of Iranian terrorism although its cause was not known at the time and there was never evidence of Iranian involvement.[79] ILSA passed both houses of Congress unanimously and was signed by President Clinton on 5 August 1996. It targeted foreign firms investing more than $40 million annually ($20 million after one year) in Iran's energy sector. The president had to choose at least two from a menu of six penalties, which included bans on (1) Export-Import Bank assistance; (2) the issuance of export licenses, (3) loans over $10 million over a twelve-month period from U.S. financial institutions, (4) financial institutions being designated primary dealers in U.S. debt instruments, serving as agents of the U.S. government, or holding U.S. funds, (5) procurement of goods and services by the U.S. government, and (6) licenses to import U.S. goods. ILSA provided some flexibility with two ninety-day waiver provisions—section 4(c) provides a blanket waiver for firms from countries that curb investments in Iran; section 9(c) extends project-specific waivers for reasons of national interest.[80]

The passage of ILSA provoked sharp international condemnation, particularly from the EU, which saw itself as ILSA's principal target. European objections were made on both legal and policy grounds. In terms of the former, the EU's arguments on ILSA paralleled those on Helms–Burton. Its ambassador to the United States denounced the act as an "extreme case of extraterritorial legislation because sanctions could be imposed if persons are located outside the U.S." with no connections to the United States in terms of ownership, technology, or financing.[81] As a result, ILSA was added to Helms–Burton in the EU's blocking legislation and its complaint before the WTO.[82]

In terms of the latter, ILSA engaged not only matters of principle, but significant diplomatic and economic interests. Since 1992, the EU, led by Germany, has pursued a policy of "critical dialogue" with Iran. While it cooperated with Washington on the exports of arms and nuclear and dual-use technology, it did not extend that cooperation to civilian trade and investment, particularly energy. The official rationale was to engage Iran to moderate its foreign policy. This continued even when confronted by immoderate Iranian behavior, such as the assassination of four Kurdish dissidents in the Mykonos restaurant in Berlin. When a German court found the Iranian government complicit in the murders, most EU members recalled their ambassadors, but none altered its economic relationship with Iran.[83] This policy was consistent with the EU's traditional skepticism toward embargoes and its practice of insulating commerce from political condemnation—an approach that had led to recurrent alliance conflicts over East–West trade during the Cold War. Moreover, the EU imports 20 percent of its oil from Libya and Iran.[84] As with the pipeline case, extraterritorial sanctions threatened allied perceptions of national economic security as well as their commercial interests.

The United States and EU negotiated a preliminary compromise in April 1997 as part of the Eizenstat–Brittan understanding over Helms–Burton. The United States agreed to act with restraint in applying the sanctions in exchange for negotiations over terrorism, weapons of mass destruction, and a suspension of the EU's WTO grievance.[85] Nonetheless, three months earlier, the State Department published a list of eleven oil and gas "buyback" projects publicly offered by NIOC in which foreign participation could be subject to sanctions. Making good on that threat would have put at risk the fragile truce with the EU, which reserved the right to resubmit its WTO complaint if any of its firms were penalized.[86]

Through the summer of 1997, ILSA had a mixed impact in deterring foreign investment in Iran. Those deals that did not fall within a narrow reading of the sanctions were unaffected. In at least three cases, the State Department studied transactions for potential violations, but made no determination whether they were covered by ILSA. First, Turkey signed a twenty-year, $23 billion natural gas deal with Iran to transport natural gas through a joint pipeline. The State Department criticized the deal for increasing Iran's ability to earn foreign exchange. It did not penalize Botas, the primary Turkish firm involved in the project, because the firm's investments were exclusively limited to pipeline construction in Turkey and most of the gas transiting through the pipeline originated in Turkmenistan.[87] Second, Petronas, the Malaysian state oil company, invested $300 million to obtain a 30 percent share of Total's Sirri operation, but since the Sirri contract (not Petronas's participation) was entered into before the enactment of the bill, the investment was defined as outside the scope of the sanctions.[88] Finally, a German bank loan to Iran's Offshore Engineering and Construction Company was considered outside the ambit of ILSA, which was construed to apply to direct investments, not financing.[89]

The unwillingness of the administration to define the scope of the law more broadly indicated recognition of the potential risks of enforcement. Penalizing a German bank would antagonize the EU and trigger the resubmission of its WTO grievance. Applying sanctions to Turkey would undercut an economically important deal for a country that has borne considerable hardship as a result of the Iraqi embargo and the closure of its pipeline for Iraqi oil. It would also risk alienating an ally of the United States and of Israel, whose supporters were the most significant domestic constituency behind ILSA.

On the other hand, the bill initially had a chilling effect on major new investments that fell more unambiguously within its scope. In the first year of the sanctions, industry sources acknowledged a reluctance on the part of oil companies to sign Iranian contracts for fear of U.S. retaliation. There were a number of cases in which foreign firms acknowledged publicly the deterrent impact of ILSA. Australia's Broken Hill Proprietary backed out of a project to export natural gas from Iran to India and Pakistan because of its extensive U.S. holdings.[90] The president of Royal Dutch Shell acknowledged that his decision to pull out of the bidding for the South Pars offshore gas fields was because "the U.S. takes [ILSA] very seriously and makes it very difficult for international groups like ours with a big presence in the United States to do anything there."[91] Similar considerations deterred BP, which is the largest foreign investor and producer of crude oil in the United States.[92]

ILSA influenced energy firms with significant U.S. business because they recognized that this is an issue with strong congressional support and a powerful domestic constituency. Even if the Clinton administration was reluctant to invoke ILSA, its hand might be forced by domestic politics or an unanticipated event. Nor were they reassured by home country blocking legislation, which could not compensate for the opportunities in the United States denied by the sanctions. Given the uncertainties of U.S. behavior, foreign oil companies initially took a risk-averse approach and held off from Iranian contracts.

The credibility of ILSA was more seriously tested in August and September of 1997 when Iran announced two deals with foreign firms to develop offshore fields that the State Department had identified as sanctionable. The first was an agreement to develop the Balal natural gas field by Canada's Bow Valley Energy and the Indonesian state company, Bakrie Minarak.[93] The second was a $2 billion deal between Total, Petronas, and Russia's Gazprom to develop the South Pars natural gas field. This latter deal was the largest foreign investment in Iran since the 1979 revolution and was expected to yield two billion cubic feet of natural gas per day by 2001.[94]

Both deals elicited strong congressional outrage since they were the kinds of investments that ILSA was designed to prevent. Particular animus was directed at the Total deal because this was the same company that had snatched the Sirri contract from Conoco after the administration had forced it to back out.[95] This also created a dilemma for the administration. Penalizing the companies would unravel the recently negotiated understanding with the EU. On the other hand, if the sanctions were waived, one administration official noted, "every non-American energy firm on the globe is going to race in after [Total]."[96] A waiver could also trigger mandatory sanctions legislated by Congress, precipitating a major transatlantic crisis.

For the next eight months, the administration fudged the implementation of sanctions, neither punishing nor clearing the companies. It elided the law's timetable for enforcement by claiming that it was studying whether the investments were sanctionable, even though they were clearly within the scope of ILSA.[97] In reality, the administration was buying time to find a negotiated settlement that would both pacify Congress and persuade the EU to withdraw its WTO grievance.

That agreement came as part of the negotiation between the United States and the EU over Helms–Burton on 18 May 1998. The EU and Russia agreed to tighten controls on the export of technology associated with weapons of mass destruction and ballistic missiles in exchange for a 9(c) national interest waiver for the three companies involved in the South Pars project. The administration did not extend a 4(c) waiver since the EU had not taken parallel actions to curb investments in Iran. It did, however, make a political commitment to exempt comparable deals by European firms in the future.[98]

As with the expropriation disciplines, the administration cited the outcome as a vindication of discretionary sanctions that provide bargaining leverage to strengthen multilateral cooperation. The agreement, however, did not break substantial new ground. While the Russian agreement on missile technology was new, the EU accord largely reaffirmed existing cooperation in denying strategic technology.[99] In effect, the United States opted for compromise over enforcement because the latter would not have reversed the projects and would have resulted in unacceptable diplomatic repercussions.

First, the participants in the two oil deals were not vulnerable to the sanctions available through ILSA. Neither Bow Valley, Petronas, nor Bakrie Minarak had any assets in the United States, though Bakrie was forced to pull out of the Balal project due to the Asian financial crisis.[100] Total minimized its vulnerability to ILSA by selling off its largest U.S. marketing and refining operations. Even though its remaining U.S. assets comprised 3 to 4 percent of its profits, its president explained why that business was less important than maintaining a free hand in Central Asia: "When you realise that the Middle East has two-thirds of the world's oil reserves and one-third of gas reserves, I would say it is more important for an oil company to be in the Middle East than the US. Our strategic axes are really to develop in countries with fast economic growth, in particular in Asia. By 2000, we expect to generate more than 30 per cent of our results in Asia."[101] With the exception of BP and Shell, most foreign oil companies were not so dependent on the U.S. market that the threat of penalties within it persuaded them to forego the development of major new sources of supply.[102]

Gazprom appeared to be more vulnerable, particularly since it was trying to obtain credit in the United States—that is, it had signed a $750 million agreement with Eximbank, half of which had not been disbursed, and Goldman-Sachs was underwriting a $1 billion bond to finance the import of equipment for its natural gas operations in Russia and the rest of the world. Even though neither loan was designated for South Pars, the U.S. connection raised a furor in Congress. Sanctions proponents called on the administration to apply the law, particularly since two of ILSA's recommended sanctions were a denial of Eximbank loans and a $10 million limit on the amount of capital an offender can raise in the United States. Senator Mitch McConnell (R-Ky.) went so far as to threaten Eximbank with a reduction in funding if it did not suspend the loan.[103] The issue became moot when Gazprom abandoned the bond issue and canceled the remainder of its Eximbank credit. Instead, it raised $3 billion in Europe from the state export financing institutions and an international consortium, which included Citicorp and other U.S. banks.[104] In other words, the outcome demonstrated the futility of applying unilateral financial sanctions on creditworthy customers in a world of financial globalization.

Even if the projects could not have been reversed, sanctions proponents argued that ILSA should have been invoked to deter other energy firms. The administration concluded that the costs of this option were prohibitive. First, any reprisal against a European firm would trigger the resubmission of the EU's WTO grievance and risk a trade war that could weaken the international trade regime. Second, it could fray European cooperation over strategic exports to Iran, an area in which there was a transatlantic consensus. Third, it could jeopardize allied support in the UN Security Council, particularly from France and Russia, for supporting the continuation of economic sanctions against Iraq. Finally, penalizing Russia's largest private natural gas firm would be counterproductive to U.S. support for political and economic reforms in Russia, its efforts to get the Russian Duma to ratify the START II arms control treaty, and its interest in working out cooperative arrangements with Moscow in Bosnia and Kosovo.[105]

These considerations continued to override any preference for applying ILSA even though European governments interpreted the U.S.–EU understanding and the Total waiver as a "green light" for their firms "to conduct their business without the threat of sanctions hanging over their heads."[106] Washington officially tried to discourage this by declaring that it would still investigate individual transactions on a case-by-case basis. It also set down a marker, asserting that pipeline projects (as opposed to investments in energy development) were not covered by the waiver after Tehran issued a $400 million tender for pipeline construction.[107] Moreover, prospective investors had to consider the fact that congressional sanctions proponents were critical of the Total waiver and introduced legislation to strip ILSA of its discretionary authority.[108] These risks gave pause to some oil companies with extensive

U.S. holdings—for example, Shell backed out of a pipeline project in December 1998 while BP was reportedly reluctant to challenge ILSA after its merger with the U.S. oil company, Amoco.[109]

Yet political risk in the U.S. market has not had as large a chilling effect on foreign investors in Iran as it has had in Cuba—primarily because the value of access to Iranian energy reserves is more important to oil companies than the more uncertain opportunities available to investors in Cuba. In early 1999, Iran was able to secure two major investments—a $300 million joint venture between Bow Valley and Britain's Premier Oil to expand development of the Balal offshore fields, and a ten-year deal between France's Elf-Aquitaine and Italy's ENI to develop the Darood offshore oil field.[110] The administration interceded unsuccessfully with Canada, France, and Italy to block the deals. The State Department also announced it would study both projects to determine whether they were sanctionable under ILSA—a threat which the Economist Intelligence Unit observed was "no longer credible" after the Total waiver.[111] This was made plainly evident in November 1999, when Royal Dutch Shell, whose president had previously acknowledged ILSA's impact on the company's decision making, finalized an $800 million deal with Iran to develop two offshore oil fields.[112]

CONCLUSION

Helms–Burton and ILSA represented the most serious effort to reverse the lessons of the pipeline experience regarding extraterritorial sanctions. The policy had its origins in U.S. domestic politics. The hegemonic decline model predicted the opposite—that is, that interest groups and their legislative allies would mobilize against unilateral sanctions, which concentrate costs on the U.S. economy by surrendering markets to third country competitors and subject U.S. business to retaliation. There was some indication of this in the late 1970s, when Congress tried to limit the president's emergency economic powers, and the early 1980s, when it tried to reverse the pipeline sanctions and amend the Export Administration Act so as to make the use of unilateral sanctions more difficult. The Reagan administration ultimately followed the congressional lead and reined in the territorial scope of its sanctions. Since the end of the Cold War, however, Congress has tried to reverse this moderating trend, spurred on by noneconomic interest groups. Not only has the agenda of issues proliferated, but members of Congress have been less inhibited from projecting their domestic agendas abroad. When others did not follow the American lead, secondary sanctions became the tool of choice to coerce the cooperation of others.

An alternative structural explanation might see this development as evidence of a second era of American hegemony. The Clinton administration, however, was as wary of the costs and risks of coercing allies as its predecessors. It signed both bills due to election year pressures, but was reluctant to invoke them. It consequentially used waivers whenever they were available and fudged an evaluation of the facts when they were not—namely, indefinitely "studying" whether investments made foreign firms subject to Helms–Burton's visa denial or ILSA's menu of penalties. In that sense, the agreement Secretary Eizenstat brokered on 18 May 1998 can be seen as part of a strategy of dual containment. Only the targets were not Iran and Iraq, but Congress and the Europeans. Congress was offered just enough to hold off pressures for mandatory reprisals. The Europeans were mollified and withdrew a potentially damaging grievance from WTO.

Despite administration fudging and the enactment of allied blocking orders comparable to those used against the pipeline sanctions, both laws had some of the deterrent impact on foreign investment that their authors had intended. Helms–Burton led to the disappearance of new investments by major firms with significant U.S. assets. ILSA had a comparable impact during the first year of the sanctions and inhibited some firms heavily involved in the United States from finalizing deals even after the 1998 U.S.–EU accord. A survey of European investors by the European-American Business Committee one year after the passage of ILSA found that roughly two-thirds of the companies interviewed had been influenced by the passage of the secondary sanctions, causing them to forego $1.9 billion in investment opportunities.[113]

Given the administration's ambivalence, the influence of secondary sanctions on foreign companies was due primarily to U.S. domestic politics—that is, the intensity of congressional and interest group commitment to the sanctions. This made credible the likelihood of penalties if certain thresholds were crossed. Unlike the pipeline sanctions, allied blocking orders had little impact in altering corporate behavior. While they can compel the performance of legally binding contracts, they cannot mandate new investments in Cuba and Iran. Those decisions are a function of private calculations of benefit and risk and allied blocking orders cannot alter that balance by compensating for the expense of litigation from Helms–Burton or the loss of economic opportunities through ILSA.

What this analysis implies is that the chilling effect of the secondary sanctions is likely to diminish only if the domestic political equation in the United States changes in a way that makes congressional activism on this issue less likely. That clearly was not the case when both laws were passed. The Economist Intelligence Unit noted that there was "little incentive for any leading politician to espouse any approach to Iran other than the present policy."[114] A former NSC official responsible for Cuban policy wrote that those who advocated any move toward normalization with Cuba "usually became political punching bags."[115]

Those political calculations changed somewhat in the late 1990s as the domestic politics of economic sanctions became more evenly balanced. In 1997, the National Foreign Trade Council (NFTC) formed USA-Engage to begin an aggressive corporate countermobilization against sanctions.[116] Their efforts contributed to a congressional reassessment of unilateral sanctions, particularly after the Glenn Amendment's mandatory penalties against India and Pakistan after their nuclear tests in May 1998. The hastily crafted law provided no executive branch discretion and established no conditions for lifting the sanctions. Not only did this complicate diplomacy, it also mobilized agricultural lobbies, whose members could no longer export to India and Pakistan on credit, to join corporate trade associations in opposing unilateral sanctions and persuading Congress to modify the Glenn Amendment. This provided additional support for the Sanctions Reform Act, which would subject unilateral or secondary sanctions to greater scrutiny. While the bill has not yet passed, it is evidence of a "shift in the correlation of forces on the Hill."[117] It also makes it less likely that Congress will legislate reprisals in response to presidential waivers, thereby diminishing the risks associated with Cuban or Iranian investments.

Comparable developments have opened up political space for the administration to take diplomatic steps away from the total isolation of Cuba and Iran. In the former case, the Pope's visit to Cuba and the death of Jorge Mas Canosa, the long-time leader of the CANF, enabled the Clinton administration to liberalize licensing requirements for medical exports and travel restrictions without serious concern for congressional action.[118] It also emboldened business and agricultural lobbies to challenge the embargo, eliciting the support of several conservative Republicans from agricultural states, and the Republican governor of Illinois, George Ryan, who made a high-profile visit to Cuba with representatives from the business community.[119] The influence of the CANF was further weakened when the Cuban exile community overplayed its hand during the Elian Gonzales case. In the summer of 2000, both houses of Congress voted to lift the embargo on food and medicine and the House voted to prevent enforcement of the ban on travel to Cuba.[120] The bill's immediate significance may be limited by the fact that it still bans any transaction that involves U.S. private or public credits.[121] It does, however, demonstrate that the legislative momentum is in the direction of moderating the sanctions rather than expanding them. This decreases the risk that domestic pressures would force an administration's hand over Title III waivers. As a result, some foreign companies that stayed away from Cuba because of Helms–Burton are preparing to resume operations.[122]

There has been a parallel evolution of U.S.-Iranian relations. The election of a more moderate president, Mohammad Khatami, has made for the possibility of a diplomatic opening. The political space for such overtures has expanded with the defeat of Senator D'Amato in the 1998 midterm elections and the mobilization of the oil industry and some prominent members of the foreign policy establishment against dual containment and the Iranian sanctions.[123] This neutralized the political fallout from moves designed to explore diplomatic openings to Iran, as when the United States removed sanctions on non-oil imports in March 2000.[124] It may not lead to the rescission of ILSA (which is set to expire in 2001) or the 1995 executive orders. As with the Cuban case, however, it seems to have created a blocking coalition against the expansion of the sanctions. This has increased the confidence of foreign oil companies—even those as committed to the United States as Shell—to invest in Iran without the same risk of reprisal that existed when ILSA was first enacted. Ironically, domestic political change in the United States has been more significant in ameliorating the risks associated with both ILSA and Helms–Burton than the blocking orders enacted by their governments or the negotiations between the United States and the EU.

NOTES

1. *Boston Globe*, 25 June 1995, 55.

2. *New York Times*, 21 July 1996, sec. IV, 3.

3. In a speech to a religious organization in which a reporter, Elaine Sciolino, was present, President Clinton argued that mandatory sanctions legislation forced him "to fudge an evaluation of the facts of what is going on" to avoid diplomatic confrontations. It was reported in *New York Times*, 28 April 1998, A1.

4. Neff, *Friends But No Allies*, 146.

5. Andreas F. Lowenfeld, "Sauce for the Gander: The Arab Boycott and U.S. Political Trade Controls," *Texas International Law Journal* 12 (winter 1977): 28.

6. Testimony of Secretary of State Cyrus R. Vance in U.S. Congress, Senate Committee on Banking, Housing, and Urban Affairs, *Arab Boycott*, Hearings, 95th Cong., 1st sess., 1977, 427.

7. U.S. Congress, Senate Committee on Banking, Housing, and Urban Development, *Export Administration Amendments of 1977*, Report, 95th Cong., 1st sess., 1977, 21. Prior to congressional involvement, the State Department preferred not to intervene, allowing U.S. companies to respond to boycott pressures on an individual basis. See Gil Feiler, *From Boycott to Economic Cooperation: The Political Economy of the Arab Boycott of Israel* (London: Frank Cass, 1998), 150.

8. Lowenfeld, "Sauce for the Gander," 33.

9. See Morley, *Imperial State and Revolution*, 347; and *Middle East Executive Reports*, July 1986, 7.

10. Shambaugh, *States, Firms, and Power*, 133–134.

11. Mastanduno, *Economic Containment*, 277, 290–295.

12. Statement of Representative Wise (D-W.Va.) in U.S. House Committee on Foreign Affairs, Subcommittees on International Economic Policy and Trade and on Africa, *Proposed Economic Sanctions against South Africa*, Hearing, 100th Cong., 2d sess., 1988, 68.

13. *Financial Times*, 30 August 1988, 14.

14. Ellicott, "From Pipeline to Panama," 14.

15. David B. Matthews, "Controlling the Exportation of Strategically Sensitive Technology: The Extraterritorial Jurisdiction of the Multilateral Export Control Enhancement Amendments Act of 1988," *Columbia Journal of Transnational Law* 28 (1990): 759.

16. See Beverly Crawford, "Changing Export Controls in an Interdependent World: Lessons from the Toshiba Case for the 1990s," in *Export Controls in Transition: Perspectives, Problems, Prospects*, eds. Gary K. Bertsch and Steven Elliott-Gower (Durham, N.C.: Duke University Press, 1992), 264–276.

17. Dorinda G. Dallmeyer, "The Problem of Extraterritoriality in U.S. Export Control Policy," in *Export Controls in Transition*, eds. Bertsch and Elliott-Gower, 156–158.

18. *New York Times*, 21 February 1991, A15.

19. See Matthews, "Controlling the Exportation of Strategically Sensitive Technology," 753, 760; and *New York Times*, 22 February 1991, A8.

20. *Washington Post*, 11 June 1998, A1.

21. Lila Haines, *Reassessing Cuba: Emerging Opportunities, Operating Challenges* (New York: EIU, 1997), 3–5.

22. Cited in Antonio Jorge and Robert David Cruz, "Foreign Investment Opportunities in Cuba: Evaluating the Risks," in *Investing in Cuba*, eds. Suchlicki and Jorge, 19.

23. See Jorge Perez-Lopez, *Odd Couples: Joint Ventures Between Foreign Capitalists and Cuban Communists* (University of Miami, North South Center, North–South Agenda Paper No. 16, 1995), 5–15.

24. Haines, *Reassessing Cuba*, 13.

25. See Krinsky and Golove, eds., *United States Economic Measures against Cuba*, 97–103.

26. The text of these warnings is reprinted in U.S. Congress, Senate Committee on Foreign Relations, Subcommittee on Western Hemisphere and Peace Corps Affairs, *Cuban Liberty and Democratic Solidarity Act*, Hearing, 104th Cong., 1st sess., 1995, 192–193.

27. *Inter Press Service*, 4 May 1995.

28. Representative Ileanna Ros-Lehtinen (R-Fla.) likened this to "fencing stolen property." See U.S. Congress, House Committee on International Relations, *Cuban Liberty and Democratic Solidarity Act of 1995*, Hearings and Markup, 104th Cong., 1st sess., 1995, 58.

29. Mark P. Sullivan, "Cuba: Issues for Congress," CRS, 25 June 1997, 7–8.

30. U.S. Congress, House Committee on International Relations, *The Cuban Liberty and Democratic Solidarity (Libertad) Act of 1996*, Report, 104th Cong., 2d sess., 1996, 57–58.

31. See Representative Burton's remarks in *Globe and Mail*, 15 June 1995, B1.

32. Andreas F. Lowenfeld, "The Cuban Liberty and Solidarity (Libertad) Act," *American Journal of International Law* 90 (July 1996): 426–427.

33. Statement of Marc Thiessen, cited in *Globe and Mail*, 7 March 1996.

34. See the remarks of Allen Weiner, State Department Office of Legal Affairs, in U.S. House, *Cuban Liberty and Democratic Solidarity Act of 1995*, 19–20.

35. Peter Morici, "The United States, World Trade, and the Helms–Burton Act," *Current History* 96 (February 1997): 89.

36. See the testimony of Monroe Leigh in U.S. Congress, Senate Committee on Foreign Relations, Subcommittee on Western Hemisphere and Peace Corps Affairs, *Libertad Act: Implementation and International Law*, Hearing, 104th Cong., 2d sess., 1996, 29–31.

37. See statements by Representative Torricelli in *Congressional Quarterly Weekly Report*, 14 October 1995, 3157.

38. U.S. Senate, *Cuban Liberty and Democratic Solidarity Act*, 38; the State Department conceded that the effect of allied blocking orders was "minimal" and that there was "little or no adverse effect" on U.S.-European trade. (U.S. Senate, *Cuban Liberty and Democratic Solidarity Act*, 159).

39. *Toronto Star*, 17 March 1995, B1.

40. Vanderbush and Haney, "Policy Toward Cuba During the Clinton Administration," 403–404.

41. Lowenfeld, "The Cuban Liberty and Solidarity (Libertad) Act," 426.

42. Lowenfeld, "The Cuban Liberty and Solidarity (Libertad) Act," 422.

43. Preeg, *Feeling Good or Doing Good with Sanctions*, 20.

44. *International Legal Materials*, 1997, 111–117.

45. *International Legal Materials*, 1997, 125–132.

46. *Guardian*, 21 November 1996, 15.

47. *Weekly Statements of President*, 19 July 1996, 1265.

48. Those companies were an Israeli citrus company (B.M. Corp.) and telecommunications firms from Mexico (Grupo Domos) and Italy (STET). Grupo Domos was removed from the list after it sold its stake to STET. STET worked out a financial settlement with the former U.S. owner, ITT, which exempted it from Title IV. Ironically, this arrangement better served Helms–Burton's official rationale of protecting property owners rather than its actual economic warfare strategy. See Thomas W. Wälde, "Legal Boundaries for Extraterritorial Ambitions," in *Companies in a World of Conflict*, ed. John Mitchell (London: Earthscan Publications, 1998), 143.

49. *Financial Times*, 3 October 1996, 5.

50. Joaquin Roy, "Europe: Cuba, the United States, and the Helms–Burton Law," in *Transatlantic Tensions: Europe, the United States, and Problem Countries*, ed. Richard N. Haass (Washington, D.C.: Brookings Institution, 1999), 40–41.

51. Roy, "Europe: Cuba, the United States, and the Helms–Burton Law," 42–43.

52. See statement of Stuart Eizenstat, Assistant Secretary of State for Economics, Business, and Agriculture, in House Committee on International Relations, *Economic Sanctions and U.S. Policy Interests*, Hearings, 105th Cong., 2d sess., 1998, 80–81.

53. Richard Nuccio, "Cuba: A U.S. Perspective," in *Transatlantic Tensions*, ed. Haass, 23.

54. See Representative McCollum's article, "Putting Fangs Back into Helms–Burton," *Journal of Commerce,* 16 September 1997, 9(A).

55. Gerke, "The Transnational Rift over Cuba," 49–50.

56. EIU, *Cuba*, Country Report, 1997, no. 2, 10.

57. "Press Briefing by Sandy Berger and Peter Tarnoff," *M2 Presswire*, 18 July 1996.

58. *Ottawa Citizen*, 9 March 1996, 1(E).

59. *Financial Post*, 29 February 1996, 3; *Petroleum Economist,* February 1998, 40.

60. *Cuba Business*, September 1996, 5.

61. See Haines, *Reassessing Cuba*, 21.

62. *Financial Post*, 23 April 1996, 10.

63. EIU, *Cuba*, Country Report, 1997, no. 1, 21; *Cuba Business*, November 1996, 3.

64. See Gareth Jenkins, "Implications for Trade and Investment of the Cuban Liberty and Solidarity (Libertad) Act," Annex to *Cuba Business* (July/August 1996), 2; also see Haines, *Reassessing Cuba*, 15; Nomi Morris, "Cooling on Cuba," *Macleans*, 9 March 1998, 40–41; EIU, *Cuba*, Country Report, 1998, no. 2, 21–22.

65. *Financial Times*, 17 July 1996, 17.

66. S. Kern Alexander, "Trafficking in Confiscated Cuban Property: Lender Liability Under the Helms–Burton Act and Customary International Law," *Dickinson Journal of International Law* 16 (spring 1998): 535–536.

67. On the withdrawal of the Dutch bank, ING, see *Financial Times*, 24 July 1996; on the Canadian banks, see *Financial Post*, 24 March 1995, 9, and 29 June 1996, 1; for an overview, see Haines, *Reassessing Cuba*, 119–124.

68. *Financial Times*, 15 July 1996, 5.

69. See Haines, *Reassessing Cuba*, 72–73.

70. Maria Kielmas, "Sanctions Stir Up Political Risk Market," *Business Insurance*, 19 August 1996, 32.

71. *Congressional Quarterly Weekly Report*, 6 May 1995, 1252.

72. *Platt's Oilgram News*, 12 September 1995, 1.

73. U.S. Congress, House Committee on International Relations, *Trade Sanctions Against Iran and Libya*, Hearings, 104th Cong., 2d sess., 1996, 3.

74. Testimony by Tarnoff in U.S. Congress, Senate Committee on Banking, Housing, and Urban Affairs, *The Iran Foreign Sanctions Act*, Hearings, 104th Cong., 1st sess., 1995, 4–5.

75. *New York Times*, 13 December 1995, D1.

76. *Congressional Quarterly Weekly Report*, 23 December 1995, 3895.

77. *Congressional Quarterly Weekly Report*, 15 June 1996, 1699.

78. See U.S. Congress, House Committee on Ways and Means, *Iran and Libya Sanctions Act of 1996*, Report, 104th Cong., 2d sess., pt. 2, 15.

79. *Congressional Quarterly Weekly Report*, 20 July 1996, 2064.

80. U.S. House, *Iran and Libya Sanctions Act*, pt. 2, 14–18.

81. *Journal of Commerce*, 24 July 1996, 1(A).

82. *International Legal Materials*, 1997, 132.

83. Peter Rudolph, "Critical Engagement: The EU and Iran," in *Transatlantic Tensions*, ed. Haass, 75–81.

84. *Financial Times*, 7 August 1996, 4.

85. *International Legal Materials*, 1997, 530.

86. See *Oil Daily*, 10 January 1997, 5.

87. *Platt's Oilgram News*, 21 March 1997, 5.

88. *Financial Times*, 1 November 1996, 5.

89. *Oil Daily*, 20 May 1997, 1.

90. Preeg, *Doing Good or Feeling Good about Sanctions*, 63.

91. *Platt's Oilgram News*, 17 January 1997, 1.

92. *Financial Times*, 6 May 1998, 4.

93. EIU, *Iran*, Country Report, 1997, no. 4, 11–12.

94. *Journal of Commerce*, 30 September 1997, 1(A).

95. *Journal of Commerce*, 16 October 1997, 3(A).

96. *New York Times*, 16 October 1997, A1; on the bureaucratic debate over invoking ILSA, see *Washington Post,* 6 March 1998, A33.

97. *Journal of Commerce*, 15 December 1997, 1(A).

98. Rudolph, "Critical Dialogue," 85–87.

99. See Patrick Clawson, "Iran," in *Economic Sanctions and American Diplomacy*, ed. Haass, 90.

100. *Petroleum Economist*, February 1998, 40.

101. *Financial Times*, 30 September 1997, 7.

102. See Shambaugh, *States, Firms, and Power*, 190–193.

103. *Oil Daily*, 27 October 1997, 1, and 31 October 1997, 1.

104. EIU, *Iran*, Country Report, 1998, no. 1, 19–20.

105. See Eizenstat testimony (n. 52), 14.

106. Comments of Jacques Santer in *Platt's Oilgram News*, 19 May 1998, 1.

107. *Petroleum Economist*, July 1998, 3.

108. *Journal of Commerce*, 22 May 1998, 1(A).

109. EIU, *Iran*, Country Report 1999, no. 1, 15.

110. *Oil and Gas Journal*, 5 April 1999, 29.

111. EIU, *Iran*, Country Report, 1999, no. 2, 5.

112. EIU, *Iran*, Country Report, 2000, no. 1, 25.

113. European-American Business Committee, "Is the Price Too High? The Costs of U.S. Sanctions," October 1997 (the executive summary of the report can be accessed at www.eabc.org).

114. EIU, *Iran*, Country Report, 1997, no. 3, 17.

115. Nuccio, "Cuba," 9.

116. See its Web site at www.usaengage.com.

117. *New York Times*, 31 July 1998, A1.

118. *Washington Post*, 28 July 1999, A1.

119. *Cuba Business*, October 1999, 1.

120. *Congressional Quarterly Weekly Report*, 7 October 2000, 2334.

121. *Congressional Quarterly Weekly Report*, 7 October 2000, 2334.

122. *Financial Times*, 16 June 2000, 38.

123. See Zbigniew Brzezinski, Brent Scowcroft, and Richard Murphy, "Differentiated Containment," *Foreign Affairs* 76 (May–June 1997): 20–28.

124. *New York Times*, 18 March 2000, A1.

Chapter Seven

"Think Globally, Sanction Locally" Disinvestment Campaigns against Multinationals in South Africa, Burma, and Nigeria

> The South Africa story shows that . . . thousands of small acts of commitment and protest—from demonstrations to letter writing to voting shares of stock— many of them derided at the time as inconsequential, steadily accumulated into a force that altered history and brought forth justice.
>
> —Robert Kinloch Massie[1]

The preceding chapters indicate some of the difficulties in imposing effective extraterritorial sanctions. Some of the evidence supports the contention of globalization theorists that the transnational spread of business shields it from political accountability. Even when the United States was more successful in altering corporate behavior, the absence of multilateral cooperation meant that alternative suppliers could replace those firms vulnerable to political risk in the United States. As one scholar concluded from a review of U.S. efforts at extraterritorial enforcement: "[G]overnments can only assert control over transnational corporations by acting collectively."[2]

This raises the question of whether effective collective action to regulate MNCs can come not just from governments, but also from transnational civil society—that is, coalitions of nongovernmental organizations (NGOs) with churches, unions, shareholders, and consumers, committed to promoting human rights, labor, or environmental issues across national borders. In 1982, for example, the World Health Organization (WHO) and UNICEF drafted a voluntary code of conduct regulating the sale by Western MNCs of breast milk substitutes, whose misuse in many developing countries had increased rates of infant malnutrition and mortality. Corporate compliance with the code was not enforced by states; despite overwhelming approval, only seven adopted it as law. Rather, it was the result of a transnational coalition of grassroots organizations, which targeted the industry leader, Nestlé, with consumer boycotts, shareholder resolutions, and adverse publicity. By 1984, Nestlé and the rest of the industry complied with the code despite the absence of parallel pressures from governments and the opposition of the United States.[3]

The Nestlé boycott represents one of the most successful examples of what some observers have called the "new accountability" in which NGOs assert social control over MNCs without the intermediary of the state. Traditionally, NGOs have acted as advocacy networks, trying to persuade governments to ban socially irresponsible business activity. When state support is not forthcoming, citizens groups have redirected their energies away from the central authorities toward the corporations, directly pressuring them through boycotts and shareholder activism, and local governments, persuading them to condition eligibility for municipal contracts on human rights criteria. These efforts have often elicited corporate compliance with activist demands in the infant formula case and a number of human rights, labor, and environmental issues. In such cases, NGOs exercise a form of governance without governments.[4]

Some activists have used these instruments to press MNCs to move beyond social responsibility to disengagement in order to impose the equivalent of economic sanctions. Their role model is the antiapartheid movement. In his book on U.S.–South African relations, Robert K. Massie shows how citizen pressures influenced corporate boardrooms, which were initially indifferent, if not sympathetic toward apartheid. Over time, U.S. companies were persuaded first to embrace social responsibility in the workplace and ultimately to disengage. Massie concludes that these social movements contributed to a "transformation from below" since they, more than state sanctions, caused the loss of business confidence that persuaded Pretoria to accept majority rule.[5]

This chapter examines the degree to which NGOs can provide an alternative center of authority to the state in securing the compliance of MNCs with their aim of imposing extraterritorial sanctions to promote human rights. The antiapartheid model is contrasted with attempts to replicate it in the 1990s vis-à-vis oil company investments in Burma and Nigeria. The findings present a mixed picture. In each case, citizen pressures increased the costs and risks of "business as usual" with pariah states and induced some corporations either to assume social obligations or to disengage. At the same time, nonstate sanctions were limited by three factors that make the replication of the South African experience in Burma and Nigeria unlikely. First, NGOs can induce, but unlike the state, cannot command corporate behavior, which means that compliance is likely only if the size of the stake is small relative to the costs at home. Second, their success in South Africa was dependent on state policies that reinforced their aims, which did not materialize in Burma and Nigeria given the high premium Western governments have placed on the development of energy resources. Finally, the most potent source of pressure on multinationals—municipal procurement power—was predominantly limited to the United States because of its decentralized federal system, and its future availability may be narrowed by recent challenges to its constitutionality.

THE "NEW ACCOUNTABILITY": NGO PRESSURE ON MULTINATIONALS

Many grassroots organizations have seen MNCs as levers through which they can promote human rights. In some cases, they have waged campaigns for disinvestment from or boycotts of abusive regimes in order to hasten their demise. This was the strategy of the antiapartheid movement as well as the recent campaigns against oil companies in Burma and Nigeria. In other cases, they have called for codes of conduct by which MNCs accept social responsibility criteria. Targeted practices include employment discrimination in Northern Ireland, environmental damage in Indonesia, and the purchase of goods made in sweatshops in Central America or prisons in China.[6]

MNCs initially resist these pressures. They contend that their investments are politically neutral and they bear no responsibility for the practices of countries with which they do business. To abandon this apolitical role, they argue, would jeopardize their relationship with the host state and work to the advantage of less scrupulous competitors. MNCs also make a moral case for maintaining their presence in repressive regimes, claiming that their operations benefit the population as a whole and withdrawal would only add economic misery to the victims of oppression. They concede that there may be times when a regime's behavior is so odious that normal business is unacceptable, but they maintain that such a call should be made by governments, not corporations.[7]

Efforts by human rights groups to persuade states to make that call have invariably fallen short of their expectations. Governments are reluctant to restrict business with repressive regimes that are not adversaries because of the costs to diplomatic cooperation or access to investment sites, markets, and raw materials. While most condemned murderous crackdowns, such as the Tiananmen Square massacre in China, or practices, such as child labor, few have moved beyond symbolic sanctions and voluntary codes of conduct. Attempts to reverse these priorities by lobbying national legislatures are usually neutralized by the superior resources available to MNCs and foreign governments to counter them.

As a result, activists have turned increasingly to instruments and venues not traditionally associated with foreign policy. First, they have applied consumer pressure through protests and boycotts to stigmatize a company's goods in the marketplace. Second, they have used shareholder activism, persuading churches, universities, and other institutional investors to divest their stock portfolios of targeted corporations or vote for proxy resolutions to change corporate practices.[8] Finally, they have lobbied state and local governments to condition eligibility for contracts on social responsibility criteria. Since municipalities command a huge portfolio of public funds, this enables activists to link an MNC's bottom line to its conduct abroad.[9]

The aim of such measures is not just to salve individual conscience, but to assert social control over business. NGOs have been most influential vis-à-vis large diversified firms for whom the stake in question represents a small fraction of its overall operations. In such cases, grassroots pressures can alter corporate calculations by raising the costs of "business as usual." Nestlé, for example, accepted boycotters' demands because the costs in terms of sales, the diversion of executive and boardroom time, and corporate image were disproportionate to maintaining a prerogative that represented 4 percent of global sales.[10] Clothing manufacturers, such as Reebok and the Gap, implemented workplace codes of conduct and independent monitoring of their suppliers' factories because of adverse publicity regarding child labor and sweatshop conditions in factories in the Philippines and El Salvador.[11] In the environmental arena, the most celebrated case is the campaign led by Greenpeace against Shell's plans to dump the Brent Spar oil storage buoy into the Atlantic Ocean. Sizable losses at the pump from a European boycott persuaded the oil giant to reverse its plans and agree to a more costly onshore dismantling.[12]

When NGOs succeed, they challenge traditional notions of state–society relations since they try to regulate business without changing public policy, particularly if corporate compliance exceeds legal mandates or contradicts official policy. In the Brent Spar case, for example, Shell backed off from a disposal plan that was strongly endorsed by the British government. This point was made by Greenpeace activists, who called their victory as a kind of "politics without politicians," which "unsettled the very basis of executive authority."[13] Nor was it lost on critics of the "new accountability," who see it as a means by which committed minorities can usurp the policy process. One consequently defined NGOs as "modern-day non-territorial potentates" that can "constrain private behavior as effectively as sovereign commands."[14]

Yet are these pressures as influential when NGOs move beyond social responsibility to human rights sanctions? Compliance with the former is less costly to multinationals because they can legitimize their overseas activities with mobilized constituencies at home. The latter, by contrast, demands of firms the more expensive obligation of abandoning their stakes as part of a strategy of concentrating pressure on repressive regimes. The case studies that follow will explain the degree to which the antiapartheid movement was able to persuade firms to disengage from South Africa and the implications of that case for the campaigns against oil companies in Burma and Nigeria.

THE ANTIAPARTHEID MOVEMENT

The late 1980s witnessed two dramatic examples of corporate disengagement from South Africa. The first was the private credit boycott, triggered by Chase Manhattan's 1985 decision to stop rolling over its South African loans. The second was the disinvestment of over 350 (mostly U.S.) direct investors after the outbreak of political violence in 1984. Neither of these actions was mandated by governments despite the enactment of international sanctions in the fall of 1986. They were, however, long-standing goals of nongovernmental antiapartheid groups. This outcome has been cited by many observers as evidence of the potential power of grassroots organizations to influence corporate behavior independent of central governments and provide a vehicle through which activists might influence corporate conduct in future cases. This section assesses that argument, first by placing the antiapartheid movement in historical context and then by analyzing its impact on the two principal examples of corporate disengagement.

States, Multinationals, and NGOs (1959–1985)

From the origins of the apartheid system in 1948 through the mid-1980s, the United States joined with other Western governments in opposing punitive sanctions against South Africa. While it condemned apartheid and many of the practices used to enforce it, Washington defined its relationship with Pretoria in strategic and economic terms. It consequently voted with Great Britain in blocking Security Council resolutions calling for comprehensive sanctions following the Sharpeville massacre in 1960 and the repression that followed the township violence in Soweto in 1976. As a result, restrictions on U.S. business with South Africa were limited to controls on the export of dual-use technology associated with the United Nations' voluntary (1963) and mandatory (1977) arms embargoes.[15]

Since their governments imposed few restrictions, Western firms approached business opportunities in South Africa no differently than any other market. Most were either indifferent or sympathetic to the apartheid system, limiting their objections to practices that interfered with business discretion.[16] Publicly, they defended their presence by arguing that South Africa's racial politics played no role in their decisions because business is apolitical. As one

Chase Manhattan official put it, the decision to lend to a country was purely economic and "implied no concurrence with the social, or political, or economic theories of that government."[17] Both corporate and government officials buttressed this with a moral argument. Separating economic relations from human rights condemnation would allow markets to play a liberalizing role in South Africa, encouraging an evolution away from apartheid. Many publicly endorsed the Oppenheimer Thesis that economic growth would generate greater income and expectations for blacks, better enabling them to mobilize their demands for participation in the political system. This would facilitate South Africa's development into a modern industrial economy, which would find the practices of apartheid increasingly irrational in restricting the skills and mobility of labor and retarding the size of the black consumer market.[18]

An alternative strategy was advocated by the nongovernmental antiapartheid movement. These groups had their origins in the 1950s with the creation of the Anti-Apartheid Movement in Great Britain and the American Committee on Africa in the United States. In 1959, they followed the lead of the African National Congress (ANC) in calling for sanctions, arguing that only economic pressures could persuade whites to accept majority rule. From their perspective, corporate investment in South Africa was neither politically neutral nor a progressive force eroding discriminatory laws; rather, it increased apartheid's staying power and this made Western firms accomplices in the system's racial injustices.[19]

The initial goal of the movement was to act as a transnational pressure group, persuading governments to impose sanctions.[20] By the mid-1960s, however, it was clear that state sanctions were not forthcoming. Therefore, activists redirected their energies from governments to corporations. The first major efforts were campaigns in the United States and Great Britain against bank lending through enlisting some institutional investors, primarily churches, to withdraw their accounts.[21]

These efforts intensified in the 1970s. In the United States, activists discovered a new lever in shareholder activism following a 1970 decision by the Securities and Exchange Commission (SEC) to allow the submission of proxy resolutions on social responsibility issues.[22] The antiapartheid efforts were coordinated by the Interfaith Center on Corporate Responsibility (ICCR), which monitored corporate behavior and disseminated information to shareholders. Reflecting the diversity of opinion among activists, many of the demands of the initial resolutions stopped short of disinvestment, calling for nondiscriminatory workplace practices or a ban on sales to the military and police. By the late 1970s—that is, after the Soweto uprising and the repression that followed—most resolutions demanded corporate withdrawal.[23] Soweto also provided the impetus for two new arenas for pressure on corporations. First, it precipitated student campaigns in most U.S. colleges and universities to divest stock portfolios of firms with direct investments in South Africa. Second, it started a trend that would expand in the 1980s when activists persuaded the city council of Madison, Wisconsin, to give preferential treatment in bidding for city contracts to firms with no investments in South Africa.[24]

The immediate corporate response was to fall back on traditional arguments regarding the apolitical character of their operations. One Citicorp official contended that bank lending was an "agent of development to all South African peoples" and that it was not "the role of a private corporation to pass judgments . . . on sovereign governments."[25] Firms also denied an obligation to attach social responsibility criteria to their operations. IBM claimed that its South African sales were politically neutral although its computers were used in the enforcement of the Pass Laws.[26] A Ford official testified that it would be inappropriate to challenge apartheid because "the modern corporation is not an institution which is empowered to confer rights on people."[27] Others argued that staying out of local politics was necessary for survival in an ideologically diverse world. As an official at Royal Dutch Shell averred, "We will always serve under the government whatever it is. . . . There's one thing you must never ask a multinational to do: to choose."[28]

As public pressure increased in the late 1970s, MNCs needed a more credible way to deflect pressures for withdrawal. This meant that they had to go beyond the argument that market forces by themselves would ameliorate racial discrimination and affirmatively attach social responsibility criteria to their South African operations. The hallmark of this strategy was the adoption by the most prominent U.S. investors of a code of conduct developed by Reverend Leon Sullivan, a former civil rights leader serving on the board of directors of General Motors. The Sullivan Principles obliged signatories to adopt nondiscriminatory hiring and workplace practices and an improvement of working and living conditions for their black employees. Compliance with the code was subject to external auditing and public reports from the Arthur D. Little Corporation.[29] The need to combat pressures at home also persuaded U.S. firms to be the first in South Africa to recognize black trade unions, beginning with Ford in 1979.[30] Finally, to make the case more effectively that their business was not strengthening apartheid, many MNCs ended their dealings with the South African government. For example, IBM and GM agreed to stop selling technology to the military and police while a number of major banks, such as Chase Manhattan and Citicorp, ended their loans to the South African state.[31]

These changes fell short of the core aim of the antiapartheid movement. From its perspective, corporate social responsibility might improve conditions for some blacks, but they represented a tiny fraction of the workforce.

On the other side of the ledger, a continued corporate presence would, in the words of ICCR Director Timothy Smith, "directly assist the staying power of South Africa's white rulers."[32] It strengthened apartheid economically through taxes, technology, fuel, and economic growth. It also sent whites a powerful signal that they need not change because whatever the West says about its abhorrence of apartheid, it will always see South Africa as an acceptable business partner. Consequently, activists intensified their pressure for economic disassociation.[33]

The corporate approach prevailed in Western capitals. Even after Soweto, Western restrictions were limited to strategic sales. Foreign investment, guided by codes of conduct, was still characterized as a progressive force. This strategy of increasing economic ties with South Africa was strongly endorsed by the Reagan administration in the early 1980s, whose strategy of "constructive engagement" saw cooperation rather than public pressure as the best way to encourage an evolutionary process of reform.[34]

Events in South Africa made this strategy politically untenable. The escalation of violence in late 1984 and the declaration of a state of emergency in June 1985 shifted state preferences from engagement to sanctions. In 1986, most countries imposed sanctions against South Africa, including the United States when the Congress overrode President Reagan's veto of the Comprehensive Anti-Apartheid Act (CAAA). While these laws were debated in cabinets and legislatures, a parallel battle was waged against corporate involvement in South Africa away from the central authorities—in state legislatures, city councils, colleges and universities, at annual shareholder meetings, and in the marketplace. Since the two most visible examples of corporate retrenchment—namely, the private credit boycott and the wave of disinvestments—exceeded that required by law and coincided with many of the demands of the antiapartheid movement, this raises the question of whether these venues had more influence over MNCs in South Africa than did Washington.

The Private Credit Boycott

It is generally agreed that the most damaging source of external economic pressure on Pretoria came from the private credit boycott. South Africa's financial crisis began in July 1985, when Chase Manhattan chose not to roll over its South African loans as they came due and froze all unused lines of credit. This triggered a panic in which other banks followed suit, producing massive capital flight and a severe weakening of the rand. The hemorrhaging of South Africa's economy stopped on 1 September, when Pretoria imposed exchange controls and declared a moratorium on the repayment of $14 billion in private debt.[35] The result was that South Africa was cut off from private

capital markets and transformed into an exporter of capital. Given its dependence on foreign loans, the economy was unable to achieve the growth necessary to create political stability.[36] As the *Economist* remarked, "[T]he market achieved in a few telecommunicating seconds the sort of damage that
proposers of sanctions had reckoned would take years."[37]

These actions were not mandated by governments. In fact, Chase's decision preceded legislated financial sanctions by more than a year. As a result,
the CAAA's ban on new lending merely ratified what had already taken place
in the market. Moreover, EC sanctions recommended, but did not require, an
end to new lending. This not only exempted European banks from the sanctions, but U.S. banks as well if they operated through their offshore branches
and subsidiaries. Given the fungibility of capital, no regulations could have
prevented European banks from evading the CAAA by borrowing from their
U.S. counterparts to make loans to South Africa.[38]

To a degree, the bankers' decisions can be attributed to market conditions
and political risk inside South Africa. First, South Africa had an unstable debt
structure. It had become increasingly dependent on foreign loans in the late
1970s and early 1980s, and its banks borrowed short-term on international
markets to lend the money longer term within the country. Consequently,
from 1980 to 1985, South Africa's external debt increased by 50 percent to
$24 billion, with $14 billion due over the next year.[39]

Second, this lending was premised on the assumption that Pretoria was in
control of events. The growing township violence in the mid-1980s and the
resistance of South Africa's president, P. W. Botha, to reforms, undermined
that assumption and increased private calculations of financial risk. Many
opponents of sanctions concluded that the private credit boycott represented
the "sanctions of the marketplace" applying its "checks and balances" to
apartheid's irrationalities.[40] As one Citibank official testified: "It [the private
credit boycott] came about because capital will not go where risks exceed reward. South Africans now understand that they cannot fully access the
world's capital markets until the government shifts the risk/reward balance in
its favor by eradicating apartheid."[41] Administration officials also used this
line of argument. Chester Crocker testified that sanctions were unnecessary
because "the marketplace is reaching its own conclusions and sending its sig-
nals and they are being heard."[42] Arguing retrospectively, Herman Nickel, the
U.S. ambassador to South Africa from 1982 to 1986, took issue with those
who attributed the fall of apartheid to sanctions by stating that "the markets
had already decided that South Africa under P. W. Botha was not the place to
put—or keep—your money."[43]

Yet the magnitude of the banks' withdrawal cannot be explained simply by
market forces. Until 1985, South Africa had a spotless repayment record,

large reserves, a strong balance of payments surplus, and a relatively low debt service ratio. When faced with debtors whose prospects for repayment were dimmer, the international financial community opted for a more orderly strategy of rescheduling and refinancing.[44] Nor had international bankers ever linked South Africa's creditworthiness to its political system. After Sharpeville and Soweto, for example, there was initial capital flight, but that was reversed when Pretoria restored political order through repression and economic order through the IMF.[45] Therefore, the banks' assertion that the end of apartheid was necessary for economic normalization reveals that they were concerned not only with its impact on the balance of risk and reward in South Africa, but in their home markets as well.

The principal reason why the home market was vulnerable was the ability of antiapartheid activists to exact a price for conducting business with South Africa. First, by mid-1985, they persuaded fifty-eight cities, fourteen states, and nine counties to enact depository bans on banks that loaned money to South Africa. These included major municipalities, such as the city of New York, and put at risk sizable deposits of pension funds.[46] Second, there was a marked increase in the number of proxy resolutions filed at annual meetings by a broader range of institutional investors. As in the Nestlé case, this contributed to a "hassle factor" whereby banks were forced to devote a disproportionate share of executive and board time to a small portion of their overall operations. South Africa represented an average of roughly 0.5 percent of the international loan portfolio of U.S. banks, diverting resources away from more salient problems, such as the Latin American debt crisis. The *Financial Times* noted that these pressures "allowed shareholders, depositors, and the public directly to impose an economic sanction without having to persuade their Government to do so."[47]

Yet the political factors that influenced bank decision making did not come exclusively from nongovernmental sources. The movement toward state sanctions in the mid-1980s also influenced the banks—not so much by legally enjoining them but by magnifying private perceptions or risk. These risks had been assuaged in the early 1980s. With Ronald Reagan and Margaret Thatcher setting Western policies, creditors saw sanctions as a remote possibility. In addition, if South Africa fell into financial trouble, they assumed that the West would help. This view was confirmed in November 1982 by an unconditional $1.1 billion loan from the IMF's Compensatory Finance Facility to rectify payments difficulties resulting from a steep decline in the price of gold. The United States played a key role in pushing through the loan, despite objections from several executive directors that it should have been conditioned on ending South Africa's system of influx control because of the severe constraints it imposed on labor mobility.[48]

By the mid-1980s, it was clear that Western governments could no longer play this supportive role and might actually enact punitive sanctions. First, Congress prevented the Reagan administration from supporting another financial rescue package by a 1983 amendment to the IMF Replenishment Act that mandated a vote against loans to "any country that practices apartheid."[49] Since the 1982 loan required strong U.S. support to overcome considerable opposition, this effectively removed the safety net from the banks when South Africa went into crisis and contributed to the financial panic in the summer of 1985. Second, private creditors had to factor the likelihood of sanctions into their projections of South Africa's ability to service its debt, particularly after President Botha's "Rubicon" speech in which he refused to make conciliatory moves necessary to defuse antiapartheid pressures at home.[50]

In sum, grassroots pressures, combined with changes in state policy, transformed banks into instruments of economic pressure, both through the private credit boycott and the linkage of new credits to political reform. The antiapartheid movement tried to achieve parallel success in debt-rescheduling negotiations that followed. Activists called on banks to hold out for the toughest terms possible on the $14 billion of private debt that the South African government had frozen in the standstill net in 1985. Demanding rapid repayment, they argued, would augment the payments constraints facing Pretoria and ratchet up the pressure on the regime to end apartheid.[51]

Unlike the private credit boycott, however, the banks' strategy did not coincide with that of apartheid opponents. From 1986 to 1989, they negotiated three interim accords that postponed and stretched out the debts owed by South Africa within the standstill net, thereby alleviating some of the pressure on the South African economy. A clause (Section 12) in the second of these accords afforded Pretoria additional breathing room by allowing banks to convert their short-term loans into long-term (9.5-year) loans outside the standstill where principal payments would not begin until the last 2.5 years. The attraction of this option to foreign banks was that they would be guaranteed repayment over a longer period without the stigma of continuous negotiations with Pretoria. According to the Investor Responsibility Research Center (IRRC), $4 billion of the $13 billion remaining in the net in 1989 was converted through this device. U.S. banks, facing stronger pressure at home, used Section 12 to cover $1.7 billion or 70 percent of their $2.4 billion in outstanding loans.[52]

Activists denounced the banks for "provid[ing] a mechanism for South Africa to alleviate its debt burden."[53] In the United States, campaigners targeted Citicorp, which transformed its entire $670 million in loans through Section 12, through protests, shareholder resolutions, and municipal depository bans.[54] These efforts were unable to alter the bankers' calculation of self-interest as with the private credit boycott. One distinction between the two cases is that the campaigners were trying to punish banks for a single-shot decision already made rather than an ongoing relationship. Another was that nonstate actors could not induce banks to equate their interest in protecting their assets with the movement's overall aims. On lending, antiapartheid pressures reinforced the banks' interest in repatriating capital out of South Africa and not throwing good money after bad. On rescheduling, the banks' primary interest was to get their money out of South Africa. This was best achieved through negotiations that spread out the repayment of debt to what the government believed it had the capacity to pay. By contrast, a tough policy designed to cripple South Africa's economy could push it into default and force creditors to write off their loans. The same factors influenced the banks' willingness to attach political strings to economic normalization. The resumption of new credits required political reform because the removal of a sanctions environment was necessary for South Africa's creditworthiness; no such linkage was made vis-à-vis any of the rescheduling accords.[55]

Direct Investors and the Disinvestments of the Late 1980s

A second area of corporate retrenchment was the wave of disinvestments following the eruption of political violence in late 1984. As with the private credit boycott, governments did not mandate this. Neither the United States nor the EC extended sanctions to direct investors. In fact, both rejected the calls for disinvestment and continued to encourage MNCs, guided by codes of conduct, to act as a progressive force within South Africa.[56]

While disinvestment can be attributed to economic conditions and political instability within South Africa, the scale of corporate withdrawal was more pronounced than it had been in comparable circumstances elsewhere. A complete explanation has to account for the efforts of nonstate actors to compound political risk in South Africa with growing costs in the home market. By the end of the 1980s, the U.S. campaign to divest stock portfolios of firms with direct investments in South Africa had enlisted twenty states—including California's $11 billion state pension fund—and seventy-two colleges and universities.[57] There was also a marked increase in shareholder activism. This contributed to a hassle factor comparable to that for the banks because South Africa represented only 1 to 2 percent of the global sales or assets of most American investors. Since most resolutions focused on direct investments, disinvesting enabled firms to devote fewer resources to defending a decreasingly profitable part of their overall operations.[58]

The most important source of nonstate pressure on multinationals came from state and local governments in the United States. By the end of the antiapartheid campaign, 164 municipalities enacted either stock divestment ordinances or selective procurement rules linking eligibility for municipal contracts to various levels of noninvolvement (usually disinvestment).[59] The latter represented the most costly development for U.S.-based MNCs because many did considerably more business with cities and states than they did with South Africa. Such measures were passed in five states, fourteen counties, and fifty cities, including major markets, such as New York, Los Angeles, San Francisco, and Chicago.[60] Surveys by the U.S. embassy and consulates in South Africa found that municipal procurement power was the most significant external pressure on U.S. firms to disinvest.[61]

Nonstate actors were not the only source of external political pressure on corporate decision making. Governmental sanctions, both actual and potential, became more salient as multilateral support for constructive engagement eroded. When Western governments opposed sanctions, *Business International* advised its readers that they were "a remote possibility for the foreseeable future."[62] The supportive stance of home governments combined with economic growth in South Africa persuaded MNCs that they could safely ignore the antiapartheid movement. Consequently, foreign investment in South Africa increased sharply in the early 1980s.[63] As noted by one respondent to a survey of corporate managers: "South Africa is a classic case of people who want something done they *can't* get through government."[64]

By the mid-1980s, investors could no longer make that assumption. Although no Western country mandated disinvestment, state sanctions convinced many firms that it was the best alternative given their impact on business confidence. U.S. companies were confronted with an additional cost after the passage of the Rangel Amendment in December 1987, which denied tax credits to direct investors. Several firms, most prominently Mobil, attributed their departure to this law.[65] MNCs also had to account for the possibility that states might require disinvestment if conditions worsened or even stayed the same. This was of particular concern in 1988 when the House of Representatives (but not the Senate) passed the Dellums–Wolpe bill ordering U.S. investors to dispose of their South African investments.[66] This would have placed them in the position of forced sellers to South Africans who would have little incentive to pay anything resembling market price. As a result, many firms sold their South African assets in anticipation of worst-case scenarios.

Disinvestment, however, imposed only minimal costs on South Africa's economy. Almost all the departing firms sold their equity stakes to local management or third parties and maintained an ongoing licensing relationship to provide services, technology, and trademark rights to the new South African enterprises. This shift to nonequity ties minimized the costs to white South

Africans, who maintained the access to the departing firms' goods. Moreover, it had a negative impact on social responsibility goals since the new firms were no longer bound by workplace codes of conduct.[67]

This outcome parallels the antiapartheid movement's inability to translate its influence over lending to rescheduling. In both cases, nonstate pressures increased the costs and risks of business as usual to a point where withdrawal became a self-interested option. Once they achieved that goal, MNCs were free to choose the form of retrenchment that best served their interests, even if that diverged from the activists' goals.

This is evident in corporate responses to mounting pressures for withdrawal as political conditions in South Africa deteriorated. MNCs initially defended their presence by more aggressively assuming the mantle of social responsibility. In 1985, for example, the number of Sullivan Principles signatories grew from 129 to 178.[68] Investors increased contributions to community development programs in education, housing, training for small business, and the provision of free legal assistance to black employees who ran afoul of the apartheid laws.[69] Many MNCs went further when, in 1985, Reverend Sullivan implored them to engage in "corporate civil disobedience" by challenging apartheid laws. Rather than fall back on traditional arguments about noninterference, the president of the American Chamber of Commerce in South Africa stated that the time had come for U.S. firms to "take a stand against apartheid."[70] In October 1985, ninety-two U.S. companies took the unprecedented step of signing a full-page ad in South African newspapers calling for an end to discriminatory laws and for negotiations with the ANC.[71] In order to make the case more effectively that their presence eroded apartheid, many firms housed their black employees in white areas in defiance of the Group Areas Act. They also protested and lobbied against a law that would have required them to assist the government in quashing a rent strike in state-owned housing by deducting withheld rent from employee paychecks.[72]

The principal reason why MNCs adopted a more political role was to deflect antiapartheid pressures—defusing those from nongovernmental sources and persuading governments to stick with the "progressive force" argument. These obligations did entail an economic cost as well as the risk of antagonizing Pretoria. This was accepted as the price of blunting home country pressures for withdrawal, which at the time was seen as a more costly option.

While these efforts were applauded by home governments, they provided no respite from the antiapartheid movement. Activists charged that the benefits these obligations conferred upon a limited number of blacks were overwhelmed by corporate contributions to strengthening apartheid. At shareholder meetings, proponents of disinvestment resolutions pointed out that while U.S. firms provided $27 million for community development in 1985, they paid $752 million to the South African government in taxes.[73] Consequently, they escalated pressure on multinationals to withdraw. This strategy was given a boost when, on 3 June 1987, Reverend Sullivan joined the calls for disinvestment.[74]

Yet once domestic costs and risks persuaded corporations that disinvestment was the less costly option, the creation of nonequity ties best served the corporate bottom line. First, MNCs continued to earn income from South Africa through an arms-length trade relationship. Second, they maximized their returns from the sale of their assets and equipment, which would be worth considerably less to the new owners without parts, technology, and trademark rights. Finally, under South Africa's two-tiered exchange rate system, foreign firms were required to repatriate the proceeds of any sale through the artificially depressed financial rand. By contrast, payment for technology and services took place at the much higher commercial rand. Firms, therefore, had an incentive to discount the price for the formal sale of assets and make up for it through higher licensing fees.[75]

The negative consequences for social responsibility goals can be similarly understood in terms of the economic interests of the new company and the departing MNC. The former had to pay more attention to the short-term balance sheet since it could no longer sink into the deep pockets of the global parent. It therefore had a strong incentive to free itself of costly social obligations, such as funding projects that did not yield income or foregoing strategic sales. The latter's interest in leaving behind an economically viable company that maximized cash flow meant that few conditioned the sale on social responsibility—an obligation assumed primarily to legitimize South African investments at home.[76] GM's sale of its manufacturing plant to its South African partner, Delta, provides a case in point. Delta's first actions were to cut wages and lay off workers. When black trade unions responded by going on strike, Delta fired the workers and ordered the police to remove the picketers. Moreover, to maximize cash flow, it slashed its contributions to community development programs and resumed sales to the military and police.[77]

Antiapartheid groups denounced these developments as "corporate camouflage" and targeted nonequity ties. These efforts produced mixed results because they had to come back to universities and municipal governments to persuade them to triple the number of companies that had to be blacklisted from contracts or stock portfolios. By 1989, only one university expanded its divestment policy to cover nonequity ties.[78] On the state and local front, Los Angeles and San Francisco were the only major municipalities to follow the movement's lead.[79] Activists were more successful in persuading institutional investors to include this practice in their proxy resolutions—eighty were filed in 1990—because such actions were less costly.[80] These efforts registered some successes in the early 1990s. In 1991, the year in which President Bush lifted the CAAA, fifteen firms decided to sever their nonequity ties, including major firms such as Xerox, Motorola, and General Electric.[81] This demonstrates that subnational pressures influenced some MNCs even after federal policy changed. Nonetheless, most firms that disinvested and maintained nonequity ties were relatively unaffected by NGO pressures.

Another constraint on effectiveness of the antiapartheid movement was the fact that the most potent weapon used to pressure MNCs—municipal procurement power—was largely a U.S. phenomenon. Washington occasionally tried to reverse state and local sanctions. For example, the Senate version of the CAAA had a federal preemption provision, but that was removed in conference with the House.[82] In 1986, the Department of Transportation threatened to withhold highway funds to New York City because its selective procurement rules violated federal laws conditioning such funds on open bidding procedures.[83] After waiving the CAAA in 1991, the Bush administration initiated a study of "the legal implications of state and local governments carrying out their own foreign policy toward South Africa." In each case, Washington backed down after protests from governors and mayors.[84] Therefore, state and local South African ordinances were shielded by American federalism and its tradition of strong local government.

European activists were less able to enact comparable measures. Britain's antiapartheid movement did persuade roughly forty municipalities to attach South African conditions to procurement and stock holdings.[85] In contrast to the Reagan administration, Prime Minister Thatcher was able to protect her policy of constructive engagement by getting Parliament to enact a law that prohibited the use of noncommercial criteria for local contracts.[86] In both Norway and Canada, the courts struck down city ordinances blacklisting Shell in Oslo and Vancouver on the grounds that the laws discriminated against a single company and did not serve a legitimate municipal purpose.[87]

As a result, the most potent weapon of antiapartheid NGOs in Europe was the consumer boycott—the most prominent examples of which were the British campaigns against Barclays and Standard Chartered Bank and the European boycott of Shell. These campaigns persuaded many firms to accept codes of conduct and, in some cases (most notably, Barclays), tipped the scales in favor of withdrawal. Their inability to extend that pressure to local governments, however, meant that disinvestment was predominantly a U.S. phenomenon. From 1984 through 1989, 202 of 313, or 65 percent, of U.S. investors withdrew, as contrasted with 63 of 297, or 21 percent, of British investors. Outside of Britain and the United States, only an additional sixty-eight firms withdrew from South Africa. The same pattern is evident in the shift from direct investment to nonequity ties. Of the 290 U.S. firms that were still doing business with South Africa in 1990, 176, or 61 percent, did so through an indirect relationship as opposed to 22 percent (132 of 587) for non-U.S. foreign investors.[88]

In contrast to the infant formula campaign, municipal procurement ordinances played a larger role in influencing corporate behavior. In the former case, NGOs confronted a single industry and targeted a boycott on its leader. The focus on a single target combined with strong transnational support enabled activists to persuade Nestlé to adopt the code of conduct. Since the antiapartheid campaign faced several hundred corporations, boycotts were less likely to succeed. That required the availability of instruments, such as the municipal procurement laws, which cast a wider net over a large number of firms. Since this feature was mostly limited to the United States, NGOs were most successful in influencing U.S. firms—first to accept social responsibility and finally, to disinvest in larger numbers than their non-U.S. counterparts.

BURMA (MYANMAR)

Myanmar, formerly known as Burma, has been dubbed the "South Africa of the 1990s" since it has been the target of the most extensive nongovernmental campaign for human rights sanctions since the end of apartheid. Since the late 1980s, the country has been ruled by a military regime known as the State Law and Order Restoration Council (SLORC).[89] It became a priority for the human rights community in 1990 when the regime refused to accept the landslide victory of its democratic opposition, the National League of Democracy (NLD) and placed under house arrest its leader, Aung San Suu Kyi, who would later be awarded the Nobel Peace Prize. That concern was intensified in the spring of 1996 following a crackdown on the NLD, the arrest of over 260 of its leaders, and the reimposition of a quarantine around Aung San Suu Kyi.[90]

Repression in Myanmar triggered the creation of the Free Burma Coalition—a transnational coalition of human rights and environmental organizations, churches, labor unions, and socially responsible investors. As in the South African case, these groups advocated economic sanctions, particularly after July 1996, when Aung San Suu Kyi called on multinationals to stop their dealings with the SLORC.[91]

The central target of the Free Burma Coalition has been the oil companies, who have been active in Burma since the SLORC opened its natural resources to foreign development in the early 1990s. The most significant and controversial energy deal was the $1.2 billion joint venture between UNOCAL

(U.S.), Total, and the Thai and Myanmar state-owned energy companies to develop the Yadana offshore natural gas fields and construct a 260-mile pipeline to Thailand.[92] Activists charge that the project brings substantial revenues to the regime, strengthening its hold on power. They also hold the companies responsible for the use of forced labor, environmental damage in the construction of infrastructure associated with the project, and of the forced relocation of villages to clear territory for the pipeline. UNOCAL and Total have denied the charges, contending that the alleged abuses are not associated with their investments. Moreover, they defend their right to stay regardless of the political practices of the host country. As the president of UNOCAL noted: "We are a global energy company, not a political agency. We will not assert ourselves in the internal debate of sovereign nations."[93]

The Free Burma Coalition appealed to governments to assert themselves by imposing punitive sanctions. None was willing to go beyond diplomatic condemnation and modest sanctions. The United States imposed the strictest measures. A bill introduced in 1995 by Senator Mitch McConnell (R-Ky.) proposed a comprehensive embargo and mandatory disinvestment. The prospect of passage triggered an intense corporate lobbying campaign. This resulted in the passage of the Cohen–Feinstein Amendment that limited sanctions to new investments, thereby exempting preexisting contracts such as the Yadana project. Even these measures were discretionary, subject to a determination every six months as to whether repression had increased or Aung San Suu Kyi had been harmed, imprisoned, or exiled.[94]

President Clinton waived the sanctions in October 1996, but invoked them in April 1997.[95] Their impact on U.S. investments has been minimal. They did force UNOCAL to drop plans to explore two offshore fields, but did not affect its Yadana operations. Moreover, the sanctions left unclear whether injecting new capital into existing ventures represented a new investment. Since Treasury made no definitive determination of this, the companies interpreted the regulations as if reinvestment were not covered.[96] Finally, the administration let it be known it planned to apply the sanctions several months before their actual imposition. Companies considering investments in Myanmar saw this as a window of opportunity to get in ahead of the new law. The *Financial Times* reported that February 1997 alone witnessed $300 million in new U.S. investments, primarily in the energy sector, more than doubling the total of fixed U.S. investments in Myanmar.[97]

Given this reluctance to enjoin corporate behavior, activists concentrated their efforts on pressing corporations directly or through subnational actors. First, they used demonstrations and the Internet to publicize human rights abuses to direct social pressure at corporations.[98] Second, they persuaded individuals and private institutions, particularly colleges and universities, to boycott goods from firms that did business with Burma.[99] Third, shareholder resolutions demanded that UNOCAL and other oil companies appoint a committee of independent auditors to investigate allegations of forced labor and environmental abuse and assess the costs to the company of continued investment in Burma in terms of political risk and international boycotts.[100] Finally, campaigners in the United States pressed states and localities to tie eligibility for municipal contracts to the severance of trade and investment ties. By the end of 1998, selective procurement ordinances were passed by one state (Massachusetts), one county, and twenty-one cities, the most significant of which were New York, Los Angeles, and San Francisco.[101]

These techniques have influenced corporate decision making. Adverse publicity surrounding involuntary labor and other human rights abuses induced several prominent retailers and garment and footwear makers to stop sourcing goods from Burma, impeding the country's efforts to diversify its exports.[102] The loss of lucrative contracts on college campuses persuaded PepsiCo to sell its 40 percent share in a bottling plant and then sever all links with its Burmese distributor.[103]

As in the South African case, state and local ordinances had the greatest impact on corporate withdrawals. Apple Computer and Motorola, for example, liquidated their Burmese operations to maintain contracts with Massachusetts and San Francisco.[104] These ordinances even had an impact on non-U.S. corporations. Of the 150 firms blacklisted by the Massachusetts ordinance, 110 are non-American.[105] Two Dutch banks withdrew their bid to buy the Bank of Boston because their Burmese ties would have precluded them from state business. U.S. subsidiaries of Mitsubishi (Japan) and Ericsson (Sweden) were deemed ineligible for contracts in San Francisco because of their parents' ties with Burma.[106] In some cases, foreign firms severed their Burmese ties to maintain their business in major municipalities. For example, the Dutch firm, Phillips Electronics, pulled out of Burma to protect its business in Massachusetts, and Sweden's ABB Asea Brown Boveri canceled a Burmese joint venture by its German affiliate in order to clear the way for a bid on an airport construction project in San Francisco.[107]

These pressures were most successful when an MNC's vulnerability in the U.S. market was disproportionate to its Burmese stakes. For example, PepsiCo's withdrawal was cited by the Free Burma Coalition as one of its major successes. Although Burma was one of the few Asian markets where Pepsi outsold its chief competitor, Coca Cola, its 1995 sales were only $4 million, a small fraction of its global sales of $10 billion. Moreover, PepsiCo owned a number of affiliates, such as Taco Bell and Pizza Hut, all of which risked exclusion from an increasing number of college campuses if the company chose to stay.[108] For PepsiCo and other departing firms, pulling out was a small price to pay to insulate themselves from risks in the U.S. market. Yet what made these firms vulnerable to NGO pressure also made their withdrawal less costly to the SLORC.

Oil investments, by contrast, are more central to the SLORC's economic plans and less susceptible to citizen pressures.[109] The Yadana fields, estimated to contain 5.7 trillion cubic feet of gas, are major investments for UNOCAL and Total. In the 1990s, UNOCAL pursued a conscious strategy of staking its future growth in exploration in Southeast and Central Asia and sold off many of its downstream operations in the United States to finance this effort. San Francisco's decision to exclude the company from a municipal fuel contract only accelerated this strategy. Given increasing pressures at home, UNOCAL moved much of its operations and management to Asia and established a second corporate headquarters in Malaysia to enable it to pull out of the United States should sanctions regulations go too far in impeding its development plans.[110]

Yet pressures from municipal sanctions, the instrument most costly to the corporate bottom line, are likely to diminish as a result of challenges in international institutions and the U.S. political and legal system. First, the Massachusetts Burma Law created more international friction than the antiapartheid ordinances because the WTO's liberalization of government procurement regulations in the 1990s meant that more non-U.S. firms lost business due to municipal blacklists. The EU and Japan consequently condemned municipal sanctions as secondary boycotts no different from Helms–Burton or ILSA. They filed a grievance against the Massachusetts ordinance in the WTO, claiming a violation of the 1994 Government Procurement Agreement that prevents the attachment of any criteria unrelated to those necessary to fulfill a contract.[111] The Massachusetts state government countered that it has a right to control its own procurement practices and that the ordinance does not discriminate between U.S. and non-U.S. firms who do business with Myanmar. The Clinton administration initially sided with the EU and tried to discourage Massachusetts from passing the law. After its passage, it agreed to defend Massachusetts before the WTO in exchange for working with the state in drafting future laws (there was a pending bill on Indonesia) so they were consistent with international trade agreements.[112] Despite efforts to work out a compromise, the EU pushed ahead with its grievance and the WTO agreed in December 1998 to convene a dispute resolution panel, proceedings that were put on hold until legal challenges in the United States were to be resolved.[113]

Second, municipal Burma sanctions were opposed by corporate trade associations, particularly the NFTC, as part of its strategy of opposing unilateral sanctions.[114] Its first attempt to invalidate subfederal sanctions was through the Sanctions Reform Act, introduced to make it more difficult to impose unilateral sanctions. The initial version of the bill would have preempted all state and local sanctions laws. That provision was later withdrawn to maximize the chances for the bill's passage.[115]

In May 1998, the NFTC shifted its focus to the federal courts by filing suit against the Massachusetts Burma Law on behalf of its members. It claimed the law was an unconstitutional usurpation of the federal government's right to conduct foreign policy. Its aim was to establish a precedent that could be used to invalidate comparable efforts by municipal governments to regulate corporate conduct abroad. On 4 November 1998, a federal judge declared the Massachusetts Burma Law to be unconstitutional. Since it seeks to "change Burma's domestic policy," Judge Joseph L. Tauro ruled that it "impermissibly infringes on the federal government's power to conduct foreign affairs."[116] The sweeping constitutional judgment called into question the legality of all subfederal laws aimed at regulating corporate conduct abroad. Massachusetts appealed the verdict. By the time it made its way to the Supreme Court, the Clinton administration shifted from neutrality to open support for the NFTC's challenge to the law, contending that it was "a wholly unnecessary irritant" in relations with trading partners.[117]

On 19 June 2000, the Supreme Court unanimously struck down the Massachusetts Burma Law. Its ruling was narrower than Judge Tauro's, sidestepping the constitutional question. Instead, it based its decision on conflicts with federal statute, which (1) granted the administration flexibility over implementation while the state ordinance was more rigid; and (2) exempted pre-existing contracts, which were targeted by the state's procurement rules.[118] The decision did not rule on state and local sanctions where there is no federal law. Nonetheless, it significantly narrows the continued utility of municipal procurement power as a lever vis-à-vis MNCs in Burma and elsewhere.

NIGERIA

A second effort to replicate the antiapartheid movement was the campaign against Western oil companies in Nigeria. Nigeria was subjected to widespread condemnation in 1993, when General Sani Abacha annulled elections, imprisoned the winner, banned political parties, and dissolved elected bodies. The Abacha regime's practices were placed at the top of the human rights agenda after 10 November 1995 when it executed the playwright Ken Saro-Wiwa and eight Ogoni activists who had protested Shell's activities in Ogoniland in what was almost universally condemned as a "show trial."[119]

Human rights activists targeted Royal Dutch Shell because it was the largest investor in Nigeria and was seen as complicit in the regime's abuses, particularly the execution of the Ogoni Nine. Shell was forced to suspend operations in Ogoniland in January 1993 after protests by the Movement for the Survival of the Ogoni People (MOSOP) against the company's environmental practices and attacks on the company's staff and equipment. Western human rights activists called on Shell to accept MOSOP's demands to clean up oil spills and allocate a greater share of oil revenues to the impoverished Ogoni region. Shell responded that these were responsibilities of the Nigerian government, not of a private corporation, and it would be inappropriate to intervene in local political struggles.[120] Instead, it asked the government for assistance in protecting its operations, a request that activists equated with responsibility for the repression that followed. When the Ogoni Nine were sentenced to death, Shell was asked by NGOs, such as Amnesty International, to use its influence with the government to spare their lives. Shell's response was comparable to that made vis-à-vis MOSOP's demands: "It is not for a commercial organization to interfere with the legal processes of a sovereign state."[121]

After the executions, human rights NGOs focused their attention on Shell. These pressures increased after internal company documents were leaked, revealing that Shell had imported weapons for the Nigerian police and was responsible for environmental damage.[122] Shell not only refused to withdraw, but recommitted itself to a $3.6 billion natural gas project only three days after the executions. Its Nigerian general manager justified the irrelevance of human rights to the economic opportunities in blunt terms: "For a commercial company trying to make investments, you need a stable environment. Dictatorships can give you that."[123] Shell's home office was somewhat more diplomatic, arguing that business should be separated from human rights condemnations and that a pullout would hurt the Ogonis more than it would the regime.[124]

Having failed to persuade Shell and other oil companies to suspend operations, human rights groups called on their governments to impose an oil embargo and mandate disinvestment. Oil was seen as the key area of vulnerability since it accounted for 80 percent of the government's revenue and 90 percent of its foreign exchange. U.S. sanctions were considered to be particularly important because the United States imported 588,000 barrels of Nigerian oil per day or 40 percent of its output.[125]

Traditional lobbying efforts were unsuccessful. Congress did introduce a sanctions bill to freeze the government's assets and ban new investments, but it was defeated by an effective lobbying campaign by corporate trade associations and the Nigerian government.[126] The Clinton administration pledged to adopt those measures by executive order if it could negotiate a multilateral consensus. The EU, however, opposed these limited measures, let alone an oil embargo. To European governments, sanctions jeopardized important economic interests. Restricting Nigeria's exports would impede its ability to service its $30 billion debt owed mostly to European and Japanese banks. An asset freeze risked the retaliatory expropriation of oil company assets and the role of Great Britain, France, or Germany as international financial centers.[127] EU sanctions were consequently limited to the suspension of development aid, cultural and sports contacts, and visas for members of the regime.[128] The British Foreign Office even reassured Shell that there would be no repercussions for its oil business in Nigeria.[129]

Given the unwillingness of states to impose sanctions, NGOs concentrated their efforts directly on MNCs. First, European activists sought to stigmatize Shell's Nigerian operations through demonstrations at its service stations and the erection of gallows outside several of its corporate offices.[130] Second, Greenpeace tried to recreate the successful consumer boycott that persuaded Shell to drop its plans to dump its Brent Spar oil rig into the Atlantic Ocean.[131] Third, shareholder resolutions were filed in London and the Hague against Shell, and in the United States against Mobil and Chevron, the two largest U.S. firms in Nigeria.[132] Finally, U.S. activists tried to use municipal sanctions to ratchet up the pressure to suspend operations. By October 1997, Nigerian ordinances had been passed in four U.S. cities and were being considered in larger municipalities, such as New York.[133]

These pressures persuaded some MNCs to make concessions in the area of social responsibility. Mobil and BP agreed to work with shareholders in providing reports on their Nigerian operations.[134] Shell retreated publicly from its initial insistence that social issues were outside of its purview. While continuing to defend its presence in Nigeria, it conceded responsibility for environmental damage and for importing arms for the Nigerian police, although it contended that paying for protection from state security forces was a common practice for oil companies in the developing world. It also assumed some environmental and social responsibility, committing itself to a $100 million per year for the cleanup of oil spills for five years as well as community investments in Ogoniland.[135] In March 1997, its Statement on General Business Principles pledged to consult with NGOs and use its influence to "express support for fundamental human rights in line with the legitimate role of business." The *Financial Times* referred to this as a "belated recognition of the influence on multinationals of international public opinion."[136]

It was also a demonstration of the limits of world opinion. First, no Western oil company was willing to abandon its access to crude oil or natural gas because of political risk at home. This was particularly true for Shell since Nigeria was the second largest source of crude after the North Sea. To have acceded to activist demands in Nigeria would have entailed a far greater sacrifice than accepting Greenpeace's demand for the onshore dismantling of the Brent Spar oil rig.[137]

Second, these pressures did not deter new energy investments. The Abacha regime's arbitrary rule and reputation for graft had poisoned business confidence. Offshore oil exploration, defined by the regime as essential to maintain the country's long-term reserves (and its own staying power), was insulated from these practices.[138] Although most foreign firms stayed away, oil MNCs saw Nigeria as a prime area for long-term development and increased their investments. From 1996 through 1998, Nigeria maintained its oil production well over its OPEC quota of two million barrels per day.[139] While the death of General Abacha in June 1998 paved the way for a transition to civilian rule, external economic pressures on the oil companies had no impact on the outcome.

CONCLUSION

This chapter began by posing the question of whether nonstate human rights groups can exercise extraterritorial regulation of corporate conduct abroad. The three cases examined provide some supportive evidence. In each, MNCs were pressured to assume ethical obligations beyond those required by law. In South Africa, investors adopted workplace codes of conduct and bans on loans and sales to the government. Similarly, Shell increased the resources expended on environmental and social projects in Ogoniland despite its initial insistence that these were government responsibilities. These actions were undertaken primarily to assuage nongovernmental pressures for withdrawal and, as such, were opposed by most activist groups. They nonetheless represented a change from the traditional corporate insistence that business is politically neutral and that social concerns are outside their responsibility.

In some cases, NGO pressures tipped the scales in favor of disengagement. In South Africa, private lending stopped fifteen months before financial sanctions were enacted and many firms disinvested although their home governments favored codes of conduct. While no government banned trade with or ordered its firms out of Burma, consumer pressures dissuaded many firms from importing Burmese goods and municipal ordinances persuaded others to withdraw. Aung San Suu Kyi endorsed these measures as an indication of the growing importance of "consumer power," noting that "it's better to have the people of the world on your side than the governments."[140]

Some observers concur, inferring from this a serious challenge to sovereign notions of governance. NGO successes in the antiapartheid campaign, the Nestlé boycott, and many of the battles over labor and environmental practices, are harbingers of a new accountability imposed on MNCs not by governments, but by a form of global civil society. One legal scholar consequently concluded that when an NGO succeeds in persuading consumers, institutional investors, and local governments to share its preferences, its impact can "secure the same result as it could have with a regulatory victory."[141]

There is, however, an important difference between an NGO success and a regulatory victory. NGOs rely on *inducements*—namely, creating penalties for socially irresponsible behavior that cause firms to redefine what they calculate as profitable. They cannot exercise *commands*, compelling a firm to act against its economic self-interest. Only states can do that.

This inability to command corporate behavior explains the mixed record of the antiapartheid case. Grassroots pressures influenced international bankers and many foreign investors to equate their self-interest with the private credit boycott and disinvestment. In both cases, however, MNCs retained the autonomy to choose the form of disengagement that best served their interests. For banks, this involved spreading out South Africa's payments. For departing firms, it meant nonequity ties and the scaling back of social responsibility obligations. In sum, without the exercise of public authority, NGOs could augment the pressures on MNCs to withdraw, but could not insure that they did so in a way that comports with the NGOs' agenda.

This exclusive reliance on inducements also means that NGO influence diminishes proportionate to the size of the stake in question. This makes it unlikely that the antiapartheid movement's successes can be replicated by the Burmese and Nigerian campaigns. In the first case, the most costly private action was triggered by the U.S. banks, whose stake in South Africa was relatively small. And given the impact of their actions on South Africa's creditworthiness, even banks more exposed in South Africa were induced to comply with the sanctioners' demands.

If Myanmar and Nigeria had a comparable Achilles' heel, it was the oil industry. Yet, oil and other resource firms are less susceptible to NGO pressures than are banks, manufacturers, and retailers. As one observer explained, the former "must extract what they need and cannot quarrel with geography" while the latter "can retreat from investments and markets if the situation becomes too difficult."[142] Moreover, given the importance of Nigeria to Shell and the heavy investments by several firms in exploration and development in both countries, activists are unlikely to be able to exact a price high enough to elicit compliance with their demands. That would require the direct exercise of public authority, demonstrating a key difference between an NGO success and a regulatory victory.

This leads into a second caveat to the generalizability of the antiapartheid movement—that is, the role played by government policies in its success.

While it is difficult to disentangle the different factors that triggered corporate retrenchment from South Africa, the change in state policies in the mid-1980s played a key role. When the activists' agenda was resolutely opposed by governments, MNCs saw little need to respond to their entreaties. That changed once it became clear that Western governments would no longer play a supportive role. Chase Manhattan's decision to pull the plug on South Africa's debt was influenced not only by the hassle factor or deposits lost from state and local laws, it was also based on the recognition that the political climate and the congressional ban on IMF loans precluded the kinds of rescue packages necessary to ameliorate South Africa's financial crisis.

This dependence of NGO successes on at least a degree of state support weakens the applicability of the South African model to Myanmar and Nigeria. While Western governments stigmatized both regimes, an oil boycott or mandatory disinvestment were remote possibilities. The central reason for this is the high premium placed by Western governments on promoting energy investments. Unlike creditors and investors in South Africa, Western oil companies can discount the possibility that sanctions would make their decision to stay a risky alternative. Moreover, unlike South Africa's foreign creditors, business confidence in Nigeria and Myanmar is not dependent on supportive state policies, such as the availability of financial rescue packages. Therefore, a political climate that would make it difficult for states to provide assistance does not pose the same kinds of risks for oil companies in Myanmar and Nigeria as it did for creditors in South Africa.

Finally, the most potent instrument available to NGOs—municipal procurement power—depended on decentralized political structures that insulate local decision making from national control. In the 1980s and 1990s, American federalism shielded this instrument from legal challenge. Yet given the more centralized political structures in other industrialized democracies, alliances between NGOs and local governments were predominantly, if not exclusively, a U.S. phenomenon. This limited their transnational reach and impact on those firms not extensively involved in the United States.

American practice, however, may be less exceptional in the future. The Supreme Court's decision on the Massachusetts Burma Law narrows the ability of activists to use municipal budgets and pension funds to pressure MNCs. This indicates the fragility of several weapons in the NGO arsenal since they are dependent on the political and legal decisions of governmental actors. For example, SEC rulings facilitated shareholder activism against apartheid in the 1970s by granting wide latitude to social responsibility resolutions and constricted it in the 1990s by requiring that all resolutions must be connected to the company's fiduciary responsibilities. More recently, activists have used the Alien Tort Claims Act, passed by Congress in 1789 to allow civil actions for violations of the "law of nations or treaties of the United States," to enable Burmese refugees to file a class action suit against UNOCAL for its alleged use of forced labor in the Yadana project.[143] This strategy of using the judiciary to reach corporate conduct abroad was given a boost in 1997 when a federal district court ruled that it had jurisdiction over the case. That decision, however, could be overturned on appeal or by an act of Congress.[144] As Kenneth Waltz wrote, "[W]hile states may interfere little in the affairs of non-state actors for long periods of time, states nevertheless set the terms of the intercourse . . . [and] when the crunch comes, states remake the rules by which other actors operate."[145] The recent Supreme Court decision and the executive branch's shift from neutrality to outright support for the NFTC suit may indicate that the "crunch" is coming as governments try to remove what they see as irritants to economic globalization.

NOTES

1. Robert Kinloch Massie, *Loosing the Bonds: The United States and South Africa in the Apartheid Years* (New York: Doubleday, 1997), 695.

2. Peter Willetts, "Transnational Actors and International Organizations in Global Politics," 295.

3. Kathryn Sikkink, "Codes of Conduct for Transnational Corporations: The Case of the WHO/UNICEF Code," *International Organization* 40 (autumn 1986): 814–840.

4. See Peter J. Spiro, "New Global Potentates: NGOs and the 'Unregulated Marketplace,'" *Cardozo Law Review* 18 (December 1996): 958–963; Paul Wapner, "Politics beyond the State: Environmental Activism and World Civic Politics," *World Politics* 47 (April 1995): 311–340; and Simon Billenness, "Beyond South Africa: New Frontiers in Corporate Responsibility," *Business and Society Review* 86 (summer 1993): 28–31.

5. Massie, *Loosing the Bonds*, 695–696.

6. See Control Risks Group (CRG), *No Hiding Place: Business and the Politics of Pressure* (McLean, Va.: Control Risks Group, July 1997).

7. See CRG, *No Hiding Place,* 3–4; and "Multinationals and Their Morals," *Economist*, 12 December 1996, 18.

8. David Vogel, *Lobbying the Corporation*, ch. 1.

9. Earl H. Fry, *The Expanding Role of State and Local Governments in U.S. Foreign Affairs* (New York: Council on Foreign Relations, 1998), 94.

10. Sikkink, "Codes of Conduct for Transnational Corporations," 825.

11. Douglas Cassell, "Corporate Initiatives: A Second Human Rights Revolution," *Fordham International Law Journal* 19 (June 1996), 1963–1984.

12. CRG, *No Hiding Place*, 18–22.

13. Robin Grove-White, "Brent Spar Rewrote the Rules," *New Statesman*, 20 June 1997, 17–19.

14. Spiro, "New Global Potentates," 963.

15. See William Minter, *King Solomon's Mines Revisited: Western Interests and the Burdened History of Southern Africa* (New York: BasicBooks, 1987), 238–239; Robert K. Massey, *Loosing the Bonds*, ch. 3.

16. See Massey, *Loosing the Bonds*, 169, 193, 267–271.

17. *New York Times*, 20 March 1965, 11.

18. See Anthony Sampson, *Black and Gold: Tycoons, Revolutionaries, and Apartheid* (New York: Pantheon, 1987), 140.

19. George W. Shepherd, *Anti-Apartheid: Transnational Conflict and Western Policy in the Liberation of South Africa* (Westport, Conn.: Greenwood Press, 1977), ch. 3.

20. Shepherd, *Anti-Apartheid*, 140–141.

21. Shepherd, *Anti-Apartheid*, 145–148; Massey, *Loosing the Bonds*, 218–221.

22. Richard W. Hull, *American Enterprise in South Africa: Historical Dimensions of Engagement and Disengagement* (New York: New York University Press, 1990), 279.

23. Vogel, *Lobbying the Corporation*, 178–179.

24. Les De Villiers, *In Sight of Surrender: The U.S. Sanctions Campaign against South Africa* (Westport, Conn.: Greenwood Press, 1995), 49.

25. Testimony of George Vojta in U.S. House, *U.S. Policy Toward South Africa*, 531, 575.

26. Vogel, *Lobbying the Corporation*, 172.

27. Statement by William Broderick in U.S. House, *U.S. Private Investment in South Africa*, 136.

28. Anthony Sampson, *Black and Gold*, 25.

29. Desaix Myers III, *U.S. Business in South Africa: The Economic, Political, and Moral Issues* (Bloomington, Ind.: Indiana University Press, 1980), 93–95.

30. Hull, *American Enterprise in South Africa*, 312.

31. Hull, *American Enterprise in South Africa*, 308.

32. Cited in Vogel, *Lobbying the Corporation*, 179.

33. Massie, *Loosing the Bonds*, 443.

34. See Chester Crocker, "South Africa: Strategy for Change," *Foreign Affairs* 59 (winter 1980–1981): 323–351.

35. Sampson, *Black and Gold*, 29–31.

36. Robert M. Price, *The Apartheid State in Transition: Political Transformation in South Africa* (New York: Oxford University Press, 1991), 222–233.

37. *Economist*, 13 September 1986, 13.

38. See Alison Cooper, *International Bank Lending to South Africa* (Washington, D.C.: IRRC, September 1988), 329–333.

39. Richard Knight, "Sanctions, Disinvestment, and US Corporations in South Africa," in *Sanctioning Apartheid*, ed. Robert E. Edgar (Trenton, N.J.: Africa World Press, 1990), 81.

40. Testimony of John D. Zutter, Manufacturers Hanover Trust, in U.S. Congress, House Committee on Foreign Affairs, *Legislative Options and United States Policy Toward South Africa*, Hearings, 99th Cong., 2d sess., 1985, 170.

41. U.S. Congress, *Legislative Options and United States Policy Toward South Africa*, 164.

42. U.S. Congress, *Legislative Options and United States Policy Toward South Africa*, 71.

43. *New York Times*, 15 May 1995, sec. IV, 14.

44. *American Banker*, 2 October 1985, 14.

45. Minter, *King Solomon's Mines Revisited*, 319; Hull, *American Enterprise in South Africa*, ch. 6.

46. Knight, "Sanctions, Disinvestment, and US Corporations in South Africa," 80–81.

47. *Financial Times*, 19 February 1986, 16.

48. *Financial Times*, 22 November 1983, 4.

49. Richard Leonard, "Business and South Africa: Pressures against Apartheid Mount in the USA," *Multinational Business* 3 (1984): 15–17.

50. Massey, *Loosing the Bonds*, 586–587.

51. Knight, "Sanctions, Disinvestment, and US Corporations in South Africa," 85.

52. IRRC, "U.S. Banks and South Africa," Banking Report B, Supplement C, 12 March 1991, 4; on the U.S. banks, see *Financial Mail* (South Africa), 13 October 1989, 32.

53. IRRC, "U.S. Banks and South Africa," 12.

54. See *American Banker*, 13 September 1989, 6, and 5 October 1989, 7.

55. *Financial Times*, 22 September 1989, 4.

56. Martin Holland, "Disinvestment, Sanctions, and the European Community's Code of Conduct in South Africa," *African Affairs* 88 (October 1989): 529.

57. See William F. Moses, *A Guide to American State and Local Laws on South Africa* (Washington, D.C.: IRRC, August 1992), 14, 145–146; and Jennifer D. Kibbe, *Divestment on Campus: Issues and Implementation* (Washington, D.C.: IRRC, 1989).

58. See De Villiers, *In Sight of Surrender*, 55–57; and Massey, *Loosing the Bonds,* 613.

59. Moses, *Guide to American State and Local Laws on South Africa*, 1.

60. Moses, *Guide to American State and Local Laws on South Africa*, 13.

61. Crehan (Johannesburg) to Secretary of State, "Update on Divestment," 30 October 1987, Johannesburg 02287 (DOS/FOIA).

62. Business International, *A Fresh Look at South Africa*, 5.

63. Stephen R. Lewis Jr., *The Economics of Apartheid* (New York: Council on Foreign Relations, 1990), 109.

64. Allan R. Janger and Ronald E. Berenbeim, *External Challenges to Management Decisions: A Growing Business Problem* (New York: The Conference Board, 1981), 22 (emphasis in original).

65. IRRC, *South African Reporter*, June 1989, 17.

66. *Financial Times*, 9 June 1988, 2(S).

67. For an overview, see David Hauck, "What Happens When U.S. Companies Sell Their South African Operations," IRRC, South Africa Review Service, May 1987.

68. Hull, *American Enterprise in South Africa*, 334.

69. Hauck, "What Happens," 9.

70. *New York Times*, 20 March 1985, 14.

71. Business International, *Critical Issues Monitor*, April 1986, 30.

72. IRRC, "U.S. Business in South Africa," 1990 Analysis C, 29 December 1989, 3–7.

73. IRRC, "U.S. Business in South Africa," 6.

74. *Wall Street Journal*, 4 June 1987, 2.

75. Keith Ovenden and Tony Cole, *Apartheid and International Finance: A Program for Change* (Victoria, Australia: Penguin Books, 1989), 157.

76. The IRRC reported that only one former affiliate allowed external monitoring of its workplace practices and that the average contribution of such firms to community development had declined by 50 percent. See Jennifer Kibbe and David Hauck, "Leaving South Africa: The Impact of U.S. Corporate Disinvestment," IRRC, South Africa Review Service, July 1988, 18–20.

77. IRRC, "Withdrawal of U.S. Companies from South Africa: GM Corporation," Social Issues Service, Proxy Investor Reports, 1988, Analysis A, 28 April 1988, 484–486.

78. Kibbe, *Divestment on Campus*, 19–20.

79. IRRC, "Withdrawal of U.S. Companies from South Africa and Ending Non-Equity Ties," 1989 Analysis C, 13 December 1988, 14–17.

80. IRRC, "Withdrawal of U.S. Companies from South Africa and Ending Non-Equity Ties," 1990 Analysis C, 2 January 1990, 1.

81. IRRC, *South African Reporter*, March 1991, 6, and June 1991, 5.

82. Moses, *A Guide to State and Local Laws*, 7.

83. Business International, *Critical Issues Monitor*, August 1986, 36.

84. Moses, *A Guide to State and Local Laws*, 7–8; the Justice Department concluded a comparable study in 1986 finding divestment ordinances to be constitutional and advising against filing suit against them or filing an amicus brief on behalf of those who challenged them. See Department of Justice, Office of Legal Counsel, "Constitutionality of South African Divestment Statutes Enacted by State and Local Governments," 9 April 1986.

85. Business International, *Critical Issues Monitor*, December 1985, 13.

86. Business International, *Critical Issues Monitor*, April 1987, 16.

87. IRRC, *South Africa Reporter*, March 1988,11; Craig Forcese, "Municipal Buying Power and Human Rights in Burma: The Case for Canadian Municipal Selective Purchasing Policies," *University of Toronto Faculty of Law Review* 56 (spring 1998): 268–271.

88. Data derived from IRRC, "Facts and Figures on South Africa: Answers to 12 Frequently Asked Questions," August 1990, 3, and February 1993, 30–31.

89. In 1997, the SLORC was renamed the State Peace and Development Council.

90. Donald Seekins, "Burma in 1998: Little to Celebrate," *Asian Survey* 39 (January–February 1999): 12–19.

91. IRRC, *Corporate Social Issues Reporter*, February 1997, 14.

92. IRRC, *Corporate Social Issues Reporter*, April/May 1996, 9.

93. *Multinational Monitor*, June 1996, 6.

94. *Congressional Quarterly Weekly Report*, 27 July 1996, 2131, and 5 October 1996, 2877.

95. *New York Times*, 22 May 1997, 1(D).

96. *Oil Daily*, 22 May 1997; and *Platt's Oilgram News*, 2 July 1997, 3.

97. *Financial Times*, 4 April 1997, 3.

98. See the Free Burma Coalition's Web site at www.freeburmacoalition.org.

99. *BusinessWeek* (22 April 1996, 53) reported that seventy-five U.S. colleges and universities have boycotted movements associated with Burma.

100. Unlike the apartheid case, proxy resolutions calling for disinvestment or the suspension of investments until the restoration of democracy or the release of political prisoners were ruled out of order by the SEC as unrelated to the fiduciary responsibilities of the companies. Hence, proxy resolutions had to be more directly connected to the company's fiduciary responsibilities. See IRRC, *Social Issues Reporter*, January 1996, 6.

101. Organization for International Investment, "State and Local Sanctions Watch List," 11 May 1999 (reproduced on the USA-Engage Web page at www.usaengage.com).

102. EIU, *Myanmar*, Country Report, 1997, no. 1, 10.

103. *Financial Times*, 28 January 1997, 6.

104. See *Washington Post*, 4 March 1997, C1; *Los Angeles Times*, 19 June 1997, D1.

105. *Financial Times*, 24 April 1997, 9.

106. *Financial Times*, 6 February 1997, 6.

107. IRRC, *Corporate Social Issues Reporter*, December 1996, 14, and March 1997, 11.

108. *Economist*, 8 February 1997, 32.

109. Two U.S. oil companies (Arco and Texaco) withdrew after the initiation of the campaign. The former left after disappointing results (*Platt's Oilgram News*, 12 August 1998, 3). The latter had a more significant stake and may have been influenced by public relations in the United States, particularly after allegations of racial discrimination jolted the company. Nonetheless, the withdrawal had little impact on Myanmar since it sold its $260 million stake to its U.K. partner, Premier Oil (*Financial Times*, 23 September 1997, 33).

110. IRRC, *Corporate Social Issues Reporter*, April–May 1996, 10; *BusinessWeek*, 5 May 1997, 40.

111. IRRC, *Corporate Social Issues Reporter*, February 1997, 13.

112. *Journal of Commerce*, 2 May 1997, 3A, and 23 July 1997, 5(A).

113. *Journal of Commerce*, 28 December 1998, 1(A).

114. See *Washington Post*, 4 March 1997, 1(C).

115. *Journal of Commerce*, 8 September 1997, 6(A).

116. IRRC, *Corporate Social Issues Reporter*, November 1998, 20.

117. *New York Times*, 23 March 2000, 20(A).

118. *New York Times*, 20 June 2000, 23(A).

119. Bronwen Manby, *The Price of Oil: Corporate Responsibility and Human Rights Violations in Nigeria's Oil Producing Communities* (New York: Human Rights Watch, 1999), ch. 8.

120. Manby, *Price of Oil*, 161–162.

121. *New York Times*, 3 December 1995, sec. IV, 14.

122. *Financial Times*, 16 December 1995, 3.

123. *Times* (London), 21 November 1996, 31.

124. *Oil Daily*, 18 December 1995, 4.

125. *Oil Daily*, 29 December 1995, 3.

126. For a detailed reporting on the failed sanctions effort, see *Washington Post*, 24 November 1996, C1.

127. *New York Times*, 12 March 1996, A1.

128. EIU, *Nigeria*, Country Report, 1996, no. 1, 8–9.

129. *African Business*, January 1996, 17.

130. *Reuters Business Report*, 13 November 1995.

131. *Inter Press Service*, 14 November 1995.

132. IRRC, *Corporate Social Issues Reporter*, January 1997; *New York Times*, 15 May 1997, D4.

133. IRRC, *Corporate Social Issues Reporter*, October 1997, 12.

134. IRRC, *Corporate Social Issues Reporter*, March 1997, 12.

135. EIU, *Nigeria*, Country Report, 1996, no. 3, 19.

136. *Financial Times*, 18 March 1997, 24.

137. *African Business*, January 1996, 18.

138. *Offshore*, May 1997, 36.

139. EIU, *Nigeria*, Country Report, 1998, no. 2, 21.

140. *Montreal Gazette*, 4 August 1998, B1.

141. Spiro, "New Global Potentates," 959.

142. Martin Woollacott, "Are Businesses Forced to Keep Bad Company?" *Business and Society Review* 95 (fall 1995), 45.

143. Robert J. Peterson, "Political Realism and the Imposition of Secondary Sanctions," *University of Chicago Law School Roundtable* 5 (1998): 291–292.

144. In August 2000, the UNOCAL case was dismissed not because of the inapplicability of the law, but because UNOCAL did not directly participate in the abuses. As of this writing, the decision is being appealed. See Elizabeth Amon, "Coming to America," *National Law Journal* (20 October 2000): A1.

145. Kenneth N. Waltz, *Theory of International Politics* (Reading, Mass.: Addison-Wesley, 1979), 94.

Conclusion

This book began by trying to explain a paradox. Why did we see the resurgence of extraterritorial sanctions in the 1990s, a decade after the most spectacular failure of this instrument? That episode had generated a scholarly and policy consensus that such measures do not work. Most observers predicted that comparable sanctions would not be enacted in the future and that American multinationals would be freer to promote their global economic interests regardless of the impact on public strategies of economic statecraft. Subsequent sanctions, however, have not only attempted to reach MNCs more often than in the past, they have also elicited a greater degree of corporate compliance than was predicted after the pipeline case.

These outcomes raise two questions about the generalizability of the pipeline experience. First, do they refute the theoretical perspectives that inform the conventional wisdom regarding extraterritorial sanctions? The answer is a qualified yes. The evidence indicates that much of the globalization literature exaggerates the degree to which MNCs have freed themselves from their parent states, at least in the area of economic sanctions. The hegemonic decline explanation overstates the ability of the United States to enforce its preferences in the early Cold War era and understates the potentially coercive impact of denying access to the U.S. market today. Domestic politics — namely, the intensity of interest group, public, and/or congressional commitment to the sanctions — was a better predictor of the use and influence of extraterritorial sanctions than was the position of the United States in the world economy. The impact of international rules and institutions as a restraining influence of extraterritorial coercion correlated more strongly with the intensity of societal and congressional support for the sanctions than with the structural position of the United States in the world economy.

Second, should the challenges to the theory lead to a reevaluation of the prescriptive case against extraterritorial sanctions in a post–Cold War environment that some have characterized as a second era of American hegemony? The answer to that question is mostly no. In some limited cases, policymakers blocked strategically significant transactions. For the most part, success involved corporate behavior that was either of marginal importance or readily replaceable by competitors. Whatever inconvenience this imposed on target states must also be balanced against the costs to alliance relations and international institutions on which the United States increasingly depends. To illustrate these points, the concluding chapter assesses the implications of the case material for both the globalization and hegemonic decline models.

MULTINATIONAL CORPORATIONS
AND THE LIMITS OF GLOBALIZATION

One of the principal findings of this study is that MNCs are less free of parent state control than is indicated by much of the literature on transnational relations and globalization. Those theories are most successful in explaining changes in the corporate mind-set away from an ethnocentric identification with U.S. foreign policy aims. When confronted with the prospect of sanctions, most firms tried to separate business from politics, even in dealing with adversaries. If there were conflicts between home and host countries, corporate preferences were aligned with the latter. Direct investors in target states sought to protect their assets by maintaining their political neutrality and lobbying for normalized relations. Foreign subsidiaries in third countries sided with their hosts in opposing the extraterritorial extension of American law.

In theory, this change in corporate worldview suggests that MNCs were more willing to use the cracks between jurisdictions to insulate their offshore operations from political accountability. In practice, they were less willing to use "regulatory arbitrage." Foreign subsidiaries in third countries did not avail themselves of blocking legislation when extraterritorial sanctions were invoked and often held back from transactions that were technically legal when they were not. Direct investors in target states at least initially followed Washington's lead during confrontations with host countries. Some MNCs even modified their behavior in response to pressures from grassroots organizations and state and local governments. In other words, aspiring to statelessness in the area of sanctions is not the same thing as escaping political accountability.

MNCs were often inhibited from pursuing their economic interests with target states in the face of intensely held state or societal pressures because of calculations of political risk. One reason why these risks were compelling is because MNCs are more dependent on their home markets than is suggested by some globalization theorists. This is the conclusion of a number of recent studies that have taken issue with the "strong version of the globalization thesis" that views MNCs as "nationalityless"[1] and the state as relatively powerless to hold them accountable. They found that MNCs are still closely tied to their home states, which is where they locate most of their assets and employees, recruit most of their top managers, and do the bulk of their research and development. In addition, most shares are owned by nationals and institutions of the home state, vesting control in persons subject to U.S. jurisdiction. This dependence on the home market and the liability of U.S. shareholders enables the state to continue to exercise governance over MNCs, calling into question the purported emergence of a "new era of state denial."[2]

This ability to exercise governance was evident in the cases. It was unambiguous when the United States asserted direct extraterritorial jurisdiction. Foreign subsidiaries in both third countries and target states complied with U.S. directives unless the host country used its territorial sovereignty to force the issue. None solicited host country blocking orders, which were designed to protect their business with target states from U.S. law. To do so would have risked criminal penalties if U.S. citizens or the home office were involved and severe fines if they were not. The subsidiary would risk denial of access to the U.S. market, a penalty that might jeopardize its viability. These risks were usually compelling even when the reach of the law was imprecise. In fact, some regulations were intentionally crafted ambiguously to chill investment without alienating allies. The resulting uncertainty, notes Thomas Walde, means that few firms will "sail close to the legal wind."[3]

Even without the formal exercise of jurisdiction, MNCs were reluctant to maintain ties with adversaries in ways that violated intensely held state preferences. In Iran and Libya, most notably, oil companies held back from opportunities that were technically legal and potentially profitable. Direct investors often tried to enforce Treasury directives beyond the letter of the law. Public officials may have been less able to rely on moral suasion by appealing to a shared belief in anticommunism, as in the early Cold War era. Corporations nonetheless did not want to alienate the federal government, on whom they depended to promote their interests through a variety of services, such as export assistance, negotiations over market access, and eligibility for government contracts. This creates a relationship that policymakers can use to increase the congruence between private behavior and public interests. As Ethan Kapstein noted, "[M]ost firms know who their home government is, and they recognize the importance of maintaining a good relationship with it."[4]

Another reason for corporate sensitivity to U.S. foreign policy is the impact of diplomatic hostility on the environment in which they do business. Escalating confrontations between Washington and prospective target states create uncertainties regarding a wide variety of political risks—such as, political instability, financial insolvency, or the risk of future sanctions that might mandate disinvestment or create a conflict of jurisdictions. Unless the target state has a lucrative resource such as oil, most investors will stay away or limit their exposure until the uncertainties are resolved. These uncertainties also create incentives for withdrawal in anticipation of worst-case scenarios, as evidenced in the departure of Castle & Cooke from Nicaragua, Exxon and Mobil from Libya, and two-thirds of U.S. direct investors from South Africa.

The uncertainties were compounded if a country's creditworthiness depends on external factors that the United States can influence, either through trade and aid sanctions or denial of access of international financial institutions (IFIs). For example, relatively favorable diplomatic approaches toward Nicaragua, during the Carter administration, and South Africa, in the early Reagan years, facilitated pragmatic adjustments in the former case and an expansion of lending to the private sector in the latter case. The expectations of creditors were rewarded by the Carter administration's support for MDB loans to Nicaragua and the Reagan administration's support for the 1982 IMF loan to South Africa. As U.S. foreign policy became more hostile, lenders could no longer forecast continued assistance and had to factor into their projections the likelihood that U.S. policies would deliberately attempt to impair the debtor's economic and social stability. The end result was that the private creditors never fully normalized their relationship with Nicaragua and investors and lenders preemptively repatriated capital from South Africa when conditions deteriorated.

These risks were also compelling if there was strong societal support for the sanctions, even if the executive branch was ambivalent. MNCs may view such sanctions as less legitimate because they "are produced for reasons of short-term political interest and agitation, destroy significant business opportunities, and even pass on hard-won gains to foreign competitors."[5] When political pressures are intense, however, defiance of the spirit of the sanctions could trigger more punitive legislation (as in the case of Conoco in Iran) or pressure on the executive branch to administer the law more rigorously (as in the case of foreign subsidiaries and the CDA). Controversial investments can also create problems with workers, shareholders, and customers, particularly in emotionally charged cases such as South Africa during the apartheid era or Libya after Lockerbie. This reluctance to make oneself a target not only provides public decision makers with the leverage of adverse publicity, it also enables NGOs to influence corporate decision making by mobilizing protests, boycotts, shareholder resolutions, and municipal sanctions.

How then can we explain those cases in which MNCs ignored these risks and maintained their ties with target states? A few caveats are therefore necessary to establish the conditions under which political actors can influence corporate decision making.

First, extraterritorial sanctions failed when they overtly collided with the blocking powers of host countries. Daniel Drezner notes that states, unlike MNCs, are more likely to risk economic retaliation if sovereignty issues are engaged. Their intervention "stiffen[s] the backbone of corporations" by transforming the conflict into an interstate dispute.[6] The case studies indicate that the deterrent impact of blocking actions was effective only when compliance with extraterritorial directives was visible—either because it required the abrogation of contracts (the *Fruehauf* and Dresser cases), mandated overt violation of the law (ordering subsidiaries to refuse to pay taxes in Panama or supply oil in Haiti), or was publicized and engaged the prestige of the host country (Wal-Mart in Canada).

Second, those cases in which MNCs preserved business ties with target states coincided with ambivalent executive branch policies and the absence of strong countervailing societal pressures. For example, foreign subsidiaries increased their Cuban trade in the 1980s because the Reagan administration saw few coercive benefits in targeting hard-currency trade for widely available goods (mostly food) and there were no strong societal pressures to alter this calculation until the early 1990s. Foreign investors who stayed in Nicaragua and oil companies who expanded their operations in Angola were never asked to leave since policymakers concluded that the private costs of disinvestment exceeded its contributions to economic statecraft. Oil companies collaborated with South Africa in circumventing the oil embargo of Rhodesia only after it was clear that Washington and London were not committed to the sanctions. U.S. contractors in Libya transferred their operations from their U.S. to European offices, while U.S. oil companies did not, because government pressure was placed on the latter, which was seen as resource-generating, as opposed to the former, which was seen as resource-absorbing.

Third, since informal pressures rely on inducements rather than commands, their influence is a function of the importance of a particular stake for the MNC. Those companies that voluntarily policed their subsidiaries or withdrew in response to increasing political conflict were generally large diversified firms for whom the question represented a small fraction of their global operations. Those firms most willing to stay in politicized environments (e.g., the independent oil companies in Libya) or "sail close to the legal wind" (e.g., Coastal Corporation in Libya) were either not part of a larger multinational structure or were more dependent on their local operations.

This finding has implications for both secondary and nongovernmental sanctions, both of which rely on inducements rather than commands—the former, since it cannot assert jurisdiction over foreign entities; the latter, since it does not control the regulatory apparatus in Washington. These pressures were most compelling when the stakes were low relative to the risk of the penalties in the U.S. market. As a result, Helms–Burton and ILSA deterred several MNCs with significant assets in the United States. Antiapartheid pressures persuaded many corporations and banks to disengage because the costs imposed in terms of board time and lost municipal contracts exceeded stakes that represented a small fraction of global sales, assets, and loan portfolios.

A corollary to this is that inducements were least influential when the size of the stake exceeded the costs and risks of penalties in the United States. Secondary sanctions were unable to reverse the most significant investments in Cuba (Sherritt's nickel operations) or Iran (Total's South Pars deal). Similarly, attempts to replicate the antiapartheid movement vis-à-vis Myanmar and Nigeria had little influence over energy investments, which have been the most significant generators of revenue for both regimes. In other words, those stakes that were most critical to the staying power of target states were least susceptible to strategies of inducement.

Fourth, the ability to affect business confidence is limited to those cases in which a target state's creditworthiness is vulnerable to U.S. action. What Nicaragua and South Africa had in common was that they were heavily dependent on foreign borrowing and their creditworthiness was critically linked to access to IFIs. In both cases, the United States could attack their creditworthiness, through its financial veto of MDB loans to Nicaragua and the congressional ban on supporting IMF rescue packages to South Africa. If business confidence in the target state is less susceptible to U.S. action, there are limits to U.S. influence. Angola's creditworthiness, for example, was not as vulnerable to U.S. policy. Although the United States denied Eximbank credits and blocked Angola's entry into the IMF, oil companies had little difficulty obtaining private credits because of Angola's expanding oil production in the 1980s. Similarly, the political storm over the Eximbank loan to Gazprom following its participation in Total's South Pars deal in Iran was irrelevant because the Russian company could raise comparable financing in European capital markets.

In sum, there were circumstances in which political actors were able to defy globalization and influence not only the foreign subsidiaries of U.S. firms, but foreign corporations as well. Supporters of extraterritorial sanctions often defend their utility by citing these cases of corporate compliance. This is a claim one should treat with caution. It is true that in a few cases (e.g., Operation Exodus, bank lending to South Africa), these efforts did inflict significant economic costs on target states. In most cases, they did not.

Formal sanctions and informal pressures persuaded foreign subsidiaries to cut their ties with Cuba and Iran but could not prevent foreign competitors from picking up those contracts to sell agricultural goods to Cuba or develop Iran's energy resources. Secondary sanctions deterred many non-U.S. firms from investing in Cuba and Iran; they also provided opportunities for firms not actively involved in the United States and were ineffective vis-à-vis the most economically significant investments. Direct investors in target states were initially willing to follow Treasury directives. Asking them to act as fifth columns, however, placed them in an impossible situation vis-à-vis the sovereign powers of state on whose territory they were operating (as in Rhodesia, Panama, and Haiti). Forcing them to disinvest meant abandoning valuable assets to the target state, providing it with an unintended windfall, as the Reagan administration learned in Libya. Multinationals may be less footloose than the globalization literature implies, but controlling their behavior is not the same as successful economic statecraft.

THE LIMITED EXPLANATORY POWER
OF THE HEGEMONIC DECLINE MODEL

The evidence also raises questions about the hegemonic decline model, which has difficulty explaining the reluctance to use coercion in the early Cold War era and the expanded reach of U.S. sanctions in the 1990s. Domestic politics provides a better explanation of both the use of extraterritorial sanctions and their ability to elicit corporate compliance. In addition, interdependence considerations, particularly the corrosive impact of coercion on multilateral institutions, inhibited executive branch enforcement during the entire period under review, though their influence was inversely correlated to the intensity of societal and congressional support for sanctions. These points will be illustrated by dividing the case analysis into three periods: (1) enforcement of the Chinese and Cuban embargoes in the 1950s and 1960s; (2) the retreat from extraterritorial sanctions in the 1970s and 1980s; and (3) the return of extraterritorial sanctions in the 1990s.

First, the United States eschewed unilateral coercion when it was economically dominant. Outside of reexport controls on strategic technology, it rejected proposals for the systematic blacklisting of firms that traded with adversaries and sought discreet compromises in conflicts of jurisdiction over foreign subsidiaries. One reason for this restraint was the cost of enforcement to international institutions. The hegemonic model assumes that concentrated resources translate into economic leverage and interdependence goals play a limited role for the hegemon, which is capable of promoting its interests through self-help. This argument ignores the liberal character of U.S. policy and the premium it placed on maintaining durable international institutions that would outlive American dominance. John Ikenberry notes that one consequence of this was that "there were real limits to the coercive pursuit of the American postwar agenda."[7] This logic informed U.S. restraint on extraterritorial coercion, which could have damaged the cohesion of NATO, weakened Co-Com's consensus on strategic export controls, and undermined U.S. leadership in liberalizing world trade through the GATT.

Restraint was also seen as necessary to insulate diplomatic relations from anti-American sentiment abroad. The hegemonic model discounts this issue, presuming that states are unitary rational actors and that bargaining is a function of relative power positions. Yet in democratic states, societal forces can shape and constrain foreign policy behavior. Thomas Risse-Kappen notes that the need not to alienate European public opinion—something allies often wielded in negotiations—set limits on American unilateralism within NATO.[8] Projections about political repercussions abroad also dissuaded policymakers from exercising extraterritorial coercion. Overtly applying foreign subsidiary sanctions in Canada could have aroused economic nationalism, which would have created a climate less hospitable to U.S. investment and poisoned bilateral relations. Comparable concerns led to a discreet retreat from enforcement in Europe after the *Fruehauf* case. As the U.S. ambassador to France recommended, it was "prudent to withdraw quietly from a position of questionable value" because using U.S. firms as instruments of foreign policy will incite Gaullist attacks on U.S. investment as "economic colonialism."[9]

Why, then, did these regulations stay on the books despite the fact that they led to recurrent conflicts with allies and resulted in waivers in the majority of cases? The answer lies in U.S. domestic politics—that is, the intensity of anticommunism in the American political system and its representation in Congress. If an administration was seen as indifferent to allied "trading with the enemy" there were many policy entrepreneurs in Congress who would try to politicize the issue. That could lead to legislation mandating reprisals and eliminating the flexibility the executive branch had in implementing the sanctions. These concerns also inhibited public confrontations with allies over the enforcement of foreign subsidiary sanctions since this might raise public expectations and increase the likelihood of congressional activism if those expectations were not realized. As a result, policymakers preferred discreet compromise to overt enforcement.

Nonetheless, the intensity of anticommunism in the American political system deterred foreign subsidiary trade with China and Cuba because of the credibility of reprisals in the U.S. market. Even though the administration routinely pursued a risk-averse policy in issuing waivers, there were few applications and many licensed transactions were never consummated. In staying away, firms had to consider not only the risk of alienating Washington, but also the risks in the U.S. market from consumer boycotts and public campaigns. In this sense, there were parallels between anticommunist societal pressures in inhibiting East–West trade in the 1950s and 1960s and the antiapartheid movement in inducing significant corporate withdrawal from South Africa in the 1980s.

Second, the retreat from extraterritoriality in the 1970s—particularly the removal of third country sanctions from the Cuban embargo—was not due primarily to the decline of U.S. economic dominance. After all, the United States had not coerced allied cooperation in the early postwar era. Allies and MNCs were more aggressive and successful in challenging extraterritorial strictures because anticommunism was a less-compelling frame of reference in the 1970s, changing the domestic political landscape. Societal pressures were more strongly arrayed against the Cuban embargo—that is, a public opinion more open to détente with communist states, a post-Vietnam/Watergate Congress more skeptical of Cold War policies and executive branch power, and a business community emboldened to press for a liberalization of East–West trade. These changes decreased the credibility of reprisals against allies and foreign subsidiaries for challenging the Cuban embargo. They also created an incentive for the administration to rein in the scope of its controls since, in contrast to the earlier era, conflicts with allies were more likely to elicit congressional rescission of the sanctions, rather than mandatory reprisals.

The Reagan administration tried to reverse this trend through the pipeline sanctions. This effort, however, represented a departure from traditional diplomatic priorities, not a nostalgic return to a bygone era of American hegemony. It failed not because the United States lacked the economic clout to influence corporate decision making; Dresser and most of the foreign licensees caught in the sanctions net were initially willing to comply with U.S. directives.[10] Rather, it failed because compliance required the abrogation of binding contracts on the territory of sovereign states that were strongly committed to their performance. Unlike its predecessors, the Reagan administration dismissed the costs of enforcement to multilateral institutions and the stimulation of anti-American public sentiment in Europe. Ultimately, those costs persuaded it to rescind the pipeline sanctions and exempt foreign subsidiaries from all subsequent sanctions. It was this retreat, not extraterritorial coercion, that represented the return to the practices of an earlier era.

As in the Cuban case, domestic politics was a restraining force on unilateral coercion during the pipeline sanctions.[11] Those sanctions differed fundamentally from the foreign subsidiary sanctions of an earlier era because their impetus came from "grand strategy" not from societal pressures. The business community was more aggressive in lobbying against the pipeline sanctions and, subsequently, the wide discretion granted to the president through the Export Administration Act. Its allies in Congress came closer than ever before to setting limits on the executive branch's export control authority. The administration's concern about the fraying consensus behind export controls was one of the reasons why it was more circumspect in the scope of its post-pipeline sanctions. In explaining the territorial limits on subsequent sanctions, one legal scholar noted that "a generation of congressional and Executive Branch policymakers received an education on some of the limits of unilateral sanctions in terms of efficiency and cost."[12]

Finally, the hegemonic decline model understates the potential of the United States to influence corporate conduct abroad even if it no longer occupies the same position it did immediately after World War II. The United States is still the largest and most open economy in the world. The threat of denying access to it or penalizing behavior within it represents a compelling risk to foreign subsidiaries and many non-U.S. firms significantly involved in the United States. Host countries may be able to block the nullification of contracts on their territory; they are less able to prevent their MNCs from factoring into their calculations the risk of penalties in the U.S. market.

This was evident in Operation Exodus, in which the Reagan administration strengthened extraterritorial controls over the reexport of U.S. computer and telecommunications technology. The key difference between this effort and the pipeline sanctions, according to George Shambaugh, was the European firms' dependence on U.S. suppliers, which dominated the market.[13] EC firms objected to the conditions attached to imports of U.S. technology, but nonetheless complied. European governments protested the enforcement of U.S. regulations on their territory, but did not interfere with these arrangements. If they did, conceded one U.K. official, British industry would be "denied access to U.S. technology not available elsewhere."[14]

Blocking legislation was similarly irrelevant to corporate compliance with the extraterritorial sanctions of the 1990s. The CDA, the first extraterritorial sanction since the pipeline case, virtually ended foreign subsidiary trade with Cuba. Canadian and British blocking orders could have prevented the voiding of contracts in their jurisdiction or intervened in visible cases. They could not reverse decisions by subsidiaries to terminate their Cuban trade quietly so as not to expose their parents to liability. Helms–Burton and ILSA initially had a chilling effect on business confidence because they held foreign firms' U.S. assets hostage. EU and Canadian blocking orders could not assuage the risk of indeterminate litigation from Helms–Burton or lost business opportunities through ILSA.

One of the central reasons why these sanctions influenced foreign corporate behavior was because of the potency of interest group and congressional constituencies behind them. This made credible the imposition of costs for proscribed behavior—namely, criminal and/or civil penalties for the home office if its subsidiary trades with Cuba, the likelihood of indeterminate litigation as long as Helms–Burton remains on the books, the risks of being penalized in the U.S. market for investment in Iran's oil industry. The weakening of the domestic consensus behind the Cuban and Iranian embargoes in the late 1990s has decreased the likelihood of penalties. That change in U.S. domestic politics has been more significant than host country blocking orders in decreasing the risks attached to Cuban and Iranian investments.

Some observers have seen the resurgence of extraterritorial sanctions as evidence of a continuing or resurgent American hegemony. That premise is implicit in the congressional rationale for secondary sanctions, which assumes that U.S. market power is so overwhelming that foreign MNCs have little choice but to comply with U.S. law. According to one international lawyer, the end of the Cold War augments Washington's economic clout because the disappearance of a superpower adversary reduces the need to subordinate enforcement to alliance cohesion.[15] Some critics of American unilateralism have adopted a parallel argument. Referring to Helms–Burton, one Canadian scholar wrote: "[T]he United States can engage in such presumptuousness because it is a superordinate power. Other governments will grumble at American arrogance, but in the end they will fold . . . when all is said and done, states value their links with the United States more than the little trade they are able to squeeze out of [the Cuban] economy."[16]

Some defenders of extraterritorial sanctions have also seen them as part of a bargaining process designed to strengthen third country compliance with international law in areas in which consensus is limited and enforcement mechanisms are weak.[17] The United States has often used unilateral sanctions to bolster multilateral regimes. For example, the threat of congressional retaliation after the Toshiba case enabled the Reagan administration to persuade Japan to upgrade its enforcement of CoCom rules. Unilateral and secondary sanctions through the Marine Mammals Protection Act (which were found to be contrary to GATT) led to the negotiation of the Panama Declaration, which limited the number of collateral dolphin deaths from tuna fishing.[18] In a "one-superpower" world, the United States is purportedly more capable of playing this role than in the past. Thus conceived, the unilateral threat of sanctions under Helms–Burton and ILSA has been characterized as a successful example of coercive diplomacy, moving the EU closer to U.S. positions on investing in expropriated property and exporting strategic technology.[19]

The evidence presented in this book provides reasons for skepticism toward these claims. First, as noted in the previous section, increased corporate compliance with extraterritorial sanctions has not usually translated into the imposition of significant costs on adversaries. Cutting off foreign subsidiary trade imposed some transitional costs, but that was quickly replaced by wholly foreign corporations. Helms–Burton and ILSA deterred new investments from firms with substantial U.S. assets. They could not reverse the most strategically significant foreign investments or deter joint ventures by firms not as heavily involved in the U.S. market. The only exception to this was Operation Exodus, which limited the diffusion of strategically significant exports. The lesson that should be drawn from this is that extraterritorial sanctions ought to be limited to those critical technologies where U.S. industry occupies a dominant position.

Second, the most recent third country sanctions are not examples of "rational governments pursuing rational foreign policy objectives against equally rational governments."[20] Neither the Bush nor the Clinton administrations welcomed them as opportunities for hegemonic coercion and only reluctantly signed the bills for domestic political reasons (not coincidentally, in election years). Rather, their origins lie in societal forces that were represented in the Congress. As in the early Cold War era, the aim of deterring Congress from legislating more punitive reprisals provided the impetus behind U.S. negotiations with allies.

This is why it is probably misleading to characterize the 1998 U.S.–EU accord as a successful exercise in coercive diplomacy. The expropriation disciplines—the EU's most significant concession—are contingent on congressional revision of Title IV of Helms–Burton, an unlikely outcome as long as Jesse Helms and Fidel Castro are still alive. EU commitments on WMD exports do not differ substantially from previous agreements. Given the risks of both a damaging WTO grievance procedure and congressional pressures for a more punitive policy, the 1998 accord is better understood not as substantive cooperation, but as cooperation to contain the conflict and avoid loss.[21]

A final argument against extraterritorial sanctions is their impact on interdependence goals. Economic globalization magnifies the salience of these goals because the promotion of national interests increasingly requires stronger multilateral institutions, the need to sustain international rules governing the world economy, and the maintenance of a reputation for reliability as an economic partner. It is the damage that Helms–Burton and ILSA do to these goals—not the purported liberation of MNCs from the nation-state—that makes the case that globalization renders such policies counterproductive.

First, extraterritorial coercion weakens international institutions designed to assert political accountability over international business activity. This is because allies are less likely to view U.S. actions as law enforcement (as Japan may have in the Toshiba case since it was a member of CoCom), but as lawless efforts to impose preferences not shared by others. As a result, coercion in areas of divergent interests is likely to complicate multilateral agreements when there is an attainable consensus (e.g., a business code of conduct and human rights linkages to foreign aid in Cuba, establishing conditions for debt rescheduling or enacting stronger strategic export controls vis-à-vis Iran).

Second, there are reciprocity costs by ignoring rules the United States prescribed for others. Secondary sanctions compromise its leadership in the world economy by using instruments condemned when practiced by the Arab League against Israel. This, in turn, sets precedents to which the United States might object if practiced by China against Taiwan. Similarly, public repudiation of WTO jurisdiction undermines the credibility of stronger dispute resolution mechanisms that the United States was instrumental in creating.

Third, extraterritorial sanctions impose reputational costs in line with George Shultz's warnings about "light-switch diplomacy." Extending sanctions to foreign subsidiaries makes it difficult for them to obtain national treatment because they can be commanded to follow U.S. political preferences at the expense of host state economic interests. Retroactively asserting jurisdiction over technology sales calls into question the reliability of U.S. firms as business partners and creates incentives for non-U.S. firms to look elsewhere. Holding foreign assets in the United States hostage to secondary sanctions increases the risks attached to the United States as a site for foreign investment.

Congressional proponents of extraterritorial sanctions dismiss these costs. In part, this is because they are influenced by interest group politics in which demonstrating a zealous defense of their constituencies is more important than the international repercussions of legislation. Yet this approach implicitly presumes a unipolar view of world politics that sees multilateral institutions as less necessary for U.S. foreign policy. The United States need not concern itself with the costs to alliance relationships and international institutions because other countries are more dependent on the United States rather than the reverse. Reciprocity arguments are less compelling since other countries do not put U.S. foreign investors at risk through secondary sanctions or try to compel U.S. subsidiaries to ignore U.S. law. The economic costs of developing a reputation for frequent use of extraterritorial sanctions are seen as minor since U.S. companies are so dominant and the U.S. market so important that the additional risks associated with extraterritorial sanctions are marginal. Or to use George Shultz's metaphor, the American "light-switch" is powered by a source of energy so vast that it can absorb whatever costs unilateral sanctions impose on it.

There is a plausible case to be made for these arguments because the United States has not been subjected to specific retaliation for its actions. It has, however, incurred significant diffuse costs. Extraterritorial sanctions against Cuba, Libya, and Iran have compelled the expenditure of diplomatic capital in relieving transatlantic tensions rather than in broadening substantive cooperation. Foreign subsidiary sanctions have deployed OFAC's enforcement apparatus against such strategically insignificant items as the sale of Cuban polyester pajamas in Canada. The precedents set during the Helms–Burton/ILSA controversy legitimized the EU's extraterritorial assertion of antitrust jurisdiction on the merger between Boeing and McDonnell-Douglass and its decision to ignore WTO rulings regarding its preferential system for importing bananas and its ban on hormone-treated beef. They have also placed U.S.-based MNCs in untenable conflicts of jurisdiction, tarnishing their image as "good corporate citizens" in their host countries and undercutting their reliability as business partners. The fact that these costs are not immediately visible does not make them any less real. Successive administrations, for the most part, have recognized this. Congressional supporters of sanctions and their domestic constituencies have not. As long as the latter are powerful enough to legislate their preferences, international institutions are unlikely to matter and extraterritorial sanctions will pose credible risks to business ties between pariah states and any multinationals actively involved in the United States.

NOTES

1. Ohmae, *The Borderless World*, 185.

2. See Paul Q. Hirst and Grahame Thompson, *Globalization in Question: The International Economy and the Possibilities for Governance* (Cambridge, U.K.: Polity Press, 1996), 13; and Louis W. Pauly and Simon Reich, "National Structures and Multinational Corporate Behavior: Enduring Differences in an Age of Globalization," *International Organization* 51 (winter 1997): 1–30.

3. Wälde, "Legal Boundaries for Extraterritorial Ambitions," 177–178.

4. Kapstein, "We Are Us," 59.

5. Wälde, "Legal Boundaries for Extraterritorial Ambitions," 130–131.

6. Daniel W. Drezner, *The Sanctions Paradox: Economic Statecraft and International Relations* (New York: Cambridge University Press, 1999), 316.

7. G. John Ikenberry, "A World Economy Restored: Expert Consensus and the Anglo-American Postwar Settlement," *International Organization* 46 (winter 1992), 320.

8. Thomas Risse-Kappen, *Cooperation among Democracies: The European Influence on U.S. Foreign Policy* (Princeton, N.J.: Princeton University Press, 1995), 37–38.

9. Bohlen to State, 12 March (NARS/D/CFP, 1965–1967, Box 3638, STR 12-3 Chicom-France).

10. Shambaugh, *States, Firms, and Markets*, 97.

11. The Reagan administration also recognized that congressional sentiment in the early 1980s favored relaxation of the Cuban embargo. It therefore played a key role in creating the CANF in order to provide a source of countervailing pressure. See Vanderbush and Haney, "Policy Toward Cuba in the Clinton Administration," 391. Ironically, the

CANF would later mobilize congressional pressure on the Bush and Clinton administrations to impose extraterritorial sanctions.

12. Barry E. Carter, "Unilateral Economic Sanctions," *American Society of International Law Proceedings*, vol. 91, 1997, 336.

13. Shambaugh, *States, Firms, and Markets*, 145–150.

14. Shambaugh, *States, Firms, and Markets*, 132–134.

15. S. Kern Alexander, *Third Country Liability under United States Economic Sanctions: The Extraterritorial Legal Framework* (Ph.D. diss. in law, University of London, 1999), ch. 1.

16. Kim Richard Nossal, "'Without Regard to the Interests of Others': Canada and American Unilateralism in the Post–Cold War Era," *American Review of Canadian Studies* 27 (summer 1997): 193–194.

17. See Brice M. Clagett, "The Cuban Liberty and Solidarity (Libertad) Act," *American Journal of International Law* 90 (July 1996): 434–440.

18. David Vogel, *Barriers or Benefits? Regulation in Transatlantic Trade* (Washington, D.C.: Brookings Institution, 1997), 43.

19. The most systematic exposition of this argument is in Alexander, *Third Country Liability Under United States Economic Sanctions*. For an application of this model to municipal sanctions, see Peterson, "Political Realism and the Imposition of Secondary Sanctions," 292–293.

20. Wälde, "Legal Boundaries for Extraterritorial Ambitions,"126.

21. On the issue of cooperation as loss-avoidance, see Janice Gross Stein and Louis W. Pauly, eds., *Choosing to Cooperate: How States Avoid Loss* (Baltimore, Md.: Johns Hopkins University Press, 1993).

Abbreviations for Primary Government Documents Used in Notes

DDRS	Declassified Documents Reference System, Washington, D.C., Carrollton Press, 1975
DEA	Classified File No. 37-16-1, "Foreign Trade—Commercial Relations—Cuba," vols. 1–10, 1963–1975, Canada's Department of External Affairs, obtained from Canada's Department of Foreign Affairs and International Trade, Ottawa, Ontario
DOS/FOIA	Department of State, Freedom of Information Act
Ford/KSF	Kissinger–Scowcroft Files, Gerald R. Ford Presidential Library, Ann Arbor, Michigan
FRUS	*Foreign Relations of the United States*, 1948–1964, U.S. Department of State Office of the Historian, Washington, D.C., GPO, 1974–1998
JFK/POF	President's Office Files, John F. Kennedy Library, Boston, Massachusetts
LBJ/NSF	National Security Files, Lyndon B. Johnson Presidential Library, Austin, Texas
NAC	National Archives of Canada, Ottawa, Ontario
NARS/D/CFP	U.S. National Archives and Records Service, Diplomatic Branch, Central Foreign Policy Files, College Park, Maryland

Bibliography

Adler-Karlsson, Gunnar. *Western Economic Warfare, 1947–1967: A Case Study of Foreign Economic Policy.* Stockholm: Almqvist & Wiksell, 1968.

Alexander, S. Kern. "Third Country Liability under United States Economic Sanctions: The Extraterritorial Legal Framework." Ph.D. diss. in Law, University of London, 1999.

Baldwin, David A. *Economic Statecraft.* Princeton, N.J.: Princeton University Press, 1985.

Behrman, Jack N. *National Interests and the Multinational Enterprise: Tensions among North Atlantic Countries.* Englewood Cliffs, N.J.: Prentice Hall, 1970.

Berman, Harold J., and John R. Garson. "United States Export Controls—Past, Present, Future." *Columbia Law Review* 67 (May 1967).

Born, Gary. "A Reappraisal of the Extraterritorial Reach of U.S. Law." *Law and Policy in International Business* 24 (1992).

Carter, Barry E. *International Economic Sanctions: Improving the Haphazard U.S. Legal Regime.* Cambridge, U.K.: Cambridge University Press, 1988.

Cohen, Benjamin J. *In Whose Interest? International Banking and American Foreign Policy.* New Haven, Conn.: Yale University Press, 1986.

Crawford, Beverly. *Economic Vulnerability in International Relations: The Case of East–West Trade, Investment, and Finance.* New York: Columbia University Press, 1993.

De Mestral, A. L. C., and T. Gruchalla-Wesierski. *Extraterritorial Application of Export Legislation: Canada and the U.S.A.* Dordrecht, Netherlands: Martinus Nijhoff Publishers, 1990.

De Villiers, Les. *In Sight of Surrender: The U.S. Sanctions Campaign against South Africa.* Westport, Conn.: Greenwood Press, 1995.

Drezner, Daniel. *The Sanctions Paradox: Economic Statecraft and International Relations.* New York: Cambridge University Press, 1999.

Ellicott, John. "From Pipeline to Panama: The Evolution of Extraterritorial Trade and Financial Controls." In *Private Investors Abroad—Problems and Solutions in International Business in 1988,* edited by Cecil J. Olmstead. New York: Matthew Bender, 1989.

Funigiello, Philip J. *America–Soviet Trade in the Cold War.* Chapel Hill, N.C.: University of North Carolina Press, 1988.

Gladwin, Thomas N., and Ingo Walter. *Multinationals under Fire: Lessons in the Management of Conflict*. New York: Wiley, 1980.

Griffin, Joseph P., and Michael N. Calabrese. "Coping with Extraterritoriality Disputes." *Journal of World Trade* 22 (June 1988).

Haass, Richard N., ed. *Economic Sanctions and American Diplomacy*. New York: Council on Foreign Relations, 1998.

Haass, Richard N., ed. *Transatlantic Tensions: Europe, the United States, and Problem Countries*. Washington, D.C.: Brookings Institution, 1999.

Hennessy, Alastair, and George Lambie, eds. *The Fractured Blockade: West European-Cuban Relations during the Revolution*. London: MacMillan, 1993.

Hufbauer, Gary Clyde, Jeffrey J. Schott, and Kimberly Ann Elliott. *Economic Sanctions Reconsidered: Supplemental Case Histories*, 2d ed. Washington, D.C.: International Institute of Economic Studies, 1990.

Hull, Richard W. *American Enterprise in South Africa: Historical Dimensions of Engagement and Disengagement*. New York: New York University Press, 1990.

Jentleson, Bruce W. *Pipeline Politics: The Complex Political Economy of East–West Energy Trade*. Ithaca, N.Y.: Cornell University Press, 1986.

Kaplowitz, Donna Rich. *Anatomy of a Failed Embargo: United States Sanctions against Cuba*. Boulder, Colo.: Lynne Rienner, 1998.

Kapstein, Ethan B. "We Are Us: The Myth of the Multinational." *National Interest* 26 (winter 1991–1992).

Keohane, Robert O. "The Theory of Hegemonic Stability and Changes in International Economic Regimes, 1967–1977." In *Change in the International System*, edited by Ole R. Holsti, Randolph M. Siverson, and Alexander George. Boulder, Colo.: Westview, 1980.

Kobrin, Stephen J. "Enforcing Export Embargoes through Multinational Corporations: Why Doesn't It Work Anymore?" *Business in the Contemporary World* 1 (winter 1989).

Krasner, Stephen D. *Defending the National Interest: Raw Material Investments and U.S. Foreign Policy*. Princeton, N.J.: Princeton University Press, 1978.

Leyton-Brown, David Robert. "Governments of Developed Countries as Hosts to Multinational Enterprise: The Canadian, British, and French Policy Experience." Ph.D. diss., Harvard University, Department of Government, August 1973.

Leyton-Brown, David, ed. *The Utility of International Economic Sanctions*. New York: St. Martin's, 1987.

Lowenfeld, Andreas F. *Trade Controls for Political Ends*, 2d ed. San Francisco, Calif.: Matthew Bender, 1983.

Martin, Lisa. *Coercive Cooperation: Explaining Multilateral Economic Sanctions*. Princeton, N.J.: Princeton University Press, 1992.

Mastanduno, Michael. *Economic Containment: CoCom and the Politics of East-West Trade* (Ithaca, N.Y.: Cornell University Press, 1992).

Malloy, Michael P. *Economic Sanctions and U.S. Trade*. Boston: Little, Brown, 1990.

Massie, Robert Kinloch. *Loosing the Bonds: The United States and South Africa in the Apartheid Years*. New York: Doubleday, 1997.

Morley, Morris H. *Imperial State and Revolution: The United States and Cuba, 1952–1986*. Cambridge, U.K.: Cambridge University Press, 1987.

Moyer, Homer E., Jr., and Linda A. Mabry. *Export Controls as Instruments of Foreign Policy: The History, Legal Issues, and Policy Lessons of Three Recent Cases*. Washington, D.C.: International Law Institute, 1985.

Nau, Henry. *The Myth of America's Decline: Leading the World Economy in the 1990s.* New York: Oxford University Press, 1990.

Neff, Stephen C. *Friends But No Allies: Economic Liberalism and the Law of Nations.* New York: Columbia University Press, 1990.

Perlmutter, Howard V. "The Tortuous Evolution of the Multinational Corporation." *Columbia Journal of World Business* 4 (January–February 1969).

Preeg, Ernest H. *Doing Good or Feeling Good with Sanctions: Unilateral Economic Sanctions and the U.S. National Interest.* Washington, D.C.: Center for Strategic and International Studies, 1999.

Purcell, John F. H. "The Perceptions and Interests of United States Business in Relation to the Political Crisis in Central America." In *Central America: International Dimensions of the Crisis*, edited by Richard E. Feinberg. New York: Homes and Meier, 1982.

Reich, Robert B. "Who Is Us?" *Harvard Business Review* 68 (January/February 1990): 53–64.

Shambaugh, George E. *States, Firms, and Power: Successful Sanctions in United States Foreign Policy.* Albany, N.Y.: SUNY Press, 1999.

Shultz, George, P. "Light-Switch Diplomacy." *BusinessWeek* (28 May 1979).

Spiro, Peter J. "New Global Potentates: NGOs and the 'Unregulated Marketplace.'" *Cardozo Law Review* 18 (December 1996).

Turner, Louis. *Oil Companies in the International System*, 3d ed. Winchester, Mass.: Allen & Unwin, 1983.

Vernon, Raymond. *Storm over the Multinationals: The Real Issues.* Cambridge, Mass.: Harvard University Press, 1977.

Vogel, David. *Lobbying the Corporation: Citizen Challenges to Business Authority.* New York: Basic Books, 1978.

Wälde, Thomas W. "Legal Boundaries for Extraterritorial Ambitions." In *Companies in a World of Conflict*, edited by John Mitchell. London: Earthscan Publications, 1998.

Willetts, Peter. "Transnational Actors and International Organizations in Global Politics." In *The Globalization of World Politics: An Introduction to International Relations*, edited by John Baylis and Steve Smith. Oxford, U.K.: Oxford University Press, 1997.

Index

253

About the Author

Kenneth A. Rodman is the William R. Cotter Distinguished Teaching Professor of Government at Colby College. He was the founding director of Colby's International Studies Program and the Oak Institute for the Study of International Human Rights. He is the author of *Sanctity versus Sovereignty: The United States and the Nationalization of Natural Resources Investments* (Columbia University Press, 1988). His research on economic sanctions has appeared in *Political Science Quarterly*, *International Organization*, and *Ethics & International Affairs*.